COLIN E. GUNTON

Yesterday & Today

A Study of Continuities in Christology

WILLIAM B. EERDMANS PUBLISHING COMPANY
GRAND RAPIDS, MICHIGAN

© 1983 Colin E. Gunton
First published in 1983 by
Darton, Longman & Todd Ltd., London

This American edition published 1983 through special
arrangement with Darton, Longman & Todd by Wm. B. Eerdmans
Publishing Company, 255 Jefferson S.E., Grand Rapids, Mich. 49503

Library of Congress Cataloging in Publication Data

Gunton, Colin E.
Yesterday and today.

Bibliography: p. 210
Includes index.
1. Jesus Christ — Person and offices.   2. Jesus Christ
— History of doctrines.   I. Title.
BT202.G86   1983   232   83-16443
ISBN 0-8028-1974-5

For
Sarah, Carolyn, Christopher and Jonathan

CONTENTS

PREFACE

The publication of another discussion of Christology is justified only if it breaks new ground or opens up questions thought to be closed. The latter is the function of the first half of the book, which is largely concerned with method and its relation to content. As a discussion of method it is not so much a review of recent work – although major recent writings are subjected to analysis – as an attempt to isolate issues and lay bare the assumptions on which different christological positions depend. The great divide in modern theology is between those who regard modernity as throwing an impassable barrier between ourselves and our Christian past and those who would attempt to see the development of Christian thinking as an unbroken and generally developing process, albeit one which is uneven, episodic and sometimes disrupted. This is to claim neither the automatic truth of the past, as the critique in the final chapter will demonstrate, nor the equation of process with progress. It is rather to hold that real questions about the nature of Christianity are at stake, and that their centre is to be found in a major divergence of orientation to the past, a divergence which generates deep differences in what is understood to be the content of Christology.

Any modern writer must engage with this 'divided mind of modern theology' and to do so must converse with representatives of that side of the divide which is not his own. That is the intention of Chapters 2 to 5, which are designed to show that our problems of method in Christology reveal close parallels with those faced by theologians of pre-modern times. These are primarily critical and analytical chapters, but are not simply ground-clearing exercises, for in them I attempt to build cumulatively a foundation or even a ground floor for the substantive work that follows. In other words, the opening chapters are concerned with method, but with

Preface

methodological discussion which is progressively formed by and
oriented to matters of substance.

Substance and content come into the centre in Chapters 6 and 7
which are the heart of the book and where is to be found the
breaking of new ground. They are substantive in the sense that they
are intended to sketch the ontological implications of the linking of
time and eternity in Christology and to clarify the status of the
language in which this is done. Although they depend upon the
argument of the preceding chapters they could be read first or on
their own, although in such a reading something would inevitably
be lost. In the final two chapters the discussion turns, so to speak,
outwards, to Christology as it bears upon human life as it is lived
before God and in society.

The book has been many years in the making, and I am grateful
for help and support along the way: to King's College for the
granting of leave; to Geoffrey Nuttall for valuable criticism of an
exploratory paper; to Huw Parri Owen, Graham Stanton and Stewart Sutherland, who read all or part of an earlier attempt, and
contributed to a process which has involved a complete rewriting;
to Daniel Hardy whose critique was central to that process, and to
whose learning, theological judgement and continual encouragement I owe very much; to John Todd and his colleagues for encouraging the development of a rather uncertain quantity; and to
Jenny Sturtridge for her exquisite typing. Finally must go my thanks
to my wife and family, for their love, forbearance and
encouragement.

Colin Gunton
King's College, London
Autumn 1982

ACKNOWLEDGEMENT

Thanks are due to the Scottish Academic Press (Journals) Limited for permission to reproduce material from 'The Political Christ: Some Reflections on Mr Cupitt's Thesis' published in *Scottish Journal of Theology* 32 (1979), pp. 521–40.

FORM, CONTENT AND THE TRADITION

PAST AND PRESENT

Our age is in many ways like that of the Fathers of Christian theology. They lived at a time when old orders were crumbling, and found themselves not only thinking the foundations of the Christian tradition but also rethinking the nature and reality of human knowledge. Now that we face the apparent collapse of so much of the culture that the Western Fathers, and Augustine in particular, helped to construct, we find that our situation is remarkably similar. In theology itself, there is, as in the first centuries of Christian thought, a wide range of approaches to be found, some of them, as we shall see, repeating the various patterns that came to be labelled orthodox and heretical, though repeating them in a characteristically modern form. These approaches, like those of the earlier days, reflect varying degrees of relationship to, and assessment of, the contemporary culture in the context of which theology is done, and Christianity is taught and lived.

It is, however, somewhat easier to command a view of another culture than of one's own; and so a judgement on classical culture in the first centuries after Christ will help to set the scene. The central thesis of Charles Norris Cochrane's *Christianity and Classical Culture* is that in face of the contradications inherent in the classical tradition, the great Christian theologians developed a view of the world and human society which formed a victorious alternative to classicism. Historically, that is to say, Christianity conquered, particularly in the West, because in certain respects it proved itself intellectually superior to a bankrupt alternative. For example, in its development of a direction taken by Athanasius, Augustinianism 'provides the basis for a synthesis which . . . serves at least to meet the legitimate aspiration of Classicism for a principle of order; while, in its vision of process and of the goal to which it moves, it discloses worlds to which Classicism, from the limitations of its outlook, remains inevitably blind' (Cochrane, p. 400).

Not everybody will agree with the details of Cochrane's analysis, but it is none the less indisputable that historical hindsight does enable us to discern a fairly straightforward direction, in which one culture replaced another.[1] It is otherwise with our own times, and for a number of reasons. In the first place, the relation of Christianity to culture has been complicated by that very victory which Cochrane describes. What happens to Christianity when the culture it did so much to develop declines or dies? But, in the second place, how clearly can it be known whether contemporary culture is dead or bankrupt? It is an open question, for example, whether contemporary music represents a further development of that which came to flower in Bach and Mozart, or whether it reveals its final decadence. In other respects, too, there is evidence to be found by both sides of a dispute about contemporary civilization. There is much talk of the decline of industrial civilization, of the collapse of institutions and of the sheer absurdity of much artistic endeavour. And one only has to scan the pages of contemporary theology to find much evidence of loss of nerve, if of nothing worse. But, on the other hand, the recent achievements of more central pillars of modern culture, the natural sciences, scarcely bear the marks of bankruptcy. Even those who doubt the value of some technological developments cannot rationally ignore the astonishing increase in human knowledge and understanding of our beautiful and intricate universe.

And so if it is correct that our age is in many ways like that of the Fathers of our theological tradition, the picture is inevitably very complicated. No culture is monochrome, least of all for those who are part of it. But, with this proviso, a theologian who writes from and for a culture must venture some generalizations as to what kind of culture he thinks it is. And the first is as follows: if there is an intellectual direction in the culture that has developed over the last few centuries it is that which is rather barbarously labelled 'immanentism'. That is to say, the phenomenon which at once

---

1 Whether, and how far, the process involved loss of essential Christian content will form part of the discussion of Chapter 9.

characterizes a culture and sets for Christian theology its central problem is the widely accepted belief that the world can be understood from within itself, and not from any being or principle supposed to operate from without. Examples are to be found everywhere, from the characteristic modern 'experience' of being alone in the universe to the brash technocratic optimism that sees in modern knowledge the key to the solution of all problems.

In theology, especially that of Protestants strongly influenced by ways of thought developed by the Enlightenment, but now increasingly that written by liberal Catholics, this means that we are all, whether we are with them or against them, the heirs of Schleiermacher and Hegel. Of Schleiermacher because, accepting Kant's rejection of the possibility of rational knowledge of the transcendent, he stressed the experiential centre of belief and theology; and of Hegel because his God, if not entirely a function of this-worldly time and process, was conceived essentially in categories of immanence. Those who read, with a knowledge of Hegel and Schleiermacher, much recent theology, especially that written in England, will realize how much of it represents a combination of the two, though in the process of combination it tends to lose both Schleiermacher's robustly christological emphasis and Hegel's preoccupation with a rationality that reflects the prior rationality of the way things are.

The positive aspect of modern immanentist theology is its concern to be responsible to modern culture. Theology has never operated by simply casting pearls of wisdom from a great height before the feet of the swine thronging below; and although this book will attack much of the way Christology in the liberal tradition is being done, it will not reject this aspect. What it will reject is any tendency to become no more than a pale reflection of aspects of contemporary culture. To be responsible to culture it is necessary to do precisely what Cochrane saw the early theologians to be doing; that is, to contribute to the thought of the age theologically in order neither to reject nor to reflect culture, but to share in its development, from within but also from a particular and distinctive place within. And if it is correct to see in its immanentist patterns of thought a leading characteristic of modern culture, theology will have to ask, first, how far it must inevitably (as part of that culture) share those patterns and, second, how far it is possible for it (as representing a community of belief distinct from the rest of its culture) to develop modes of thought and behaviour which derive from and imply some transcendent source or authority for what is being said.

This latter consideration brings into the discussion the second conversation partner with whom theology must deal. How strong a voice must the past be given in the development of modern theology? The fact is that the very words in which the problems are discussed in large part derive from a long tradition of belief and intellectual effort. But there is in contemporary theology a good measure of breakdown of confidence in the language of tradition. One reason for this is the very cultural developments which have been sketched so briefly. But the question then has to be asked as to how far the contemporary Christian is justified in allowing the 'acids of modernity' to undermine his traditional vocabulary. On the one hand, it must be strongly asserted that it is not, and never has been possible, simply to repeat the words of the Bible, the Fathers, the Reformers or any other group of authorities. We have to use our own language, as did the Reformers, the Fathers and the biblical writers. Nevertheless, on the other hand, it is difficult to believe that we can find our own language without assistance from theirs. The fact is that the belief, the tradition, is mediated – handed on from one person or generation to another – in words, and those words cannot finally be separated from the experiences or realities about which they are speaking. This is not to say that experience is completely linguistic or that language can of itself mediate or generate an experience or the apprehension of some reality (though clearly it can sometimes achieve this). Rather it is that there is a process of reciprocal shaping between experience of the world and the language by means of which we attempt to grasp it for ourselves and express it for others. Such an interrelationship of language and experience provides one of the most serious objections to the process known as 'doctrinal criticism', at least in so far as that presupposes a stance of clear, unprejudiced contemplation of the linguistic formulations developed in the past and the contemporary experience of the believer. The chief problem is this: if we can no longer in any way appropriate for ourselves the language of the past – for example, the affirmations of the Nicene Creed – then on what grounds are we able to judge whether we share the faith of the Fathers who formulated the Creed? How can we be sure that we are doing

Christian theology at all? If we reply that we are doing theology on the basis of contemporary Christian experience of the way things are, the question reasserts itself. Can we have a Christian experience of things that is free enough from the linguistic formulations of the past for us to be able to claim this? Our experience must be mediated at least in part by language. Must this not therefore mean that any starting-point that emphasizes the difference between contemporary understanding and that of the past tends to saw off the branch on which it is seated? The question can be asked in terms of form and content. The content of Christian belief, at least until the time of the Enlightenment, was expressed in words that were for the most part common to all times – except the very earliest – and parts of the Christian world. The form of talk about Christ was that of the language of Nicaea and Chalcedon, which formed a centre for the Christology of most major Christian theologians, certainly in the West. From the time of Schleiermacher there has been a division between those who would express the content in a different form and those who believe the old forms to be indispensable *in certain respects* if the content is to be retained. The argument of this book is to be that certain changes of form entail also a change of content: and that it is very difficult to maintain a real continuity with earlier ages unless we can *at least in some ways* affirm their words as our words, even though necessarily we shall not use and understand those words precisely as they did.

THE LANGUAGE OF TRADITION

Various criticisms are now frequently made of the ways in which ancient authors, from the Bible onwards, formulated Christian teaching. They derive for the most part from the savage critique of orthodox Christian belief made during the first generations of what is known as the modern era. In recent theology they reappear in the writings of many who give allegiance to Christianity but express their discomfort with a number of features of traditional formulation. First, there is the language of Greek philosophy which was used or adapted in the early Christian creeds. This is often described as 'static', a term presumably meant to characterize not the language itself but the kind of view of reality it evokes. To take a familiar example, Nicaea's 'of one substance' might be held to

5

suggest an improperly immobile view of the dynamic historical realities with which in Christianity we are concerned. A more radical version of this complaint would be that the language of metaphysics – words dealing with orders of being – is in itself inappropriate to the essentially moral or experiential concerns of Christianity. In this case it might be argued that not only the creeds but much of the New Testament overlay with abstract theory the essentially straightforward teaching of Jesus. In this critique there is often an implicit claim to be able to understand better than the earliest writers the nature of Christianity. Of course, this may be true: the idea of progress in theology should not be rejected out of hand. But the idea that we can be right where the tradition is wrong, that truth derives from a complete denial of tradition, is a rather more questionable claim. Be that as it may, the matter of the adequacy of the language of the past will receive discussion in later chapters.

The second source of discomfort is to be found in the writings of those who describe the ancient writings or world-view as 'mythological'. This word has a wide range of meanings, and should where possible be avoided. It can be used to characterize the story form of religious texts. In crude and early usage, traces of which still remain in some writers, it was used to characterize the difference between the figurative, pictorial language of the so-called primitive mind and the conceptual forms of thought supposed to characterize the modern. This emphatic distinction between the past and the present is of a piece with those views of modern Christianity which accentuate most strongly the 'broad ugly ditch' between ourselves and our past. But there is also a use of the word which attempts to characterize the imagery in which some early statements of belief were couched: 'He came down from heaven'. How far those who used such language were aware of its metaphorical character and how far they believed in a 'three-storey' universe is a matter for debate, as is the question of whether when thinking of God we inevitably think of him as in some way vertically related to us. That the question is not a simple one becomes clear when we realize, as Professor D. M. MacKinnon has recently pointed out, that such language is not only used in the Nicene Creed but is preceded, and therefore to some extent controlled, by the technical and conceptual term *homoousios* (MacKinnon, 1982, p. 151). Thus for those who

6

share the suspicion of Greek conceptuality the problem is compounded; but mitigated for those who seek to 'demythologize' by the use of philosophical language. In one sense, demythologization began from the very beginning.

The question of mythology is, as we have seen, largely a matter of language, and should not be confused with the third area of discomfort, that of theological method. In the past, theology would begin its procedures with credal assertions like those of Nicaea, or simpler biblical affirmations like 'Jesus is Lord' or 'Christ died for our sins according to the Scriptures', and argue from there. In Christology it began with assertions of the divine origin and status of Jesus, and proceeded to elaborate their implications. This is the method of approach that has recently been described as 'Christology from above'. Methodologically, it begins in 'another world' or with God, the 'other', and moves thence to discussions of this-worldly reality. But it is widely believed, and the belief must derive in part from concern to do justice to immanentist strains in modern culture, that this is no longer possible or proper. We must work 'from below'. The debate is, as we shall see, focused particularly in Christology, and concerns the way in which we should speak of God (if at all) in connection with Jesus of Nazareth. Now it is not here being denied that there are other ways of speaking of God than the christological. But it is evident that the question there comes into a unique focus, for it centres on a figure who is particular, temporal and (apparently) belonging to the past: a this-worldly figure, understandable in the language of immanence, although traditionally associated with that of transcendence. The possibilities are immediate and attractive: may there not be found in Christology the link with God that has been lost through the development of modern culture? But the difficulties are also evident. Is it possible to reach a Christology that is recognizably continuous with that of the past? Or does the difference of method necessarily entail a difference of form and content so great that we are no longer doing the same thing as our forefathers?

Accordingly, in summarizing the points made in this section, we can say first that the traditional way in which Christology has been expressed faces us with the question of content. Did the words plundered from Greek metaphysics in any way adequately bring to speech the truth about Jesus and, even if they once did, do they any longer in our very different cultural milieu? Second, the language of mythology, and its associated talk of pre-existence, raises the question of form. Is talk of a saviour coming 'from above' any longer credible as a vehicle for Christology in an age dominated by immanent ways of thought? Third, the place in which we should begin Christology introduces considerations of method. Can we begin in eternity and proceed to time, or must the movement be otherwise? The three questions together are relativized by a fourth: if we do conclude that content, form and method must be completely – or very – different from those of the classical Christian tradition, is there any way of guaranteeing continuity with those in the past who have expressed their beliefs in the manner now being rejected?

The contention of this book is that a Christology which is true to the claims of the Christian gospel requires a greater degree of continuity with the past than is apparent in some recent essays in reconstruction. The need is not to reverse the direction of what was the mainstream of thought until the Enlightenment, but to take it further. Only by deepening the possibilities inherent in Christology for our understanding of God can theology be truly radical, reaching down to the roots of the Christian tradition in order to flower more abundantly. The contemporary movement which claims the name of radical is in fact the reverse, for it is attempting to dig altogether elsewhere, and so is repeating those very tendencies of thought which in the past obstructed the development that was required, driving apart Christology and the doctrine of God.

The first chapters of this study will therefore be largely critical, challenging the claims that are sometimes made for new directions and suggesting that they are often old directions in disguise. After that will come an attempt to build upon the foundations of the past and to indicate where, in particular central areas of interest, developments may be attempted. In the process of the discussion, the familiar landmarks will be passed: the matters of the use of the Bible, of ontology, of language and of the implications of Christology for Christian and worldly living. But it is hoped that they will be passed in a manner different enough to justify yet another book in this central but sometimes overdiscussed area.

REFERENCES

Cochrane, Charles Norris, *Christianity and Classical Culture.*
MacKinnon, D. M., 1982, 'Prolegomena to Christology' in *Journal of Theological Studies* 33, 146–60.

2

CHRISTOLOGY FROM BELOW

PREVIEW

The discussion of method and its relation to content will begin with a critical look at the current fashion for what has come to be called 'Christology from below'. It is not intended to concentrate attention here upon those whose use of the method leads them to primarily sceptical conclusions (Nineham). It would be tempting to do so, arguing that the method leads to such sceptical conclusions that its results can scarcely claim the name of Christian. But from the point of view of a study of method it is far more instructive to examine the work of some of those who claim by this alternative route to reach something very like the traditional conclusions. If orthodox or even Chalcedonian doctrines can be reached by methods more in harmony with modern assumptions and epistemology it would indeed be a great gain, achieving maximum communication with minimum loss of distinctive Christian content.

But what is Christology from below? The first point to be made is that except in very general terms there is little agreement about what is meant (Lash). These general terms involve appeal to some such principle that in the modern world it is more reasonable to ask, What is true about human beings that it is possible that one of them should also be in some manner the vehicle of divine salvation? than to ask, What is true about God that he should be able to incarnate himself in a man, without loss of his divinity or the man's humanity? Thus the general concern of Christology from below is to begin theological inquiry more on a this-worldly plane than in flights of speculation about the eternal *Logos*. Christology from below aims to ground what it has to say primarily in the anthropological or, more generally, in that which has to do with time rather than with eternity. But it is, in the theologians we shall examine, a *ground*: there is every intention and indeed expectation to leave the ground, to speak theologically as well as anthropologically, and not to remain stranded on the earth.

TRANSCENDENT ANTHROPOLOGY

Karl Rahner's programme is for a Christology from below which will yet be in continuity with that of the tradition. For him 'from below' represents a particular method of approach, beginning, that is to say, not in some theological dogma but in considerations of philosophical anthropology. But, wherever it begins, the aim is to achieve essentially the same Christology as that of the Council of Chalcedon without, however, producing the outcome which is often claimed to result from the Definition, of splitting Christ into two: stressing, that is, the 'without confusion' at the expense of the 'union between the Logos and the human nature. . .' (Rahner, 1961, p. 170, cf. pp. 179ff.). The other problem with which Rahner hopes to deal concerns the form rather than the method of early Christology. He appears to hold, though his argument is not entirely clear, that the 'static' categories in which ancient Christology was often couched make it easy to misunderstand it as holding that Christ is, so to speak, a mixture of two thing-like and incompatible entities. But that, he claims, would be to misunderstand what it is to be human. 'Human being is not some absolutely terminated quantity which . . . is combined with some other thing . . . by a wholly external miracle' (p. 183). Because traditional language and ontology distort our conception of the human it becomes inadequate for the exposition of Christology, by definition, we might say, in view of the aspects of the matter which centre on a historical human being.

By means of a different approach to both method and form Rahner hopes to avoid the misunderstandings inherent in traditional language about Christ. The improved form of Christology comes from the adoption of a different anthropology. In the light of modern philosophy he believes that it is possible to adopt a vocabulary that is more appropriate than that available to the Fathers.

In contrast to the static character of traditional formulations, we must, he argues, say that human being 'is a reality absolutely open upwards; a reality which reaches its highest perfection . . . when in it the Logos himself becomes existent in the world' (p. 183). The very beginning of theology lies for Rahner in the development of a view of human nature as necessarily open to a dimension of transcendence which is the same as that reality we denote when we speak of God (Rahner, 1978, ch. 1). It is because we can understand all human life as open to transcendence in this way that we can come to understand Jesus as a unique instance of humanity open to God. Thus a suitably modernized anthropology becomes the basis for our understanding of the divine status of the saviour, and the method – 'from below' – derives from it.

Method and form, then, belong together. But what of the content of Christology on this understanding? Rahner is insistent that what he has to say, even though he says it in different language, is the same as that of the traditional creeds. The whole enterprise of the discussion entitled 'Current Problems in Christology' is to provide a Christology that is true to the framework provided by the Definition of Chalcedon, and in particular to safeguard Orthodoxy's teaching of the uniqueness of Jesus. But it is in this latter respect that Rahner's Christology becomes at once problematic and obscure. What does he mean by saying, at the end of the sentence already cited, that human being 'reaches its highest perfection . . . when in it the Logos himself becomes existent in the world'? If he means, as some of his language suggests, that the transcendent humanity is the basis of the person of Christ, which becomes what it is by some kind of divine fulfilment ('by a free act from above', Rahner, 1961, p. 184), then he is indeed arguing strictly from below. Jesus's uniqueness consists in his being a unique and perfect example of humanity's openness to God. But to this it may be objected that unique and perfect humanity is unique and perfect humanity: the equivalent of the traditional 'sinlessness', but hardly equivalent to 'of one substance with the Father'. It is still in the realm of 'of one substance with us as touching the manhood, like us in all things apart from sin' (Stevenson, p. 337). That is to say, Rahner's anthropology may indeed be an interesting way of expressing an understanding of humanity, avoiding suggestions that humanity is

12

a closed-off reality, in no way fitted for relationship to God. It is not, however, a full account of orthodox Christology.

It is here that Rahner's argument becomes opaque. Some of his language suggests that he has already said enough to give an account of what tradition calls the divine nature of Jesus Christ. Thus he speaks of 'a man, who, precisely by being man in the fullest sense (which we can never attain), is God's Existence in the world' (p. 184). Here we have a rather Antiochene understanding of the relationship, where God's relation to the human Jesus is seen as a special case of the possibilities for grace inherent in all human existence: 'Human being is . . . a reality which reaches its highest . . . perfection . . . when in it the Logos himself becomes existent in the world' (p. 183). At other times, however, Rahner suggests a more ontological understanding of the relationship, and refers to the hypostatic union. In this case there is, corresponding to the Christology of transcendental anthropology, a movement of the Logos from above. This introduces a new aspect into the discussion, over and above the anthropological and without which Rahner's desire to be true to the intentions of Chalcedon cannot be fulfilled. Particularly in his later work there is much discussion of what it means to say that 'God became Man' (Rahner, 1978, pp. 206–28). The details of the discussion do not concern us here. What is of interest is that Christology from below is not all that we find in Rahner. Answering to the findings of transcendental anthropology is another element of a far more traditional character. The point of the anthropology is here not so much to create a Christology as to lessen the difficulties inherent in traditional language. It is to show that many of the difficulties of orthodox formulations can be avoided. *Methodologically* there is a double movement, corresponding to the human and divine *content* of christological language. Christology is both from above *and* from below.

What Rahner has achieved, then, is an attempted fusion of the tradition with a philosophical approach derived from the modern world. Marked features of the latter are the strongly Hegelian overtones of Rahner's discussion of history. History is seen by him (see especially Rahner, 1978, pp. 177ff.) as the history of the development of spirit, and it is against such a philosophical background that he then proceeds to speak of the hypostatic union. He guards very carefully against a totally immanentist Christology, in which the hypostatic union is seen as the high point of an evolution of spirit within time, and no more. He is also careful to use the language of history and evolution to protect Christology from its traditional pitfall of seeing what happened in Christ as an isolated incursion or intervention into a world totally foreign to it. But the tensions we have seen to be present in his language must leave it as an open question as to whether the rather idealist framework is too strong for the traditional language that is inserted into it; and – the same question in reverse – whether the language of hypostatic union falls like a bolt from the blue into the language of self-transcendence in terms of which Rahner expounds the nature of human reality.

This in its turn raises another interesting question about method and content. Perhaps it is a feature of all genuine language about Christ that it will come up against the limits of philosophical conceptuality. The latter cannot be avoided if we are to do the kind of thing Rahner attempted, and do Christology in a systematic way, taking seriously the task of expressing the truth. But will not the content always be too much for the form? The question then is, and it is raised in particular by Rahner's talk of self-transcendence, not of *whether* concepts are used, but of *which* ones are the best, and how they should be employed. Does Rahner's philosophical anthropology form a framework or a straitjacket? To put it crudely, is the final product true to the reality of Christ, or a projection of a particular image of humanity?

It is very important to attempt an answer to such a question if we are to have a Christology which does justice to two overwhelming aspects of the biblical picture of Jesus. The first is what might be called the very ordinariness of Jesus, at least in the impression he appears to have given to many of his contemporaries ('Is not this Joseph's son?'). If the human excellence of Jesus is stressed in the wrong way, we lose the man like ourselves, for according to the biblical testimony it would appear that one major difference between us and him as human beings lies not in the degree of self-transcendence but in the fact that where we succumb to temptation he did not. The notion of self-transcendence does not help us very much in another central area, either, where the significance of Jesus is from the beginning linked with the fact that it is through this particular human life that God's salvation becomes actual on earth.

14

Here, too, where the accent is often on the fact that it is by Jesus's lowliness that he functions as saviour, notions of self-transcendence actually obscure the heart of Christology. Rahner's weakness, then, is in his dependence upon an anthropology which, far from removing the dangers of ancient anthropology, reproduces them in another form, by creating a gulf between the New Testament picture of Jesus and forms of human self-assessment drawing heavily on existentialist and other modern traditions. This is not to suggest that such categories are of no use at all, but rather that by using them in an *a priori* and dominating manner essential aspects of Christology are lost. Thus it is precisely where it begins from below that Rahner's thought is more questionable, achieving an anthropology in severe tension with important aspects of the tradition.

DEGREE CHRISTOLOGY

There are, in Rahner's work, traces of what has come to be known as 'degree Christology'. This is an approach to the doctrine of the person of Christ which operates with something like Rahner's transcendent anthropology, but without his counterbalancing emphasis on the eternal Logos. It is therefore more accurately termed Christology from below, and attempts to develop a doctrine of the person of Christ that guarantees his cohumanity with the rest of mankind. The error it wishes to overcome is the orthodox tradition's apparent insistence on the miraculous otherness of Jesus, which, it claims, fails to do justice to his humanity. Because so much traditional Christology, it is argued, lifts Jesus out of the human sphere, it is docetic, teaching an unreal humanity, a God walking round in human clothes. We cannot then speak of the absolute uniqueness of Jesus, or of a uniqueness in kind: rather, we must teach that he is different from us only in degree. 'If one had to choose, I should side with those who opt for a "degree Christology" – however enormous the degree. For to speak of Jesus as different in kind from all other men is to threaten, if not to destroy, his true solidarity with other men. . .' (Robinson, pp. 209f.). According to this method of approach, then, Christology from below operates as follows. It sees certain characteristics to be the defining qualities of humanity, and argues that the significance of Jesus consists in his having a large, even unique, degree of these qualities.

15

Without doubt, one of the functions of Christology is to express an understanding of the way in which Jesus is supremely human, of one substance with ourselves, sin apart. But degree Christology wants to do more than this, and to say that Jesus's especial or divine significance is grounded in or demonstrated by his supreme human qualities. That is where its chief weakness is found, for it appears to presuppose that to be divine (or unique in the way a Christology asserts) is the same thing as to be successfully human. If, it seems to argue, we can discover certain immanent qualities by which Jesus exceeds other human beings, we can present him as a source of salvation or model for behaviour. The presupposition that to be divine is to be very successfully human may operate with another tacit assumption: that in some sense already to be human is to share in divinity. This is something that the theology of the modern era shares with much Greek thought, that by virtue of some feature of our being (reason, knowledge, morality or some other) we are already incipiently divine. Jesus, then, would be seen to be the one who brought this innate quality to perfection. It is in that respect that he is divine, as the supreme *degree* of what we are already, and is therefore not *in principle* different. In this way a crudely docetic Christology, in which Jesus is simply a god dressed in human guise, is avoided.

Degree Christology, in both of the forms that have been outlined, would appear, then, to depend on a belief in the inherent or incipient divinity of mankind. Its assumptions are either that Jesus's divinity *consists in* the abundant possession of certain human qualities or that, because human reality already contains the seeds of divinity, to be unique he needs to be understood as very much what we are already. The origins of such a view are to be found in some strains of classical philosophy, which were themselves revived by philosophers of the Enlightenment and, perhaps more important for our purposes, G. W. F. Hegel. It is through him in particular that such philosophical presuppositions have become operative in modern Christology. Faced with a loss of confidence in traditional ways of ascribing the source of Jesus's significance to a transcendent world, theologians in this tradition sought the divine within: in history, the human mind or, if their orientation was more to Kant than to Hegel, to human moral striving. There seems little doubt that Rahner's transcendental anthropology has received some tar from this brush. Now, we cannot at once reject such an approach without some apprehension of the way in which its representatives are engaging with modern culture's discomfort with transcendentalism. But two immediate objections must be raised. The first is that it appears to say the opposite of the teaching of traditional Christianity, as appears from Kierkegaard's jibe: 'That the human race is or should be akin to God is ancient paganism; but that an individual man is God is Christianity. . .' (Kierkegaard, 1941b, p. 84). Those who regard Kierkegaard's objection as simply positivistic, and not an argument at all, cannot evade the second objection, which is that degree Christology tends to achieve the opposite of what it sets out to do. The objection can be put in the form of a question: have not those who are most anxious to avoid docetism produced an understanding of Christ which, if not docetic, at best repeats the worst feature of docetism? If Jesus's significance is based on his superiority to us in essential human characteristics, are we not back with what was alleged to be the weakness of traditional Christology, a Jesus so different from us that he is no longer truly one of us? By putting all their eggs in the basket of an immanentist understanding of Jesus, exponents lift him far outside of our human sphere, and necessarily so, for they must either do this or abandon Christology altogether.

Let us, to illustrate this point, contrast this with one of the earliest Christologies. The Epistle to the Hebrews is noteworthy for a Christology which is, on the one hand, 'high' and otherworldly: 'a Son . . . through whom also he created the world' (1.2); and, on the other, emphatic about the humanity of Jesus: 'For we do not have a high priest who is unable to sympathize with our weaknesses, but one who in every respect has been tempted as we are, yet without sinning' (4.15). Whether the author has the right so to juxtapose time and eternity, and why he is confident that he can do so, does not here concern us. What does is the fact that because he does not seek to rise from below, by using a logical ladder from the human to the divine, the author is not compelled to take the human Jesus out of our sphere. A Christology from below whose *only* resource is some kind of transcendental anthropology seems logically bound either to do that or to concede the content of traditional Christology. Its more clear-eyed exponents have already taken the latter step. But whatever the outcome, one thing is becoming clear: in

17

Christology, matters of method and content are closely related: the way a Christology is approached cannot be separated from the kind of Christology that emerges, and a Christology from below is hard put to avoid being a Christology of a divinized man.

GROUNDS, REASONS AND BEGINNINGS

The same close relation between method and content is to be found in the Christology of Wolfhart Pannenberg, whose advocacy of Christology from below has become well known. His basis is not some kind of philosophical anthropology, as in Rahner and in degree Christology, but particular findings of historical research. Philosophical considerations do underlie his thought, but in a rather different manner, as will emerge later. Context is also provided by his view of what kind of theology is possible in the modern world. Any conception like that of Barth which makes theology into a 'science of faith', independent of the methods of contemporary historiography and science, is to be rejected as inappropriate. Rather, the theologian must use methods recognizably similar to those of other disciplines (Pannenberg, 1976, ch. 5).

In Christology this means that it is impossible to begin with some assertion of faith that presupposes the divinity of Jesus. Rather, 'This confession must be *grounded* by Christology' (Pannenberg, 1968, p. 29). By 'Christology' Pannenberg means in this context a process by which it is shown how faith in Jesus originated – what he calls substantiation. 'Only when (the) revelatory character [namely, of the history of Jesus] is not something additional to the events but, rather, is inherent in them, can the events form the basis of faith. Christology has to show just this' (p. 30). In other words, Christology is the discipline which establishes rather than supports the Christian confession of Jesus as Lord. Beginning in historical research alone it attempts to show that certain past events, accessible to empirical research because part of the immanent order of space and time, contain, of themselves, more than barely empirical significance.

Here is to be found the clue to what Pannenberg means by 'Christology from below'. As might be expected, he defines the method by contrast with the traditional approach 'from above'. As a matter of fact, there are a number of possible meanings for the

18

expression *Christology from above*, as will be argued in Chapter 3. But Pannenberg sees the matter to be fairly straightforward, as indeed from one point of view it is: 'For Christology that begins "from above", from the divinity of Jesus, the concept of the incarnation stands in the centre' (p. 33). That is to say, Christology from above is a Christology that begins with an implicit if not an explicit belief or teaching of the incarnation. The primary datum is a statement containing as its subject God, the Word or the Son. After some account of those who take this approach, Pannenberg adds that 'It is characteristic of all of these attempts to build a "Christology from above" that the doctrine of the Trinity is presupposed and the question posed is: How has the Second Person of the Trinity (the Logos) assumed a human nature' (p. 34)?

Christology from below is necessary, Pannenberg believes, because of the impossibility of such a method. He gives a number of reasons for his change of method. They are worth rehearsing because they reveal the springs of his own approach. The last of them is the weakest: 'One would have to stand in the position of God himself in order to follow the way of God's Son into the world' (p. 35). But this is unconvincing, because there are a number of reasons for identifying a phenomenon or event as divine, including the one Pannenberg has stated. The difficulty for him is that if his argument is accepted, his own case falls as well, for if to begin an argument with a confession of the divinity of Christ requires a Godlike stance, must not the same happen at the end of an argument? Indeed, it might be claimed to the contrary that an attempt to establish the divinity of Jesus by historical research is a more Promethean enterprise than – say – the acceptance of some supposed revelation. The latter may appear to be a less rational proceeding, but Pannenberg's argument here concerns the theological presuppositions of an approach, not its rationality. *Any* claim to discern God in a historical happening must, on Pannenberg's account, 'stand in the position of God himself'.

Weaknesses of Pannenberg's account are also revealed by an examination of other reasons he gives for the necessity of operating from below. 'The most important task of Christology is . . . to present the reasons for the confession of Jesus's divinity' (p. 34). But this is inconsistent with his claim that Christology *establishes* the divinity of Jesus on the basis of inquiry into this-worldly historical events. One can only give reasons for something one has already stated or assumed for the sake of discussion. If Pannenberg were saying that Christology must substantiate in whatever ways are appropriate our belief that Jesus is divine, he would be able to say what he has said here. But he is not. To give reasons for the confession of Jesus's divinity presupposes that we already believe, in some sense, in his divinity.

However, it is worth asking what underlies Pannenberg's concern for a Christology from below. It seems that he wishes to avoid a purely *a priori* Christology, one which simply presents the reader with a confession or a dogma. He is advocating a more *a posteriori* approach. One cannot, in face of contemporary concerns with historical inquiry, simply operate with abstract theological concepts. It is necessary, rather, to ground our theology in the finite and empirical, moving not from eternity to time, but the other way round. That is not, of course, the way he has put it. But supposing it to be a fair reflection of the general stance that is being adopted, we can move to an examination of what emerges from its application.

Christology from below, says Pannenberg, is Christology which 'rising from the historical man Jesus to the recognition of his divinity, is concerned first of all with Jesus's message and fate and arrives only at the end at the concept of the incarnation' (p. 33). Here the contrast with Rahner is instructive. In place of the double movement, with anthropological considerations being, so to speak, answered by a theological movement from above, Pannenberg's process of thought is continuous, a movement from the finite to the infinite. He will not even acknowledge the correctness of an approach like that of Käsemann which begins with the apostolic kerygma and then seeks to establish its continuity with the historical facts about Jesus (pp. 51ff.), for it presupposes a theological content.

How, then, does Pannenberg move from finite premises to a conclusion in which Jesus is linked with the infinite? His approach is to seek an event in Jesus's story that is *both* a possible subject of historical investigation *and* carries with it some kind of theological significance. Such is the resurrection, since 'the occurrence of the resurrection did not first need to be interpreted' for Jesus's Jewish contemporaries but 'spoke meaningfully in itself. If such a thing happened, one could no longer doubt what it meant' (p. 67). The resurrection is a possible subject of historical investigation because it is an event in the empirical causal nexus. In terms, however, of the context of the society in which it took place, 'the emergence of primitive Christianity can be understood . . . only if one examines it in the light of the eschatological hope for a resurrection from the dead. . . (A)n event that is expressible only in the language of the eschatological expectation is to be asserted as a historical occurrence' (p. 98). Because Israel expected a general resurrection, the occurrence of a single such event would immediately confer significance on the one to whom it happened in the eyes of its witnesses and contemporaries. It is, then, more than brute fact, for it carries something of its own interpretation with it (p. 73). To those who object that this is to ignore the distinction between fact and meaning, it is replied that such an objection represents a dogmatic Kantian 'positivistic understanding of the historical method according to which history establishes only "facts". However, . . . historical inquiry always takes place from an already given context of meaning . . . which is modified and corrected in the process of research on the basis of the phenomena examined' (p. 109).

Suppose, then, that this method of christological inquiry from below were successful in its aim to establish the divine significance of Jesus. It is difficult to see how it achieves what Pannenberg claims for it, and for the following reasons. (1) To claim that Jesus's resurrection carried for his contemporaries the immediate implication of his especial or even divine significance is a statement of the obvious, and scarcely has to be supported by argument. But (2) to admit that historical inquiry already takes place within a context of meaning is to invite the rejoinder that Pannenberg is doing precisely what he accused Käsemann of doing: *either* presupposing some dogmatic beliefs ('context of meaning') and thus not arguing genuinely from below at all; *or* failing to establish what is wanted, namely, the divinity of Jesus. The reason is that Pannenberg is confusing two different questions. The first is that about the significance of Jesus within the context of interpretation – what he meant to his contemporaries. The second is that concerning his significance now. To establish the credibility of the resurrection stories, as Pannenberg seeks to do, may enhance the credibility of present-day claims for Jesus's significance, but, in advance of acceptance of that framework of meaning, does not establish his divinity for faith now, only that it was a reasonable inference in its context. It may well be true that 'all subsequent church history lives from . . . the fact that at that time Jesus's resurrection and the end of the world could be seen together as a single event. . .' (p. 108). But that is a long way from establishing the doctrine of the incarnation, or even the special or divine significance of Jesus from below, as the end point of historical reflection upon the historical Jesus of Nazareth. It is a straightforward confusion between what happened in church history and what is or is not established as the result of a process of argument, between history and method. The contemporary expectation may have been mistaken and its conclusions false.

It is therefore difficult to see how Pannenberg can be considered to have established his programme to demonstrate that christological statements take their departure 'not only psychologically but also logically from the man Jesus' (p. 186). We can agree that they do so psychologically, in the sense that the resurrection gave the first disciples reasons for believing certain things about Jesus. But, as we have seen, that is not the same as producing a logical sequence of thought that begins with Jesus and ends with some conception of his more than human significance. Such a conclusion is possible only with the assistance of other premisses or warrants on the basis of which the movement from finite to infinite is made. In Pannenberg's case, the warrants derive from what is perhaps the best known of all his theological concepts, the notion of universal history. For him, all human intellectual inquiry presses towards the horizon of universal history. To inquire about any finite entity inevitably leads on to questions about the relation of the part to the whole. Accordingly, the quest for the meaning of the whole of history, for its overall and universal meaning, is part of the human intellectual process in general (Pannenberg, 1976, Part One).

This means that all thought is incipiently theological. Although the totality of meaning is something that will only be revealed at the end of history, anticipations are achievable during the course of time. The resurrection, being conceptually linked to the end time, is therefore the paradigmatic locus of meaning: establish the resurrection of Jesus, and you have established a link between a finite human being and the meaning of all reality. That is the route by which Pannenberg moves from finite premisses to a conclusion containing the word *God*. But of course it means that the premisses are not in every way finite, for, as we have seen, the fundamental assumption is that all thought is incipiently theological. Read between any meaningful lines and you will see the question of whole and part, and so of God, begin to emerge. Pannenberg's Christology from below operates within a matrix of Hegelian or idealist forms of understanding.

What, then, is the content corresponding to the idealist method and form by which christological inquiry proceeds? It is significant that, unlike Rahner, Pannenberg rejects the Christology of Chalcedon. For Rahner, the two strands of Chalcedon's Christology ('of one substance with God'; 'of one substance with ourselves') cohere reasonably well with the double movement of his thought, though in characteristic modern fashion he has inverted the order. For Pannenberg, who aims at a more continuous Christology, Chalcedon is unavoidably dualistic: 'The contradiction between God and creature is the logical starting-point for thought. . .' (Pannenberg, 1969, p. 284). Despite the translator's rather misleading title (*Jesus – God and Man* for *Grundzüge der Christologie*), a Chalcedonian duality is not at the centre of the resulting Christology. Rather, a recurring expression is 'Jesus's essential unity with God'. In place of four other ways in which Jesus's relation to God has been expressed, Pannenberg argues for what he calls a revelational unity (pp. 115, 127ff.). By this he means that any understanding of Jesus's divinity must be based upon the (immanently understood) history of his life, and not upon a concept of incarnation. The humanity is prior: 'as this man Jesus is God' (p. 283).

Despite all his careful safeguards and detailed conversation with tradition, it is difficult to see how Pannenberg can avoid an outcome similar to that of degree Christology, of making Jesus into a divinized man. Too much weight falls upon the finite premisses, too little on the gospel background of Christology: its claim that what happens on earth takes its origins in eternity, in the prevenient love of God. Questions of this kind will concern us later. But, once again, Pannenberg is aware of the dangers. He sees that current theological methods often succeed in divorcing Christology from soteriology, and he wishes to avoid such a rift. That is also the criticism being made of Pannenberg's own Christology: that unless some priority is given in it to the eternal (as it is in Rahner), certain essential soteriological dimensions of Christology will be lost. Why does Pannenberg believe that he can escape the danger? A glance at his exposition on this matter will advance our inquiry in several ways. It will enable us to see a little more clearly the difficulties raised by Pannenberg's account of christological method; and to notice the historical background of the whole enterprise known as Christology from below.

CHRISTOLOGICAL METHOD AND THE NINETEENTH-CENTURY BACKGROUND

Pannenberg's account of the relation between Christology and soteriology is closely related to his view of method in Christology. It involves a clear distinction between the two related disciplines – a distinction Pannenberg believes to have been ignored in much recent theology's tendency to reduce Christology to soteriology. It is against this tendency that he asserts that 'Christology, the question about Jesus himself, about his person, as he lived on earth in the time of the Emperor Tiberius, must remain prior to any questions about his significance, to all soteriology. Soteriology must follow from Christology, not vice versa. Otherwise, faith in salvation loses any real foundation' (Pannenberg, 1968, p. 48). The general methodological point that is being made is an important one. Unless assertions of Christ's significance are based upon beliefs or statements about what he is, a purely subjectivist theology is likely to result. Christ becomes no more than his benefits as the individual believer happens to conceive them. Pannenberg, as we have seen, wishes to avoid this pitfall by a rigorous and objective programme of historical research. Once that has been done, soteriology will follow automatically, because it will become clear, according to his theory of meaning, that the events, when found, *interpret themselves*. They are not simply facts, but facts redolent with significance for our understanding of our place within universal history.

But there is a problem, and it lies in Pannenberg's conception of Christology as an inquiry into what Jesus was. It brings us to the heart of the weakness of this approach to Christology, for it leaves us asking the question whether in this discipline we are concerned with a present or a past figure. This is a problem that Rahner's more existentialist approach does not encounter, for its beginning in present human questions rather than research into past facts gives it a rather different orientation. Here, however, for all its use of eschatological language, we have a conception that comes very near to making Jesus little more than a past figure who happens to have triggered a particular understanding of human existence. To put it another way, we must ask whether the resurrection is simply about structures of meaning or whether it is to do with a past historical figure who in that historical event is shown to belong not simply to past time but to present and future as well. According to the latter account, the resurrection is not only about Jesus's meaning but also about his status as a historical but also time-transcending reality. Moreover, a very different conception of Christology results from the two approaches: a choice is presented between Christology as an inquiry into the past and as the exploration and exposition of a present reality. Certainly, Pannenberg is concerned with present meaning, and meaning as mediated by Jesus. But his conception of Christology from below shapes his understanding of Christ into a form necessarily different from that of much traditional Christology. Content is once again seen to be closely tied up with method.

An interesting feature of this development is that it relates Pannenberg very closely to nineteenth-century theologians who, on Pannenberg's own account, are guilty of reducing Christology to soteriology. An investigation into some of their themes will be of interest here not in trying to suggest guilt by association nor in arguing that Pannenberg is just the same as they, but to indicate something of the historical background of recent developments in Christology. Pannenberg's manifest intention is to avoid Kantian theories of meaning which divorce fact from meaning. But his immediate antecedents lie in Kantian theologians who built upon certain hints from the work of Luther. Pannenberg, as we shall see, belongs in the tradition of liberal and Kantian Christology, but it is a tradition he wishes to transform from within.

'Impulses in [the] direction [of a Christology from below] were made in the ancient Church, in the Middle Ages, and by Luther. . .' (p. 36). Although Pannenberg is no more specific than this, there is no doubt that in mentioning Luther he has indicated a fountainhead. The *locus classicus* was cited by Wilhelm Herrmann in 1892: 'Therefore we can have no certain proof of the deity of Christ unless we enfold and enclose our hearts in the sayings of the Scriptures.

For the Scriptures begin very gently, and lead us on to Christ as to a man, then afterwards to a Lord over all creatures, and after that to a God' (Herrmann, p. 165). One manifest feature of this passage is its difference from Christology from below in Pannenberg's sense. Clearly, Luther is referring to the human Jesus of biblical witness, and not to the product of historical research, as the phrase 'to Christ as to a man' demonstrates. To suggest anything else would be anachronistic, and in any case the 'humanity of Christ' is a theological concept in the way that 'the Jesus recoverable by historical research' is not. But it remains true that there are in Luther 'impulses' to Christology from below, as is suggested by the metaphor of ascending in another passage cited by Herrmann: '*After this, I rise up from the Son to the Father, and see that Christ is God*' (p. 166). But once again, it is not a question of historical research: the movement is, so to speak, inner-trinitarian, from Son to Father.

If, then, there are impulses in Luther, the real development is to be found in the nineteenth-century theologians, beginning with Schleiermacher, who operated in the atmosphere created by Kant. Luther's Christ, we might say, inhabits the noumenal world from the outset. But after Kant it can no longer be assumed that the noumenal or transcendent world is ready to hand; it has to be fought for. That is the real impulse to Christology from below, the urge to find in this world, not in some assumed transcendent realm, the starting-point for Christology. Kant had found the link in practical reason; Schleiermacher, attempting to widen the area, had developed a conception of experience which formed a third capacity of the person beyond Kant's theoretical and practical. Their successors, Ritschl and Herrmann tried in different ways to find a route from below to a belief in Christ's transcendent significance.

Ritschl began his crucial christological chapter (A. Ritschl, 1900, ch. 6) with an acknowledgement, or rather interpretation, of Luther who, he claims, avoided a purely theoretical account of Christ's divinity by introducing the Godhead of Christ as 'a judgement of value. . . (T)he chief point is that in his exertions as a man His Godhead is manifest and savingly effective' (pp. 392f.). Ritschl then proceeds to quote the dictum of Melanchthon which has served, whether fairly or not, as the source of that very reduction of Christology to soteriology that Pannenberg wishes to avoid. 'To know Christ is to know his benefits, not to contemplate his natures and his modes of incarnation, as the scholastics teach' (p. 396). In that passage Melanchthon was protesting against the excessive objectivism of the scholastics in order to teach a Christ who is not simply an object of knowledge, but is what he is in the meaning he has for believers. In post-Kantian thought this Lutheran tendency to elevate the significance of Christ 'for me' over his significance in himself tended, as Pannenberg sees, to degenerate into subjectivism, in which his significance is almost made to depend on the believer, or at least on the believer's mode of apprehension. So it is with Ritschl: 'If Christ by what he has done and suffered for my salvation is my Lord, and if, by trusting for my salvation to the power of what he has done for me, I honour him as my God, then that is a value judgement of a direct kind.' And: 'The nature of God and the Divine we can only know in its essence by determining its value for our salvation' (p. 398). Christology on this account must be subordinate to soteriology, because only that is conceded which derives from Christ's supposed benefits. As a consequence, it may happen that truth is made subordinate to meaning and Christology deprived of any basis in fact.

The movement from below is similar in the case of Herrmann, except that whereas Ritschl's 'below' is the ethical life of Jesus, Herrmann turns to the moral sublimity of Jesus's inner life. Like Ritschl he reveals the influence of Kant. 'Luther once said that he would argue no more with any man who did not recognise Holy Scripture as the Word of God. . . We ought rather to say that we will argue with every man, and will only lay down our arms when we see that men have no sense of unconditional obligation. . .' (Herrmann, p. 108). Deep speaks to deep; the inner reality of the one moves the inner reality of the other. Indeed, there is no point at all in speaking of Christ's mediation of the forgiveness of sins except in so far as the tradition about Christ 'takes hold of our inner life as a reality'. Forgiveness is not 'a demonstrable doctrine. . . It is a religious experience' (p. 141). We thus move from the traditions about Jesus's inner life as they take hold of us ('below') to an ascription to him of deity. 'It is what we experience in the man Jesus that first gives definite content to the confession of the deity of Christ' (p. 128).

The reluctance of these two nineteenth-century theologians to speak of the divinity of Christ except in so far as it is a function of the believer's experience of his life undoubtedly owes much to the fact, already mentioned, that they operated within the same tradition of post-Kantian German thought. Ever since Augustine, Western theology has operated with a conceptuality in which the otherness of time and eternity has been strongly accentuated (D. Ritschl, p. 6). What Kant did was to develop even further their otherness, as well as to stress the temporal limitations of all human knowing. Christology from below can be seen to be in large measure an attempt to wrestle with the problems raised by this conceptuality and its Kantian presuppositions.

The hard-line Kantian will have no truck with such a method, and Van Harvey, for example, has argued that Schleiermacher was mistaken in his own application of his method. Being true to his starting-point that statements about God should be no more than statements about the religious consciousness would have meant the renunciation of all God-language. There can be no Christology, only anthropology (Harvey, 1962, pp. 165ff.). But, as we have seen, Pannenberg is not a hard-line Kantian. He believes, with Schleiermacher, that experience of God can in some sense be given along with experience of the world. The difference from Schleiermacher is that added to his influence is that of Hegel. Underlying all that Pannenberg writes is a view of the meaningfulness of universal history released, by anticipation, so to speak, in the resurrection of Jesus of Nazareth. The attempt to establish the truth of the resurrection takes place within a particular theoretical framework, which is parallel to those of Ritschl and Herrmann but different. In place of their tendency to moralism comes one to an idealist theory of meaning. But that, as it operates in Pannenberg, is a kind of soteriology, a way of expressing the human quest for and reception of meaning. Is it, then, any more likely that he will avoid the reduction of Christology to soteriology that he wishes to avoid? Will the outcome be very much different from the reflection of the face of neo-Hegelian man in the well of universal history? That is the central weakness of a Christology from below which establishes no more than a revelational unity of the man Jesus with God: that he may finally reveal no more than we want him to. It is for this reason that a more careful examination must be made of whether the soteriological aspects of Christology belong with it intrinsically, rather than being brought to it in the framework of understanding

28

with which it is approached. In other words, has Pannenberg too narrowly limited soteriology to matters of meaning, at the expense of those aspects of salvation customarily associated more closely with the cross than with the resurrection of Jesus?

INTRINSIC INTELLIGIBILITY

Where has this long discussion of contemporary Christology from below and its historical background taken us? It has been argued that recent claims for the superiority of this method over the supposed alternative fail to take full account of the complexity of the issues involved. We cannot solve the problems inherited from the past simply by a change of method. If we believe that we can, we shall unwittingly repeat the errors attributed to theologians of the past. There are two problems in particular. First is the fact that to begin the process of argument or discovery with immanent phenomena *simpliciter*, whether they be general matters of anthropology or particular facts about Jesus of Nazareth, is no guarantee of freedom from docetism. The humanity of Jesus can be etherialized and disappear from view more easily by this method than by one beginning more straightforwardly in the transcendent. Because it is eternalized rather than conceived as coming from the eternal, the humanity tends to be lost in a process in which too much weight is loaded upon it. By contrast, as reference to the Christology of the Letter to the Hebrews indicated, a more robustly transcendental Christology, holding the immanent and the transcendent in tension, need not fall into this error.

The second problem was noticed by Pannenberg but not solved. Unless there is room for a distinction between Christology and soteriology, between what Jesus is in himself and what he is for us, there is a loss of essential Christian content to a theology. Pannenberg realizes that the weakness of his Kantian predecessors was that they failed to ground the significance of Jesus for salvation in reality; in the way things really are. But what he fails to realize is that his more Hegelian approach contains an equally serious defect. The reason for this is that the salvatory elements of Christology, those features of Jesus's reality which are conceived to set right what is wrong with human life, are precisely those which transcend our immanent forms of life and understanding. Salvation comes from God, and to attempt simply to read it from what is merely immanent may be to impose upon Jesus our time-conditioned estimate of what we feel he ought to be. That happened in the nineteenth century, as Pannenberg realizes, but it happened by virtue of the very features of the method which he wishes to retain.

Accordingly we must conclude that a Christology from below which attempts to evade, or to postpone consideration of, the explicitly theological content of talk about Jesus, has not been shown to be successful. This is especially true at the very place where it claims most stridently to eradicate the weaknesses of traditional Christology. By using the method it is hoped to do justice to a supposedly neglected part of the content of Christology: that Jesus is 'consubstantial' with our humanity, sin apart. But neither is the content better conceived (there is an almost unavoidable docetism) nor is the form of Christian teaching better expressed (the relation of Christology and soteriology is confused, not clarified). The suspicion must remain that claims for the new method are greatly exaggerated, and that the question of Christology from above must therefore also be considered.

Nevertheless, there are, in Pannenberg's theology possibilities for what may be called a purified Christology from below, in which the defects of his over-rationalist approach are avoided. In this respect his work has more to offer than Rahner's, whose overmastering concern, certainly in the earlier work of *Theological Investigations 1* is with the theologian's relationship with the Formula of Chalcedon. While it may be true that some loyalty to the insights contained in the Formula are indispensable to a Christology that is continuous with that of the tradition, such a concern must surely remain secondary to the kind of question Pannenberg asks. Rahner's attempt to develop a conceptuality that is true to Chalcedon appears to be rather abstract, presumably because it must remain an open question whether the Definition is itself true to the biblical Christ.

By contrast, Pannenberg holds that it is on the foundational historical events that theological inquiry must centre. If there is to be a Christology which concerns itself with the theological significance of Jesus of Nazareth, its relation to the story which the New Testament at once tells and expounds must be a prior concern, for the simple reason that, as Pannenberg rightly sees, that is where the traditions about Jesus take their origin. But the question to him is whether his Christology is sufficiently from below. Does he really begin with the New Testament Jesus or, in his haste to fit him into a framework of universal history, does he not himself impose a rational mould 'from above'? Whatever the answer to that question, however, his aim is surely the right one. The central quest of his Christology is for the *intrinsic meaning* of Jesus and his resurrection. His insistence that event and meaning belong together suggests that he is seeking for something that is there, to be found within the history for those who seek. In its turn, this appears to imply that Christology is not an unaided ascent from below, by historical research or any other method. Something is given to one who listens. That is not to suggest that Christology is from above in the almost authoritarian sense that transcendent data or facts are simply given, directly and without mediation. On the contrary, the gift is given in, with and through this-worldly, immanent factors.

Accordingly, the chief methodological question raised by this chapter is that of the relationship between the human mind and that which it seeks to interpret. Christology from below, whether in the form of transcendent anthropology, or of degree Christology or of the employment of a Hegelian framework of meaning, may easily take the form of a denial of the fact that theological knowledge, like all knowledge, must derive at least in part from that which is to be known. Unless the object, in this case God as we claim to know him through Christ, gives himself to be known; unless, further, the events on which we centre our interest have some intrinsic meaning over and above their bare happening within a historical causal nexus, the theologian is open to the charge of simply projecting his wishes or his tradition on to the events, of simply idealizing them. That is the danger of Christology from below, the danger that the form of the procedure will impose its framework on the content, denying the latter the right to shape the form of our knowledge. Hence, far from being *a posteriori* in character, the method can be viciously *a priori* simply in view of the fact that its own ideological commitments are concealed or unacknowledged. Unless something is sought that is there already and able to alter our perception of the subject-matter, we are likely to perceive only what we want to perceive and thus to build a Christology after the pattern of our own alienated humanity.

REFERENCES

Harvey, Van A., 1962, 'A Word in Defence of Schleiermacher's Theological Method' in *Journal of Religion* 42, 151–79.

Herrmann, Wilhelm, *The Communion of the Christian with God. Described on the Basis of Luther's Statements*, Eng. trans. J. Sandys Stanyon.

Kierkegaard, Søren, 1941b, *Training in Christianity*, Eng. trans. Walter Lowrie.

Lash, Nicholas, 'Up and Down in Christology' in *New Studies in Theology I*, eds. Stephen Sykes and Derek Holmes, pp. 31–46.

Nineham, Dennis E., 'Epilogue' in *The Myth of God Incarnate*, ed. John Hick, pp. 186–204.

Pannenberg, Wolfhart, 1968, *Jesus – God and Man*, Eng. trans. Lewis L. Wilkins and Duane A. Priebe.

Pannenberg, Wolfhart, 1976, *Theology and the Philosophy of Science*, Eng. trans. Francis McDonagh.

Rahner, Karl, 1961, *Theological Investigations*, vol. i, Eng. trans. Kevin Smyth.

Rahner, Karl, 1978, *Foundations of Christian Faith: An Introduction to the Idea of Christianity*, Eng. trans. William V. Dych.

Ritschl, Albrecht, 1900, *The Christian Doctrine of Justification and Reconciliation: The Positive Development of the Doctrine*, Eng. trans. eds. H. R. Mackintosh and A. B. Macaulay.

Ritschl, Dietrich, *Memory and Hope: An Inquiry Concerning the Presence of Christ*.

Robinson, John A. T., *The Human Face of God*.

Stevenson, J. (ed)., *Creeds, Councils and Controversies: Documents Illustrative of the History of the Church A.D. 337–461*.

3

CHRISTOLOGY FROM ABOVE

PRELIMINARY CONSIDERATIONS

As we have already seen, Christology from above is the method of doing Christology which is often contrasted with Christology from below. Both descriptions are highly metaphorical, though not necessarily the worse for that. However, metaphors are slippery, and for the sake of clarity the different senses in which this spatial language is used require elucidation. First of all, the metaphor may denote what Pannenberg calls 'the structure of the concepts – the descent of the Son from the world above' in which early Christology was sometimes couched. Here, although Pannenberg proceeds to contrast it with what he believes to be 'the process of development of primitive Christian traditions . . . in the course of which the unity of the man Jesus with God became recognised. . .' (Pannenberg, 1968, p.33), it is clear that we do not here have a matter of method so much as of the kind of language ('mythological'?) in which the events of Jesus's life were expounded. To say that Jesus came 'from above' is to speak of his divine and supratemporal significance in spatial language. It may bear upon, but does not necessarily prescribe, the way in which we come to believe in or argue for his particular significance. We shall, therefore, leave this aspect on one side, and turn to the second way of understanding the matter, which is provided by Albrecht Ritschl.

In his well-known essay on 'Theology and Metaphysics' Ritschl engages in polemics with an opponent who, he says, 'wants to understand the issues "from above", through general concepts, before he gives himself to the scrutiny of individual entities as they actually exist. . . (H)e dealt first with the idea of the Good in general and only subsequently with the Christian idea of Good' (A. Ritschl,

1972, p. 188). We can see that Ritschl's concern is strictly with method. He wishes to dispute any approach to theology that determines, in advance of its discussion of content, the meaning of concepts, and then proceeds to classify or interpret particular facts, persons or events under them in a procrustean manner. How would this apply to matters christological? We might say that Christology from above is the method which begins with a concept of God and his relations to the world and then fits into it the human and historical elements provided by the New Testament. Everything is methodologically determined by the meaning of the word *God*, which is thus supposed to be understood in advance of historical particularities. Thus, for example, if it is true that Arius believed in the absolute simplicity and transcendence of God, it would follow that any other being must necessarily be understood as belonging to the temporal and creaturely realm. Or again, if God is absolutely impassible, he who suffers on the cross either does so merely as human or because he is less than fully God. Here Christology is *conceptually* from above.

It is probable that no theologian who wished to be called Christian has allowed *a priori* philosophical beliefs about God totally to determine his Christology. Those whose names appear in the histories of dogma as 'heretics' may be the ones who were judged to allow this to happen to such an extent that their teaching damaged essential Christian tenets. But there seems little doubt that the dividing line is not completely fixed, and that many who ended on the 'right' side were also often strongly influenced by their philosophical presuppositions. If, therefore, we are to examine examples of this kind of Christology from above, it must be with the help of those considered to be near the borderline, in danger of succumbing to philosophical temptation. Such are, from the ancient and modern worlds respectively, Origen and Hegel. Their work will advance our inquiry into the relation between form and content in Christology, illuminating different aspects of what can be called Christology from above, Type A, in which fundamental concepts, and especially the concept of God, are determined or heavily conditioned by philosophical considerations that operate independently of the particular elements of Christology.

CHRISTOLOGY FROM ABOVE, TYPE A: ORIGEN

'(I)n Christ there is one nature, his deity, because he is the only-begotten Son of the Father, and another human nature, which in very recent times he took upon him to fulfil the divine purpose' (Origen, 1936, p. 15). So goes the central dogmatic assertion of the opening section of the chapter 'Christ' in Book I of Origen's *De Principiis*. The chapter is almost entirely devoted to the 'one nature, his deity', and it proceeds by identifying Christ as the eternal Wisdom of God, existing in some measure of otherness from the Father ('hypostatically'). The stress is on his full and eternal divinity. He is, like the Father, without beginning, and the 'truth and life of all things that exist' (pp. 16f.). It is to be observed that Origen is here not concerning himself with the incarnation, but with the eternal Son's unity with the Father. None the less, it might seem remarkable that none of the ways in which he is described appears to have any reference to the historical events on which Origen's Christian faith is founded. As the divine Wisdom, Christ could not 'possibly possess bodily characteristics. . .' (p. 15), nor with any of the other titles 'is there the least reason to understand anything corporeal. . .' (p. 17). Moreover, the eternal Son is not, in the words of the Letter to the Colossians, 'the image of the invisible God'; rather Origen must gild the lily, making him 'the *in*visible image. . .' (p. 19, cf. p. 110).

Surely here are to be seen traces of that dualism between the sensible and intelligible realms that so vitiated much ancient Christology. If the two worlds are so utterly contrary in nature, it is difficult to bring them together in any way, least of all in a particular historical person. It is, says Origen in his chapter on the incarnation, beyond our capacity to understand 'how this mighty power of the divine majesty . . . can be believed to have existed within the compass of that man who appeared in Judaea. . .' (p. 109). And so he does not so much essay an explanation of how it could happen as provide a speculative scheme of cosmology within which such an event could begin to make sense. All rational creatures, goes the well-known theory, were originally granted by God freedom and a participation in himself. When that freedom was wrongly exercised and 'variety and diversity had taken hold of individual souls',[1] only

---

1 Page 110, another clear echo of the dualism of sensible and intelligible.

the soul to which Jesus laid claim clung to God in indissoluble union. 'This soul, then, acting as a medium between God and the flesh . . . there is born . . . the God-man, the medium being that existence to whose nature it was not contrary to assume a body' (p. 110). Origen affirms that the outcome of this transaction was indeed fully human, with a human soul, though one that was without the possibility of sin (pp. 112f.). But, as in the earlier chapter, there is no real filling out of the doctrine by reference to the ministry, cross and resurrection of Jesus. The incarnation is a historical event, but is conceived rather in abstraction from the gospel accounts of Jesus's life.

Thus, if it is a mark of Christology from above that it prefers to take its content more from *a priori* philosophical or theological considerations than from the particularities of the biblical story, Origen's Christology is rightly so described. And a glance at the work of a number of commentators on the wider features of his thought will serve to confirm the initial impression. The first such feature is the context of Origen's Christology and in particular the cosmological scheme within which the teaching of the *De Principiis* is set. This would appear to have more in common with cyclical theories of history than with biblical eschatology, and has been described by Hans Jonas as 'A "Divine Comedy" of the Universe' (Jonas). Though he rejected the Stoic doctrine that there will be innumerable identical worlds, Origen toyed seriously with the view that ours is but one of a series of similar aeons. Jonas also describes the central principles of Origen's system as being the necessary faultiness of diversity as such, the combination of doctrines of a gnostic 'fall' with those of biblical creation (pp. 311f.), the consubstantiality of all rational creatures including Satan and Christ (p. 315), and the essentially educational conception of Christ's function (p. 322). There is, says Arnold Gilg, to be found in Origen a 'Logos doctrine in the full sense of the term'. There is a strong element of cosmological speculation and 'one can read Plotinus in Origen and Origen in Plotinus' (Gilg, pp. 45f.).

This apparent dependence of Origen upon philosophical speculation is related to a second feature of his theology, the stress upon the divine transcendence and unknowability. 'He regards the nature of the Father as being utterly incomprehensible and transcendent', says Grillmeier (Grillmeier, p. 142). The result of this is that because it is impossible to hold that the Son actually reveals the Father, the place of the Son is determined – from above – by the Neoplatonic scheme. Gilg here cites *Contra Celsum* iii. 34 as evidence that the Logos 'stands between the uncreated and the created . . . the first member in the chain of emanation. . .' (Gilg, p. 46). Harnack's interpretation of two passages from the *De Principiis* is similar: 'From God's standpoint, the Son is the hypostasis appointed by and *subordinated* to him. The Son stands between the uncreated One and the created Many; in so far as unchangeableness is an attribute of self-existence, he does not possess it' (Harnack, p. 357). The testimony of these scholars, then, is that Origen's doctrine of the person of Christ is, at least, heavily influenced by *a priori* metaphysical considerations. He has decided in advance what is and is not theologically possible – as in his parenthetical remark that 'it was not possible for the nature of God to mingle with a body apart from some medium' (Origen, 1936, p. 110) – and has then fitted Christ into the predetermined scheme.

There are also a number of features which provide a third set of reasons for describing Origen as a theorist working from above *a priori*. As we have already seen, he is less interested than he might have been in grounding his Christology in historical events. It is not, as it is for Ignatius, for example, with the historical Jesus Christ that he begins his Christology, but with the eternal Logos. Thus Grillmeier, though he wishes in general to defend Origen's loyalty to Christ's full corporeality, admits that this 'appears to lose its positive significance as a medium of revelation in the view of eternity. . .' and that Origen 'exposed himself to the charge that his system left no room for a full appreciation of the humanity of the Lord' (Grillmeier, pp. 144f., 148). Gilg and Harnack, each representing a different theological position, are less restrained, the former quoting a passage where Origen says that after the resurrection 'he ceased to be a man',[2] and the latter a number of passages from the *Contra Celsum* indicating that the historical, incarnate Logos is no longer of any account to the gnostic.[3] Christ, for Origen, he says, is 'no longer a person, but the symbol of the various

2 *Nunc homo esse cessavit.* Gilg, p. 47, citing *in Luc. hom.* 29.
3 Harnack, p. 342. The passages are *Contra Celsum* iii, 61, cf. ii, 66, 9; iv, 15, 8; vi, 68, cf. Harnack, p. 369: 'The whole "humanity" of the redeemer together with its history finally disappears from the eyes of the perfect one.'

redemptions' (Harnack, p. 369). This, to repeat, is not the whole story about Origen, only an attempt to show how much of his Christology has a very *a priori* air: '. . . though the construction of his theory proceeded from the top downwards, he could find support for it on the steps of the *regula fidei*, already developed by Irenaeus . . .' (Harnack, p. 343).

The irony of Origen's position is that there is in it, as Grillmeier has pointed out, also an element of movement from below in the account of the believer's order of knowing. The manhood of Christ is the starting-point of the ascent for the Christian, despite the fact that has already been mentioned, that with the progress of the ascent the humanity becomes more and more transparent (Grillmeier, p. 143). Thus it becomes apparent that Christology from above, at least in one of its manifestations, is far from being an alternative to Christology from below. The movement from above is a movement of thought from eternity to time in which the temporal particulars are firmly subordinated to the initial theological scheme. But corresponding to this movement and answering to it is the movement whereby the believer may ascend from what Origen clearly believes to be an inferior form of belief, that in Christ as crucified, to the more elevated belief in Christ as the Logos:

> Some have faith in that Reason which was in the beginning and was with God and was God. . . A second class are those who know nothing but Jesus Christ and him crucified, considering that the Word made flesh is the whole Word, and knowing Christ after the flesh. Such is the great multitude of those who are counted believers (Origen, 1897, p. 324).

The misuse of Paul, who plainly saw the necessity of knowing *nothing but* Christ and him crucified (1 Cor. 2), is apparent. In *Contra Celsum* iii. 62 there appears to be a similar distinction between different types of believers in which the higher class is conceived to have outgrown some aspects of Christ's saving activity. 'The divine Logos was sent as a physician to sinners, but to those already pure and no longer sinning as a teacher of divine mysteries.' Here is a 'degree anthropology' by means of which believers are placed within a kind of pyramid or on the steps of a ladder.

In Origen, then, we have Christology from above in the theologian's movement or thought, from the abstract to the concrete. But we have also Christology from below in the true believer's progress in the faith as he moves from belief in the incarnate to belief in the eternal Word. This latter movement is not in all ways the same as that found in modern Christology from below but has, none the less, much in common with it. For both movements wish to begin in the here and now and to achieve in the movement upwards some grasp of Jesus Christ's eternal significance. It may also be possible to see something in common between Origen's Christology from above and much modern Christology from below, in so far as exponents of the latter, too, begin where they do for philosophical reasons, reasons often derived from contemporary thought. In them, as in Origen, the movement from below is shaped by the conceptual framework in which it is believed Christology must take form. There is thus a reciprocity of content and method in which features of both movements mingle in a very complex manner. At least the example of Origen should make us cautious of an oversimple contrast between the two supposed methods, and between ancient and modern Christology.

But it is where ancient and modern do differ that we begin to put our finger on the moments of truth in the positions of those who would contrast modern Christology from below with ancient Christology from above. The difference is to be found in the contrast between the world after Plato and the world after Kant. Heirs of the former – and that means, without denying the influence of other philosophers, almost all the Fathers of Christian theology – believed in the existence of an eternal world which could be known. Heirs of the latter – and that means all modern theologians in the West – either do not believe in such a world, or have to fight for the means to express the belief they have. This is true also of those who would, like Pannenberg, learn from Hegel, for Hegel's eternal is very difficult to distinguish from the world of the mind or consciousness. His metaphysic, such as it is, is very much a metaphysic of immanence, widely different from that upon which Origen could draw. A glance at his Christology should at once aid our understanding of theologians like Pannenberg and provide further important insights into the relation of form and content in Christology.

ELEMENTS OF HEGEL'S CHRISTOLOGY

Hegel is often seen as a paradigm case of a philosopher who lops off the vital limbs of Christology in order to make it fit his procrustean bed. In the sense that he is often supposed to carry a heavy *a priori* philosophical load, his might appear to be Christology from above *par excellence*, at least in the conceptual form that is being examined in these opening sections. But he is also interesting for other reasons, not least his intellectual brilliance and concern for the proper relation of form and content in the approach to human knowledge (Barth, 1972, p. 393). Moreover, like Origen, he both protested his orthodoxy (Taylor, p. 493) and has some claim to be a – though not the – father of both orthodoxy and heresy in subsequent theology. He is undoubtedly a determinative figure in the development of modern liberal theology, and J. N. Findlay ascribes to him rather than to Kant the title of 'father of "modernism"' (Findlay, p. 139). On the other side, his contributions to the thought of such theologians as P. T. Forsyth and Karl Barth have yet to be assessed. More directly interesting for our purposes is that although his Christology is conceptually and methodologically from above in the sense we learned from Ritschl, it is also, in being based in a philosophy of immanence, psychologically and methodologically from below.

Hegel's *Phenomenology of Spirit* traces the progress of the reflective spirit from its first naive experience of perception to its final outcome in pure philosophical knowledge. Religion is treated towards the end of the process, and is thus regarded as one of the higher functions of reflection. But it is itself, according to Hegel's method, divided into three, with Christianity at the head, providing a synthesis of two more naive conceptions of religion that precede it. Christianity is thus for Hegel revealed or absolute religion, at once synthesizing and raising to a higher level the lower forms – the naive consciousness of natural religion and the slightly more self-conscious activity of artistic expression. This *Aufhebung* is described as follows: 'Through the religion of Art spirit has passed from the form of substance into that of Subject. . .' (Hegel, 1949, p. 750). By this Hegel means that reflection has moved from believing that God is a substance other than itself to a realization that he is in some sense continuous with itself. There is no transcendent, 'other', God, who is thus held to be 'dead' (p. 753). But this conviction that God and the subject of reflection are one and the same is still held in a prephilosophical form. Spirit *as such*, as it really is, is not yet present to consciousness: 'The mystery of bread and wine is not yet the mystery of flesh and blood' (p. 728). Only with the incarnation does the rational truth underlying religion begin to come to expression. Hegel describes this belief as follows:

> That Absolute Spirit has taken on the shape of self-consciousness inherently, and therefore also consciously to itself – this appears now as the belief of the world, the belief that spirit exists *in fact* as a definite self-consciousness, i.e. as an actual human being; that spirit is an object for immediate experience; that the believing mind *sees*, *feels* and *hears* this divinity (p. 757).

It should be noticed that this is not so much a statement of the doctrine of the incarnation as of the fact that some such doctrine came to be believed. Hegel is not stating a doctrine that is held to be true independently of the consciousness of the believer: it is a truth of the rational consciousness. Something happened objectively, to be sure, but not in history apart from the minds of those who held the belief. There is revelation, but only in a sense that is carefully circumscribed: 'Its being revealed obviously consists in this, that what it is, is known' (p. 758). Revelation consists ('obviously') not in something God does as a being other than the one who receives the revelation, but in the fact that there is an instance of human knowledge. It is thus not a transcendent gift or impartation, but a happening entirely immanent in human mental development.

There is little doubt that according to Ritschl's definition this is a Christology from above. And if we compare it with Origen's account, similarities will appear. Just as the Alexandrian showed little interest in the life of Jesus, so it is with Hegel. Despite a youthful attempt to write a life of Jesus, he came eventually to regard such enterprises as a waste of time. 'Hegel can almost literally . . . dismiss all critical-historical prying into the biography of the historical God-man as a "spiritless" pursuit' (Crites, p. 45). In the end, he is only interested in the philosophical expression of the theological content and meaning of what came to intellectual realization through Jesus. This is precisely the kind of theology to which

Ritschl took exception. And yet, considered in terms of its cultural and psychological starting-point, it is almost a paradigm case of Christology from below. The development of the doctrine of the incarnation is understood as the product of human thought and culture, not as response to some transcendent initiative but in terms of spirit's own immanent self-development. In fact, Hegel's programme is to transmute the former into the latter. 'When the death of the mediator is grasped by the self, this means the sublation (*Aufhebung*) of his factuality, of his particular independent existence; this particular self-existence has become universal self-consciousness' (p. 781). No more than Origen did Hegel wish to deny the factuality of Jesus. *Aufhebung* means, rather, the taking up of the factuality into a higher synthesis. Whether its reality is thereby abolished or allowed to retain its full force is the question to be asked of both theologians. In our terms it has to be asked whether the content is expressed or suppressed by the theological method and form.

We have, then, attempted to look at Christology from above through the writings of two philosopher-theologians who appear to conform to Ritschl's account of the method. They are both massive figures who stand on the borders of Christian orthodoxy and, though from differing perspectives, share a drive to philosophical systematization. But Hegel is a modern thinker in the way that Origen is not. While Origen's metaphysical scheme is objective, purporting to describe objective transcendent realities, Hegel is the heir to the Cartesian emphasis upon the self as the beginning of thought. Whatever in general is his success in evading the problems he saw in Kant and the Enlightenment, he has not altered things in this respect. Rather, the Enlightenment's tendency to divinize the human mind has here come to full flower. Christology is Hegel's expression of this doctrine: 'The idea of spirit means the unity of divine and human nature . . . Spirit is accordingly the living process by which the implicit unity of divine and human natures becomes actual and comes to have a definite existence' (Hegel, 1895, p. 349).

In this respect, Hegel's philosophy represents a modern (immanent) version of one major stream of Greek philosophy, which contains a tradition of thinkers who relate or even identify the human mind and the divine. It is here that we may be justified in seeing the link between Hegel and Origen. How far is it possible to see in Origen's conception of the hierarchy of types of belief and in the Hegelian progress of the spirit different versions of the same ascent of the human to divinity? Or, to put it differently, how near are we in the thought of both these speculative minds to the idea of the ascent from the material to the non-material and spiritual that is associated with the thought of Origen's near contemporary, Plotinus?

Such inquiries are not simply speculative, for they raise the related question of whether in some of its forms Christology from below, and especially degree Christology with its implied scale of reality, repeats the characteristics of Neoplatonism. If it does so, it is in characteristically modern form: the ascent without the preceding or corresponding movement of the transcendent from above. It is, as we have seen, Rahner's insistence on traditional dogmatic formulations, that preserves his theology from what would otherwise be, and has in others become, a Christology of a divinized man. But Pannenberg's attempt to move strictly from below and the Hegelian background to his thought must make him liable to some such outcome.

Thus the overall picture is a very complex one, with no clear difference between Christology from above and Christology from below yet emerging. To attempt to find one we must seek a definition of the former less in matters of philosophy and method but more in terms of the theological content of the theologian's 'psychological' or factual starting-point.

CHRISTOLOGY FROM ABOVE, TYPE B

Pannenberg's preoccupation with strictly historical procedures leads him to hold that christological method should reproduce the process by which beliefs about the divinity of Jesus came to be held in the early Church. We must begin as they did with Jesus as a man and move in thought to descriptions of him as divine. 'The historical process . . . in the course of which the unity of the man Jesus with God became recognized, runs counter to the kind of concepts that speak of God's becoming man' (Pannenberg, 1968, p. 33). However, we are here presented with a problem, for it has not usually been so.

43

Christology 'from above' was far more common in the ancient Church, beginning with Ignatius of Antioch and the second-century Apologists. It became determinative for the further history of Christology, particularly in the form of the Alexandrian Christology of Athanasius in the fourth century and of Cyril in the fifth century. . . . The christological procedure 'from above to below' is followed in modern Protestant dogmatics by Karl Barth especially.[4]

Methodologically, that is to say, the tradition beginning with Ignatius and represented in the modern era by Barth moves *from* rather than *towards* explicitly theological judgements about Jesus. This is what we shall mean by Christology from above, Type B. Despite what Pannenberg sometimes suggests, it does not entail beginning with a fully-fledged doctrine of the incarnation or of the Trinity. It is possible, for example, to begin with a relatively informed confession of faith ('Jesus is Lord') and move from there to a full doctrine of the incarnation and the Trinity. Clearly, the objections Pannenberg makes against those who attempt to support a confession of faith by historical research indicate that this, too, is for him Christology from above (see above, p. 20). Any explicitly theological premiss will be such that the procedure based upon it will be methodologically 'from above'.

This general definition of Christology from above, Type B, makes a number of clarifications possible. First, it provides a clear contrast with that method which begins with the findings of historical research alone. While the latter operates with purely empirical premisses – albeit premisses interpreted in the light of an idealist theory of meaning – Christology from above operates with premisses which already attach some theological significance or confession of faith to the Jesus of history. Second, it gives Christology something to

---

4 Page 33. A sentence omitted from that passage of Pannenberg reads as follows: 'The structure of these' [namely the New Testament] 'concepts – the descent of the Son from the world above – is the opposite of that we can gather from the process of the development of Christian traditions.' It scarcely needs to be pointed out that the structure of concepts – in this case the use of pictorial spatial metaphors – is a different matter from that of method. The point about Christology from above in this sense is that it begins *methodologically* with statements containing some form of theological assertion, with statements of faith or dogma about the divine significance of Jesus. Christology from above in this sense could be done without any metaphors of descent or ascent.

do. If, as Pannenberg suggests, Christology from above began with a fully worked out theology of the incarnation, it is difficult to see where an argument would lead, except in the production of other statements by logical deduction – a procedure possibly adopted by some medieval theologians, but certainly not by any of those Pannenberg lists as representing this approach. A less explicit definition of Christology from above therefore allows both for differences between it and Christology from below and for the variety of argument and development that are revealed by representatives of the former method. Thus the method Pannenberg rejects can be seen to begin typically with a relatively unformed statement or confession of the meaning of Jesus as Lord or Saviour, which it then expands, supports and justifies in the way that seems appropriate. We can say that Christology from above in this sense might well take the form of faith seeking understanding; of a quest for rational expression and justification of something already believed on other grounds.

The first discovery we make if we examine the matter in this way is that in this case, too, we find that it is not possible to find a Christology that is 'from above' *tout court*. Let us begin by looking at the first authors to put down their thoughts about Jesus. In the general sense of Christology from above, all of the New Testament writers come under its rubric. None of them appears to use the life of Jesus as the premiss of an argument for his divinity. They write only because they already believe in it, or at the very least in his close link with the God of Israel. This is manifestly true of Paul, the Johannine literature and the Letter to the Hebrews, as few will dispute. But, while it would be false to claim that there is anything like an explicit doctrine of the incarnation in the Synoptic Gospels, their authors, too, only write because they already believe that there is something theologically significant – and therefore from above in the sense it is being used in this section – about Jesus. Thus Luke's opening chapters prepare the way for 'thy salvation which thou hast prepared in the presence of all peoples' (Luke 2.30f.), while Mark describes Jesus as the Son of god in the eleventh, and possibly the first, verse of his Gospel; and in the closing verses of Matthew, the Son is placed alongside the Father and the Spirit as the name into which converts were to be baptized. (We are not at this stage concerned with the nature and status of such claims as Jesus made

45

for himself, but rather with the doctrines and assumptions of the gospel writers.)

These writers, then, operate with what must be called Christology from above. They write because they believe in the divine significance of Jesus and in order to commend their beliefs to others. It would be absurd to suggest that their theological content is derived from a process of argument beginning from the humanity of Jesus. Both psychologically and methodologically they operate from above. They are also, however, proceeding from below, if by that is understood the fact that they are writing about Jesus of Nazareth, the human being that they or some of their informants had known 'after the flesh'. Once again we are compelled to distinguish what Pannenberg has confused. Historically, the New Testament grew because of what happened in the life and fate of a human being. But its writers all operate from a belief which they developed after the resurrection in the transcendent significance of that human being.

It has been necessary to begin with the New Testament books in order to avoid an oversimplistic contrast between them and subsequent theology. In this respect, despite the fact that they are not the same kind of writings as those that followed them, they are continuous with the beginnings of Christian theology proper. Ignatius and his successors are in some ways doing different things from Paul and Mark. They are answering different kinds of question and serving different needs, often being concerned to defend the teaching they have received from what they believe to be distortions. But in beginning their thought about Jesus in a confession of faith in his divine and saving significance they are in no way different. A passage from Ignatius cited by Grillmeier provides an early and excellent illustration of the theme. It is Christology from above in the sense that it is openly theological. But that is not seen as a denial of the fact that theological expression derives *historically* from an earthly human life. The passage is from Ignatius's *Letter to the Ephesians*:

> There is only one physician – of flesh, yet spiritual, born yet unbegotten, God incarnate, genuine life in the midst of death, sprung from Mary as well as God, first subject to suffering then beyond it – Jesus Christ our Lord (Ignatius, p. 9G).

The translation misses some of the point of the antithetical expres-

46

sion. For example, the bald 'God incarnate' would, rendered literally, be 'in flesh becoming/God', in parallel with 'of flesh/of spirit', etc.

Ignatius provides an interesting study, not only for the simplicity and directness of his thought but for the contrast he offers to the Christology of Origen and Hegel which tends to swallow up into philosophical abstraction the historical reality of Jesus. 'The thought of Ignatius, directed to the historical (*geschichtlichen*) Christ . . . is dominated by the simple identity of the historical with the post-existing Lord. . .' (Gilg, pp. 14f.). That is not to deny the difference between his theology and that of the New Testament writers. 'Three times in John we find the designation "God" for Christ, in Ignatius it is already quite frequent' (Grillmeier, p. 87). Methodologically, however, there is little difference. The content is being further specified, and rightly or wrongly the dogmatic description of Jesus as God is coming to the centre. As the first representative of Pannenberg's category, Ignatius has been rightly classified.

Here two further points can be made, the first fairly briefly. It is that Pannenberg is as half-correct about the last member of his list as he is about the first. He has, as has been pointed out by Nicholas Lash, failed to understand what is happening in the Christology of Barth that he describes so naively (Lash, p. 36). 'The New Testament obviously speaks of Jesus Christ in both these ways: the one looking and moving, as it were, from above downwards, the other from below upwards' (Barth, *Church Dogmatics* iv/1, p. 135). The point could also be illustrated from Barth's discussion of revelation in the first volume of the *Church Dogmatics*. God reveals himself *to* men through the *humanity* of Christ (Barth, *Church Dogmatics* i/1, p. 323). For Barth theology is rooted in faith, and therefore works from above. But faith derives from immanent, worldly events, which are indeed susceptible to investigation by historical research, even though they do not give up their theological treasures simply by such means.

The second point brings us nearer to the heart of what is at stake here. If we look forward from Ignatius to Origen and the later Alexandrians, what do we find? First of all, there is a clear continuity. During a process of increasing specification through controversy Ignatius's straightforward christological assertions are replaced by an increasingly technical language, which *intends to say the same thing*. Scholars like Grillmeier can plausibly trace a straight line of development from the New Testament through to Chalcedon. And yet, second, it is clear that in some respects things have changed. An intention to be true to the basic credal propositions of the Christian faith, for example those of the story of salvation in the Apostles' Creed, by no means guarantees success in Christology. In fact it was not the creed that separated the different parties in the christological controversies of the early centuries. They disagreed not on that but on its implications for a Christian view of Christ and salvation (Meijering).

A simplistic view of the matter would hold that the problem was the use of philosophical or ontological terms, or of Greek language for a supposedly Hebraic gospel. However, the opposition of Greek and Hebrew is now almost everywhere conceded to be an impossible way of viewing the development of doctrine. Judaism and Hellenism were not two hermetically sealed systems, but rather all Christian linguistic usage of the time would develop in a world in which numerous streams of culture and influence were operating. But was it a mistake to use philosophical conceptuality at all? To this question only brief answers can be given here, though in a sense the whole of the book is meant to be a kind of answer. The first consideration takes the form of a counter-question. What other language could they use when attempting either to guard against conceptions which they held to falsify the Christian gospel to or answer the sceptical questions of educated pagans like Celsus? It was a matter of being responsible for the truth and credibility of what was believed. And this leads us to the second consideration against the suggestion that ontological or metaphysical language is inappropriate for the nature of the message. It is that all languages and systems of concepts, even those that attempt to avoid explicit ontology, carry ontological implications or presuppose some view of reality. In that sense ontology is unavoidable, especially for those who would dabble, as writers about Christology must, in matters such as history, time, humanity and God.

And so the problem does have something to do with the relation of philosophy and theology, even if not in the simplistic way that is sometimes suggested. As Meijering has pointed out, the Fathers were mostly Platonists who were not so much interpreting the creed and the Bible *for* their time as *from* it. The difference is an important one, and very instructive for contemporary theology, anxious as it is to be relevant to contemporary concerns. To hold that the Fathers interpreted *for* their time suggests too much that they were on a pedestal, elevated above the culture and thinking of their contemporaries. They were, rather, a part of it, and as a part of Hellenistic culture expressed their understanding of the person of Christ *from within* it. But it was an understanding of Christ which intended to be true to Bible and creed, not simply an understanding of philosophical culture (Meijering, p. 145).

It is here that the question of theology and philosophy can best be understood. As sharers in the tradition of Plato, the Fathers would be bound to use the language of the tradition, but not necessarily in the same way in which others used it. The term *homoousios* is a case in point: its use, Meijering claims, is incompatible with the mainstream of Platonism (p. 125). But the possibility is always there that, once used, the language will, so to speak, float loose of its historical moorings in the life and fate of Jesus of Nazareth. It has already been suggested that this is the tendency implicit in the Christology of Origen, who seems to have felt little need to fill out his systematic Christology with data culled from accounts of Jesus's life. A similar point is made by Meijering in speaking of Cyril of Alexandria's difference from the Platonists:

> They would not have identified the second Principle with Jesus of Nazareth. Cyril obviously believed that it is enough to show that the Platonists could have believed in the possibility of the second Principle incarnating itself in *a* man; the fact that this man was Jesus of Nazareth is of secondary importance to him. This shows that Cyril's theological system did not start with Jesus of Nazareth, but with a preconceived philosophical-theological scheme into which he fitted Jesus of Nazareth (p. 126).

That a charge of this kind can be made against Cyril gives reasons for being suspicious about Christology from above. But the same suspicions arise with the Christologies of Rahner and Pannenberg! The lesson to be learned is that also within the approach called Christology from above, Type B, there are differences to be found. The differences are not always easy to discern, but they have much to do with the way language is used and with its relation to the historical Jesus of Nazareth. Cyril's commitment to the humanity of the Saviour is unquestioned. What is a cause for suspicion is whether he really needs this particular humanity to say some of the things that he does.[5]

Another aspect of this very complicated matter of philosophy and theology is illustrated by the differences between Athanasius and Arius. Both operated with a Christology from above, and both wished to be true to both creed and Scripture. What, then, was the difference between them? It was *not* that one was a Platonist and the other not. It was rather that Arius appears to have undermined both the humanity and the divinity of Christ by making him a *tertium quid*, whereas Athanasius for various reasons did not do so.[6] But one should not for that reason overemphasize the difference between them. As Professor Stead has suggested, the difference derives from the fact that Athanasius, in his concern for the position of the Son, is willing to do violence to his inherited philosophical dualism (Stead, 1964, p. 23). The platonism and dualism are there, but are modified under the impact of what he believes to be the heart of the Christian gospel.

The outcome of this discussion of what happened after Ignatius is that it is no longer possible to define exactly between Types A and B of Christology from above. The reason is that it is not always easy to be certain whether a Christology is so determined by *a priori* philosophical conceptions that it is no longer Christian. The disputed places of both Arius and Origen in the history of Christian thought bear witness to this. Further, one type of Christology can slip over into the other. Yet again, the distinction, even where it can be clearly applied, is not co-terminous with that between orthodoxy and heterodoxy. One may hold firmly to both the divinity and the humanity of Christ and yet produce a doctrine strangely abstract from the concrete history of salvation. (Similarly, as we have seen, and shall see again in Chapter 5, Christology from below can produce classically heterodox conceptions of Christ.) Whatever else we have seen, it is surely that Pannenberg's distinction between

5 Not all interpreters of Cyril would accept Meijering's view of the matter. But that is not the main point at issue here.

6 I am here relying on a recent (so far unpublished) paper by S. G. Hall which seems successfully to have undermined the thesis argued by R. C. Gregg and D. E. Groh.

two ways of doing Christology produces a gross oversimplification of very complex issues.

And yet Pannenberg's listing together of figures from Ignatius to Barth is not in all respects mistaken. They do have something in common, and that is a concern methodologically to link Christology and soteriology. Ignatius speaks of 'one physician'; Barth of the Son who goes into a far country to achieve reconciliation between God and man. Because both see in the human life of Jesus the way by which God has restored human life to wholeness, their theology has the distinctive character that it does, as a particular kind of Christology from above. It is for this reason that human and divine belong together from the beginning in their christological thinking. They are concerned not to abstract from this centre in coming to terms with what they believe to be the truth about Jesus Christ. It is when philosophical and cosmological speculation (in the patristic period) and apologetic concern to prove something on the basis of what can be known about Jesus (in the modern period) expel this consideration from the centre that imbalance occurs. Of course, there are different conceptions of salvation, too. But it is surely significant that one of the issues between Athanasius and Arius was the matter of soteriology, whatever be the outcome of the debate about the nature of the latter's conception. Christology from above in this sense retains its orientation because it believes that Jesus's importance derives from his saving significance, and it is this that requires discussion of Christology that is from the beginning theological in content. But it is theology that is also bound up with the historical and human Jesus.

SOME PROVISIONAL CONCLUSIONS

Despite Pannenberg's failure to establish a clear difference between two methods of doing Christology, it is evident that modern Christology has to be different. We are not, for the most part, Platonists any more, in that it is a fact of modern culture that belief in a transcendent world can no longer be assumed in the way that it could when ancient Christology was being formed and debated. Does that mean that we cannot adopt for our own the classical expressions of the reality of Christ? If it does, we are in grave difficulties in view of the fact that the content of Christology is so closely related to its form, as we have seen. And if the form of Christology can no longer achieve the harnessing together of Christology from above (the inseparable and unconfusable theological content) and Christology from below (the content deriving from Jesus of Nazareth) it is doubtful whether it retains the same content. That is the measure of the crisis of modern Christianity since the Enlightenment destroyed the synthesis of reason and history that made Christendom possible.

As soon, however, as this characterization of the difference between ancient and modern is made, it has to be qualified. There are a number of reasons why it is wrong to posit an absolute difference between the culture of the Fathers and that produced by the Enlightenment. The first is the general point that the philosophy of Descartes, Kant and Hegel, against whose background modern systematic theology must be done, is not wholly new. It is new in the preoccupation with the immanent which it has spawned, but not in its dualism. The dualism of the ancient and modern contexts of theology will be the topic of a later chapter. Second, we have seen that there is much in common between modern Christology from below and the approach to knowledge characteristic of Platonism. The latter took the form of an ascent from earthly and temporal realities to the eternal framework of being believed to underlie them. This is very evident in Origen, and is to some extent repeated in Hegel. Accordingly, an approach to modern conditions must take into account similarities as well as differences. Kant observed that the metaphysical urge was unavoidable: what he denied was that it achieved the kind of results often claimed in the past. The outcome has been a quest to construe transcendent realities as a function or epiphenomenon of this-worldly ones, and, accordingly, Jesus's significance as a function of time and process. But post-Kantian philosophies of immanence are no more true by definition than was the Platonism of earlier times, and the question for theology remains the same: how may authentic Christology be found not *in terms of* philosophies of immanence but *in their context*?

This leads us to a third point, that *the same kind of* problems arise in the relations between philosophy and theology as arose in patristic times. If it is inevitable that we use some kind of conceptuality in speaking of Christ, Christology will draw upon the contemporary stock of language. And the pitfalls will be similar. It is significant here that the logic of degree Christology tends to produce, from below (though philosophically from above!) the same kind of Christ as that produced by Arius from above: a *tertium quid*, neither fully man because he is so superior to us, nor fully God, or only so by virtue of his superiority of immanent virtue. Degree Christology is inverted Arianism, or docetism from below: a divinized man rather than a humanized Logos. Similar problems arise when we consider the way in which our present christological language is tied to the past reality of Jesus of Nazareth. We saw how a failure to tie the two vitiated the Christology of Origen and possibly also that of Cyril. It is precisely the same with modern Christology that bases itself upon philosophies of immanence. Some time ago I wrote of *The Human Face of God* that its author, J. A. T. Robinson, 'appears to hold that the word "Christ" can be given a self-evident meaning independent of Jesus, whatever the status of the latter in bringing out the full meaning of the word: a sort of "natural Christology" ' (Gunton, 1973, p. 486). A Christology that is avowedly a degree Christology operating from below reproduces the methodological features of some ancient Christology from above.

What, then, is the main difference between the ancient and modern contexts of Christology? It is that whereas ancient thought tended to abstract Jesus Christ from history by eternalizing him – by making him, as human, a timeless theophany – modern thought tends to abstract him from eternity by making his temporality absolute. A christological method that is excessively from above runs the first risk; one excessively from below, the second. One makes eternity absolute, the other time. Both methods, made absolute, determine the content and falsify the subject-matter. Thus there are moments of truth in the arguments of proponents of both views. But, then, the main question repeats itself. How far may the element of Christology from above be retained in the midst of modern immanentist culture? That is the question for the remainder of the book. Its answer has already been anticipated in what was taken from Pannenberg in Chapter 2. Such solution as is possible must derive from a search for elements of intrinsic intelligibility in the biblical portrayal of Christ, elements that enable us to bring together both time and eternity, immanence and transcendence. Our path must, then, begin with an examination of some aspects of the interpretation of biblical Christology. Are there any features of the

New Testament's witness to Jesus that enable us to hold together both elements of what have hitherto been held to be an authentic Christology?

REFERENCES

Barth, Karl, 1972, *Protestant Theology in the Nineteenth Century: Its Background and History*, Eng. trans. Brian Cozens and John Bowden.

Barth, Karl, *Church Dogmatics*, Eng. trans. eds. G. W. Bromiley and T. F. Torrance.

Crites, Stephen D., *In the Twilight of Christendom. Hegel vs. Kierkegaard on Faith and History*.

Findlay, J. N., *Hegel: A Re-examination*.

Gilg, Arnold, *Weg und Bedeutung der altkirchlichen Christologie*.

Gregg, Robert C. and Groh, Dennis E., *Early Arianism: A View of Salvation*.

Grillmeier, Aloys, *Christ in Christian Tradition*, vol. i, *From the Apostolic Age to Chalcedon*, 2ᵉ revised, Eng. trans. John Bowden.

Gunton, Colin E., 1973, Review of J. A. T. Robinson, *The Human Face of God* in *Theology* lxxvi, 486–7.

Harnack, Adolf von, *History of Dogma*, vol. ii, Eng. trans. N. Buchanan from 3ᵉ German.

Hegel, G. W. F., 1895, *Lectures on the Philosophy of Religion*, vol. ii, Eng. trans. E. B. Speirs and J. B. Sanderson.

Hegel, G. W. F., 1949, *The Phenomenology of Mind*, Eng. trans. J. B. Baillie.

Ignatius of Antioch, 'The Letter to the Ephesians', ed. Cyril C. Richardson, *The Early Christian Fathers*. Library of Christian Classics, vol. i, pp. 87–93.

Jonas, Hans, 'Origen's Metaphysics of Free Will, Fall and Salvation: A "Divine Comedy" of the Universe' in *Philosophical Essays: From Ancient Creed to Technological Man*, pp. 305–23.

Lash, Nicholas, 'Up and Down in Christology' in *New Studies in Theology I*, eds. Stephen Sykes and Derek Holmes, pp. 31–46.

Meijering, E. P., *God Being History: Studies in Patristic Philosophy*.

Origen, 1897, *Origen's Commentary on the Gospel of John*, Eng. trans. Allan Menzies. Ante-Nicene Christian Library, additional volume.

Origen, 1936, *Origen's 'On First Principles': Being Koetscham's Text of 'De Principiis'*, Eng. trans. G. W. Butterworth.

Origen, 1953, *Contra Celsum*, Eng. trans. and ed. Henry Chadwick.

Pannenberg, Wolfhart, 1968, *Jesus – God and Man*, Eng. trans. Lewis L. Wilkins and Duane A. Priebe.

Ritschl, Albrecht, 1972, 'Theology and Metaphysics. Towards Rapprochement and Defence' in *Three Essays*, Eng. trans. Philip Hefner, pp. 151–212.

Robinson, John A. T., *The Human Face of God*.

Stead, G. C., 1964, 'The Platonism of Arius' in *Journal of Theological Studies*, 15, 16–31.

Taylor, Charles, *Hegel*.

4

THE FORM OF NEW TESTAMENT
CHRISTOLOGY AND ITS EMPLOYMENT IN
MODERN CHRISTOLOGY

METHOD IN CHRISTOLOGY AND THE NEW TESTAMENT

Much has been written in recent years on the subject of New Testament Christology. This chapter does not propose to rehearse the main areas of debate, but to attempt to find a way to give the theme of this book orientation towards this part of its legacy from the past. A particular view will be taken of what New Testament Christology is, and in its light there will be discussion of the way in which it is appropriate for it to contribute to the construction of systematic Christology. Inevitably this will involve the anticipation of topics such as that concerning the relation of faith and history. But in the main the focus will be on the epistemological and methodological aspects of the topic.

We shall begin by taking up again questions raised in Pannenberg's approach to Christology. We saw that for him Christology must begin in straightforward historical research, about whose possibilities he is optimistic, generating what would be called a 'conservative' account even of the historicity of the resurrection (Pannenberg, 1968, pp. 88ff.). But his approach is not simply historical-critical, for it is done in the light of a Hegelian theory of meaning in which the individual items of history are interpreted as parts of a whole; what he calls universal history. The bearing of such a theory on the New Testament documents is seen through the focus of the history of the transmission of traditions. The texts bear witness to their place in a history of interpretation within the wider horizon of universal history, whose meaning is understood by anticipation in the light of the resurrection. Christology, the inquiry into what Jesus was, is the discipline by which the process of interpretation within tradition is traced from its beginnings in the life of Jesus of Nazareth through to the acknowledgement of his oneness with God.

There will be widespread disagreement about the nature of Pannenberg's programme, and certainly about his Hegelian epistemology. But that there was some kind of development within the tradition is surely now beyond dispute. Christology began, as a matter of historical fact, with the man Jesus of Nazareth. That is the unavoidable moment of truth in the arguments of those who advocate Christology from below. But we are then bound to ask about the precise nature of the 'below', particularly in relation to the documents which mediate the historical beginnings of Christology. What view or views of it do they have, and how is that related to our contemporary christological enterprises? Once again we shall find that questions of content, form and method are bound up together.

THE HISTORICAL JESUS?

The view advocated by Pannenberg, and adopted by many others, particularly in Anglo-Saxon theology, is that Christology is primarily a matter of who and what Jesus was. It is thus primarily a historical exercise, concerned with discovering from the New Testament a number of facts about Jesus on the basis of which we can ascribe to him some saving or especial significance. Christology from below begins with the historical Jesus, and moves from there to any other articles of belief about him.

It should be noted from the outset that this kind of claim is different from a statement that Christology began as a result of what happened with Jesus of Nazareth. Here we must draw a clear distinction between two different meanings of 'the historical Jesus'. The first of them constitutes a reference to the human being who lived in Palestine during the first few decades of what has since come to be called the Christian era. It is with this life that the Christian Church and its intellectual enterprise known as Christology began. It must be said that even those New Testament writers who show little interest in the details of that life, and more concern

57

with expounding its dogmatic and ethical significance, still centre their Christology upon it. Thus J. D. G. Dunn: 'For Paul the Jesus of history is integral to his soteriology; it is of vital significance for Paul that Jesus actually lived and died in history' (Dunn, 1974, p. 126). The second meaning of 'the historical Jesus' refers not so much to the man as to the facts about him that can be garnered by historical research.

The distinction may appear to be of very little import, but there is in fact a world of difference, consisting in large part in the distinction between the historical (factual) figure, Jesus of Nazareth and the statements which may be made about him as a result of historical research. The difference is indicated by the fact that it is not a contradiction to hold that the factual figure may not be discovered by historical-critical methods, but that he may be by other ones. It is not logically necessary that the historical Jesus should be discovered by the methods of secular historiography alone. All depends upon who the historical Jesus was (or *is*), for facts may only be discovered by methods appropriate to their nature. It is for this reason that there is a continuing debate about the value and success of the quest of the historical Jesus, by which is meant an attempt to discover by historiography the truth about his life. The debate has thrown up a number of different positions, some of the chief of which are as follows.

1   Wide currency has been given this century to the view that the quest of the historical Jesus is self-defeating. By this is meant that it can be shown in a number of ways that *as a matter of fact* the quest has failed. This theory can in its turn be subdivided into (*a*) the view associated with Weiss and Schweitzer that a rigorous application of historical method undermines rather than supports the Christology which the earlier representatives of the quest hoped to develop and (*b*) the view associated with the Roman Catholic modernist George Tyrrell that it simply finds what it is unconsciously seeking – a reflection of its own ideology. His famous dictum is quoted by D. M. Baillie: 'The Christ that Harnack sees, looking back through nineteen centuries of Catholic darkness, is only the reflection of a liberal Protestant face, seen at the bottom of a deep well' (Baillie, p. 40). It must be noted that neither version of the criticism gives reasons to believe that the attempt to discover the facts about Jesus is *in principle* mistaken. Rather, it is suggested

that it has in fact failed. They do not rule out that a different kind of approach may one day succeed. This is clearly the view of a number of those, Pannenberg included, who have in recent times entered upon new versions of the quest.

2   The quest of the historical Jesus is a mistaken enterprise because it attempts to find the wrong kind of assurance for faith. This view, which is sometimes associated with the work of Bultmann, has much justification as a reason for the rejection of some approaches to Christology from below. It is not, in itself, based on a belief that the more incredible the gospel is, the more credit there is in believing it, as unsympathetic critics of Bultmann have sometimes alleged. Underlying it is a view, perhaps derived from Kierkegaard, of the 'infinite qualitative difference' between time and eternity. It is one thing to be a man, another to be God. How then can it possibly be established simply from the facts of Jesus's life that he is also the eternal in the midst of time? What could be discovered about any man *qua* man that would qualify him for an ascription of divinity? '(O)ne cannot, without being guilty at one point or another of a μετάβασις εἰς ἄλλο γένος, arrive suddenly by an inference at the new quality . . . God; as if the consequence or consequences of . . . a man's life might suddenly furnish the proof that this man was God' (Kierkegaard, 1941b, p. 30). Because, one might say, Christology necessarily involves paradox, there is no logical route from below to above. It is christologically a waste of time to attempt to establish historical facts. For all of its merits, however, this kind of argument runs the risk of claiming too much, of so driving apart time and eternity that they cannot rationally be held together at all. The fact is that Jesus's life was a temporal, historical life, and the documents with which we are concerned are temporal, historical texts. Any theology which appears to deny that also seems likely to invalidate any Christology, for is not Christology important precisely because it is where some attempt is made to think together time and eternity? The point is important, and will recur, but here we are limiting the discussion to the matter of christological method in relation to the New Testament documents.

3   The quest of the historical Jesus is mistaken because it radically misconstrues the nature of the New Testament documents. The latter are indeed historical, and locatable in a particular time and culture. But that is not the same as saying that they are

appropriately used as quarries for historical facts. Here two points should be made. The first is the outcome of Hans Frei's study of the history of biblical interpretation in the modern era. He shows that the historical critical method mistook the nature of the biblical narratives which are, he says, *realistic*. By this he means that they achieve their meaning by a cumulative process to which character, circumstances and action together contribute (Frei, p. 280). Modern hermeneutical theory, with its conception of meaning as reference, ignored this realism, and attempted instead to isolate a 'series of unrelated facts as that to which the narratives refer. This means, he says, that according to this theory 'the documents mean something other than they say' (p. 318). The quest of the historical Jesus, in other words, attempts to wring from the texts the kind of information that they cannot give because they do not contain it. The content of the texts is other than the content that is sought by the traditional historical quest. Methodologically, therefore, the attempt to establish a series of facts is bound to fail. It must be noted that Frei's approach does not constitute a protest of the kind associated above with Kierkegaard. The texts, he says, are history-*like*, even though we shall not understand them unless we take account of their differences from history pure and simple.

This leads into the second point. If we are to take the New Testament texts for what they are, we cannot evade the question of their theological content. All of them, though in different ways, present Jesus in some kind of relation to God. It is this that the quest of the historical Jesus attempts to evade. Its attraction is obvious: if we could establish, 'objectively' and 'scientifically', the facts about Jesus as they underlie the text, some of the objections of modern culture to Christianity could be answered. But it is a mistake, for it consists in an attempt to get behind the texts, to find something that is not there, to build upon an imposed and not an inherent authority. If we are to believe – or to disbelieve – the texts, must it not be for what they actually say? And do they not actually speak of Jesus at once in terms of time and eternity, of history and God? The sheer difficulty of interpreting New Testament Christology lies in its apparently naive admixture of 'below' and 'above'. That is the real problem we have to face, not whether or not a biography of Jesus can be written.

OF FACT AND INTERPRETATION

It must be concluded, therefore, that because the texts are about Jesus of Nazareth as he is understood within a theological framework (or theological frameworks) of understanding, we cannot find him apart from the theology. The texts view him and express his reality only through a focus provided by Good Friday, Easter Sunday and Pentecost. They are still interested in him as he was; but not only or primarily so. The documents seek to tell the truth about Jesus of Nazareth, but that truth is not told apart from its theological framework. They *do* offer us a way to the historical Jesus. But for them the historical Jesus has already become, without any loss of historical reality, also of suprahistorical significance.

But what is the status of that suprahistorical significance? Does it somehow inhere in the events themselves, or is it *merely* a subjective interpretation made by the evangelists and apostles? The problem with a christological method that attempts to find bare facts and uninterpreted biography is not only that it misunderstands the texts; it is also based upon a rather empiricist theory of fact and meaning. Simply expressed, it holds or assumes that 'facts' are individual 'things' in space and time, verifiable by a straightforward use of the senses. They are neutral, in the sense that they can be stated quite independently of interpretation. This view has received much criticism in recent years, though it dies hard. If we are truly to overcome it without falling into the polar opposite that everything depends upon interpretation, so that the historical Jesus becomes in effect superfluous, we must tread cautiously. We shall begin with another glance at Pannenberg's attempt to overcome the dualism of fact and interpretation. This theologian attempts to show that historical facts, because they are mediated by a tradition of meaning, carry their own interpretation with them. Understood from this perspective he is not simply essaying a repristination of the quest but intends rather to pursue it in a revised form. The old quest depended upon a dualism of fact and interpretation: these facts, and particularly the resurrection, carry their meaning with them.

Pannenberg's claim is of immense importance, even if many qualifications need to be made. The whole shibboleth of value-neutral fact has led to some of the wilder manifestations of recent Christology. The process of development is as follows. It is assumed that at the basis of the development of Christology lie a series of (neutral) facts: things happening in space and time that can be scientifically understood only in terms of their space–time relationships – only 'from below' and *immanently*. Anything else is 'interpretation', by which is meant not the *discerning* but the *imposition* of meaning upon the facts. All the New Testament theological language then comes to be understood not as an interpretation but as mere interpretation, the subjective projection of meaning upon the facts by the early Christian mind. As a result, the theological meaning which is given to Jesus's life, death and resurrection is seen not as something true or false (because on this account it is not a matter of 'fact'), but as true or false only relative to its cultural context. When it is said that the New Testament uses 'mythical' language, this is often what is meant. 'Demythologization' then becomes the programme of providing for our times a structure of interpretation relative to *our* culture. It thus replaces systematic Christology, which has traditionally been the discipline attempting to express the truth of the New Testament reports, with something that is, methodologically, intrinsically different. For it is one thing to attempt to express in other words what is there to be discerned; it is another to impose a structure of interpretation upon something which is supposed to be a network of bare facts prior to and relatively independent of the interpretation.

If, then, as it is in the most 'radical' accounts, the theological framework of the gospels and epistles is simply a culture-relative construction of or projection upon the facts by the minds of the early Church (Strauss, pp. 52ff.), Christology is no more than the provision of an appropriately modern framework of interpretation for such facts as we believe to be extractable from below the surface. It becomes an expression of our modern experience of Jesus, which, in its turn, is dominated by the characteristic features of modern culture, especially perhaps its ideology of immanence (and Tyrrell's liberal Protestant face as one of its manifestations). And so we return to the apparently inevitable outcome of certain conceptions of Christology from below as that takes the form of a quest of the historical Jesus. The search for theologically neutral facts cannot, of itself, provide, and even less guarantee, a theologically significant conclusion. What begins below must, on certain epistemological assumptions, end there too. Method and content imply each other.

It is for this reason that the remark is a just one that the most perceptive of the papers in the collection *The Myth of God Incarnate* is the 'Epilogue' contributed by Dennis Nineham. After reviewing some recent attempts, including those of his fellow essayists, to base doctrines of the perfection of Jesus not, with the tradition, on the hypostatic conjunction of Jesus's humanity with divinity, but on historical research into Jesus's life, he asks: 'Is it, however, possible to validate claims of the kind in question on the basis of historical evidence?' (Nineham, p. 188). His answer is that, in the absence of belief in the objective metaphysical significance of Jesus, it is not. We have, then, either to abandon Christology altogether or to raise again the question of Jesus of Nazareth as the New Testament portrays him. Are we being barred from the real Jesus not because he is not there but because we are approaching the New Testament armed with a theory of meaning that obscures rather than reveals? Have we, in the immortal words of George Berkeley, 'first raised a dust and then complain that we cannot see'?

INTERPRETING NEW TESTAMENT CHRISTOLOGY

The programme of this section is not so much an exegesis of New Testament Christology as an attempt to gather together the insights of some recent writings in order to understand the kind of claims that are being made by the texts. We shall begin with an attempt to distinguish between the general form of the biblical approach and that of the patristic and later Christology which succeeded it.

The most obvious difference between the New Testament pictures of Jesus and the expressions of later dogmatic lies in the greater abstractness of the latter. In general, the Bible is concerned to say what happened, in particular what God has brought about, while the development of dogmatics tended to attempt to interpret the events in more philosophical categories. The drive of metaphysical philosophy is towards the permanently knowable and true, and the use of its terms means inevitably that there is a shift of interest from what happened to what is true for all time about God and Jesus if the claims about what happened are true. This is not to say that there is nothing of the description of events in patristic theology, nor that the biblical writers are uninterested in the eternal status and significance of Jesus. The New Testament in many places anticipates later dogmatic developments. 'Jesus Christ is the same yesterday and today and for ever' (Heb. 13.8). 'I am the first and the last, and the living one. . .' (Rev. 1.17f.). Such verses express the permanence of Jesus's reality and significance, while it is also noteworthy that when speaking of Jesus writers like Paul do not use past tenses as frequently as they use the present, except when referring directly to Jesus's earthly ministry. 'He is the image of the invisible God, the first-born of all creation. . .' (Col. 1.15). Again, that the differences between the New Testament and later dogmatic are not as great as is sometimes made out is shown by the fact that writers like the author to the Hebrews and the fourth Evangelist anticipate later formulations in their ascription of what is manifestly a twofold reality to Jesus. In general it would not be far off the mark to say that there are in the New Testament large numbers of statements that place Jesus on one side of the division between the divine and the created, and equally large numbers that place him on the other.

This means that the difference between the New Testament and later work is largely a matter of degree. We might say, in following up the remarks about Origen and Hegel in Chapter 3, that it is always possible for the difference to slip into one of kind, when certain temporal and historical features are suppressed or overlaid. But for the most part it is not so, and an interpreter like Grillmeier is surely justified in seeing a straight line of development from the Bible through the Fathers to the Councils. Within this line of development there is a move towards greater systematization. In the Bible, claims for Jesus are set out in a relatively unsystematic and largely narrative manner. But it is only relatively unsystematic, and scarcely even that in the Fourth Gospel, whose combination of narrative and systematic exposition represents, for better or for worse, the major link between Bible and later dogmatic. It is for this reason that modern discussion, particularly as it appears in a writer like D. E. Nineham, has identical problems with Bible and early dogma. In both cases the difficulty for the modern mind lies in the difference between a typically modern theory of meaning and that of the world of the texts. Modern thought, with its tendency towards a metaphysic of immanence, will necessarily have similar difficulties with the theology of transcendence contained in Bible and Fathers alike, for all their real differences.

We proceed, then, with a reiteration: it is of the essence of the New Testament portrayals of Jesus that they place him on both the human and the divine levels of reality. But now we come to another serious problem of interpretation, for there is no single way in which this human and divine reality is understood by the New Testament. How can we even speak of New Testament Christology when it is clearly a matter of Christologies, a multitude of expressions of early Christian belief? (Dunn, 1977). Whether such a multiplicity of confession is regarded as a problem or a blessing has much to do with the methodological assumptions with which the text is approached. If we expect a monolithic unity, we shall be disappointed. But can there be discerned a unity within the diversity of expression?

The beginnings of an answer to this question are to be found in a framework of interpretation like that suggested by Werner Elert in his book on Theodore of Pharan. His starting-point is the rejection of the distinction made by Harnack between the Jesus of history (fact) and the Christ of faith (interpretation). Elert, holding that all of the New Testament is concerned to speak about Jesus of Nazareth, and to speak of him theologically, recommends the use of a less dualistic framework. There is a difference, he says, between the work of the four Evangelists (though this must exclude the Prologue of John) and that of the rest of the New Testament. The four Evangelists provide what he calls the *Christusbild*, the portrayal of Christ as they believed him to be visible to his contemporaries. However, even while they are doing it they include acclamations and confessions like those of Matthew 16.16 and John 6.69 which in their own way anticipate the declarations of Nicaea. On the other hand, the epistles are more concerned with *Christusdogma*, with reflecting upon, expounding and clarifying the belief that Jesus of Nazareth is the Lord. This includes what is said about pre-existence and exaltation (Elert, pp. 15–19). Elert is insistent that this does not provide us with an anticipation of the Chalcedonian two-nature doctrine, for the two categories do not correspond to the humanity and divinity respectively. Each is, in its different way, concerned with both. None the less, statements like those of Galatians 4.4, 1 Corinthians 2.8, Philippians 2.5ff., Colossians 2.9, Hebrews 1.3, the latter of which played a greater role in christological discussion after Nicaea than John 1, do provide the basis for doctrines both of the divine nature and of the two natures of Christ (p. 19, cf. Moule).

The value of Elert's distinction is that it resists not only the making of a false division between different parts of the canon, but also a premature one between Scripture and dogmatics. As Professor Graham Stanton has pointed out, it does not solve all problems, and in particular the Fourth Gospel cannot simply be stripped of its Prologue and treated on all fours with the Synoptics. We must rather, as before, see the Fourth Gospel as a unique link, interweaving history and theology in a way that it becomes, for our purposes, the representative of the whole New Testament. For in all that it does it intermingles history and suprahistory, time and eternity, the human and the divine Jesus. It does systematically what the other New Testament Christology does less reflectively, showing its understanding of how in Jesus of Nazareth the 'above' and the 'below' are given together. The historical event has theological meaning, and God has given himself to a portion of our time and history. In that sense, Prologue and all, the Fourth Gospel is an essay in Christology centred on Jesus of Nazareth, and to that extent Christology from below.

Here, however, it will rightly be objected that to treat the Fourth Gospel as representative New Testament Christology begs the very question we are attempting to answer, that of the diversity of New Testament language about Jesus. Are not the Christologies to be found so different that the quest for a single doctrine is doomed at the outset? Here we must say first of all that it has not been claimed that there is a single New Testament Christology, only that there appears to be unanimity of a general kind. No such anachronism as that all teach a doctrine of the incarnation or a 'two-nature' doctrine is being suggested. Rather, there are to be found various different expressions of the saving significance of Jesus, which is what seems to be at the heart of the matter.

What, then, is the status of this diversity? Is it such that the Christology of the Fourth Gospel can really be accepted as the conclusion of all the others? The first thing to be said is that on one level diversity does not matter. Geometrical order and precision are not to be expected in the interpretation of a historical figure, and no one should be surprised at the proliferation of metaphor and symbol employed in the attempt to bring out the significance of Jesus. Problems here would only arise if there were to be found a formal contradiction between different terms, and it seems reasonable to say that however great a strain on the imagination and mind it may be to see Jesus as at once temple, lamb and lord – or even as way, truth and life – there is no clear case of a formal contradiction, such as would be involved in a claim that Jesus is both *p* and *not-p* at the same time and in the same respects. There are those who claim that the simultaneous ascription of predicates implying humanity and divinity does generate a formal contradiction, and this is an important and formidable objection; but that is a problem affecting the whole of Christology and not merely the biblical categories, and must await treatment in a later chapter.

Nor are we concerned here with the origins of the various titles, and with whether, for example, the content and meaning of many of the christological titles are derived from Hellenistic or Jewish speculation. This too is an important, if somewhat specialized, area of discussion. But the origin of language is not the chief problem for the systematic theologian. Rather, the chief question concerns the relationship of the biblical ascriptions of human and divine qualities to Jesus to the more formal and abstract language of dogmatic theology, whether ancient or contemporary. Here the central systematic question arising from the diversity of New Testament Christology is the apparent discrepancy between the various time-frames into which the historical Jesus is set by his witnesses. The problem is set out clearly and schematically by John Knox. Knox argues that the New Testament contains the possibilities for three apparently contradictory Christologies. The first, which he holds to be the most primitive, is that in which the man Jesus is depicted as Lord at his resurrection, the doctrine taught by the speeches in Acts. The second form grew out of this, not in contradiction of it, but as seeking to provide a background in eternity to the earthly career. It led to a picture in which 'a divine being empties himself of his divine nature and status and becomes a man, who then . . . is exalted . . . to the same high office' (Knox, p. 14). This is kenoticism. But the doctrine of pre-existence espoused in this theory, intended only to be a prologue to the human story, began to take it over and to force a rewriting. The logical end to this rewriting was docetism, in which the eternal Lord dominates the humanity and makes it into a mere cipher. Knox does not claim that the New Testament ever reaches this stage. Rather, his point is that the refusal of the logic of the development makes it impossible to tell a clear and consistent story that will embrace all the different accounts.

The naivety of Knox's account is its most striking feature, based as it is, apparently, on the axiom that divinity and humanity are contradictory predicates. There are, he claims, only three basic possibilities in Christology (pp. 94f.). Therefore, the logic seems to run, if both humanity and divinity are to be ascribed, it can only be at separate *stages* in the history. If, for example, pre-existence is the doctrine chosen, divinity must be excluded, for it is lost by kenosis at the time of birth; if some version of adoptionism, presumably humanity is sloughed off like a skin at the onset of divinity. Similarly, but in the other direction, it is sometimes argued that the doctrine of pre-existence *must* be docetic. Jesus cannot have both pre-existence and full humanity. Clearly, this objection does not hold against *any* doctrine of pre-existence. The idea of existence after death, though fraught with philosophical difficulties of all kinds, is not usually considered to preclude the humanity of the person concerned. Nor need the doctrine of pre-existence do so. What is queried is the possibility of the consistency of divine pre-existence and full humanity. In that case, we are back to the same problem, which seems to be an assumption that the ascription of divinity, whether pre-existent or otherwise, is inconsistent with a doctrine of the humanity of Christ that is to be saved from docetism. That is an assumption that will have to be probed elsewhere. What can be stated here with some confidence is that it makes the New Testament easier to understand if it is approached with the expectation that the evangelists and apostles did not share that particular assumption.

A corollary of this is that it does not follow that Synoptic accounts of Jesus's baptism, or Paul's possibly borrowed 'designated Son of God in power . . . by his resurrection' (Rom. 1.3), of themselves entail or contain an adoptionist Christology. That Jesus was understood to have been publicly acclaimed Son at his baptism does not entail that he was not Son beforehand, nor does the elevation accomplished by the resurrection and ascension mean that beforehand he was any less Lord and God. It is equally possible to suppose that the New Testament wishes to tell us that as both humiliated and glorified he is equally God, and that it is its concern to emphasize different aspects of the one divine-human story that explains the differences of expression. It is a mistake to look at the narrative through eyes too much accustomed to think in dogmatic categories, as Knox seems to be doing in his schematization. Here we return to the fact that the biblical narratives and descriptions are relatively haphazard in their ascription of divine status. The first reason for this lies in the fact that there is for the writers no problem about the humanity. They know that they are speaking about Jesus of Nazareth who was manifestly a human being. Because for the most part his humanity had not come into question (though 1 John 4.2 and possibly Colossians suggest that this was not always so in the Church), their concern is not yet to abstract it and discuss it as a topic of interest in itself. That came later, when there arose those who, in the interests of formal systematic coherence or philosophical dogma – especially that concerning the impassibility of God – took leave to throw doubt on the full humanity of Christ.

The second reason for the relatively haphazard nature of the predications lies in the fact that there was little difficulty in ascribing divinity, either, and because of this, moments of revelation of Jesus's divine status are expressed either as arguments in support of some other point or at crucial stages in his story: baptism, Peter's confession, transfiguration, resurrection, etc. This means that the divinity of Jesus was not a problem for the New Testament as it came to be in the earliest Christian systematic theology. As a result, the ascription of some kind of equality with God is often indirect and capable of varying interpretations. When Jesus is confessed as the Christ or described as the Son of God, it does not necessarily mean that he is being given full divine status. Only in confessions like that placed by John on the lips of Thomas ('My Lord and my God', John 20.28) is the matter unequivocal.

In addition, the way in which Jesus is described by different New Testament authors does appear to have undergone a process of development. In itself, this is hardly surprising. Who would expect the full implications of so great a salvation as that ascribed to the life, death and resurrection of Jesus of Nazareth to be worked out overnight? The most recent major attempt to trace the process is that of James D. G. Dunn (Dunn, 1980). According to him there was a process of development which led to the Christology of pre-existence and incarnation of the prologue of the Fourth Gospel.

Thus far Knox's analysis is justified. But it is noteworthy that Knox and Dunn interpret the development differently. While Knox sees a stumbling into contradiction and confusion, Dunn sees a much more linear process, in which the Fourth Gospel is the crown and completion of earlier developments. But it is not the process as Pannenberg sees it. The movement is not from that abstraction the Jesus of history to the unity of Jesus with his father. It is rather a development which expands Jesus's eternal significance and reality. What begins by seeing him oriented to the future ends by conceiving him also as the incarnation of a pre-existent Word of God.

Why, then, do Knox and Dunn see matters so differently? May it not be that Dunn approaches the text with different presuppositions from those of Knox? In which case, which of the two is seeing things as they really are? Much here will depend on the status accorded to the development. According to one view, that particularly associated with the quest of the historical Jesus, the nearer we can go to Jesus's actual beliefs about himself or the beliefs of the first Christians, the more we can believe what we read. Thus the accounts which suggest that Jesus was a man elevated to divine status at the resurrection are nearer to the fountainhead than the Christology of Paul and John. An alternative view might hold the reverse: that doctrine must develop, and the truth is to be found in the more rounded Christology of John, or, to take it further into history, of Chalcedon. But it would be wise to avoid romanticisms of either kind. There is no guarantee that the primitive or the developed is of itself the guide to the truth. The one might be primitive and in need of polish; the other overdeveloped and decadent.

Here two considerations must be brought to bear, each of great importance but in need of counterbalancing by the other. The first is that we are not so much concerned here with historical primitiveness as with what is logically primitive. Two remarks made by Dr Dunn will introduce what is meant by this. He says, when detailing the step by which the New Testament moved from seeing Jesus as different in degree from the prophets to giving him a metaphysical status, that the authors show 'no consciousness of taking so dramatic a step' (Dunn, 1980, pp. 204f.). Similarly, in discussing the relation of 1 John and Revelation to the Fourth Gospel's Christology, he says that they 'perhaps show us that the

70

transition was a quite natural step to take, or at least it seems so to them *once it had been made*' (p. 247, my emphasis). As we look back over the history of development, it may be that it will appear that a natural or even necessary step has been taken.

It is sometimes remarked that a great piece of music, viewed as a completed work, has about it an impression of necessity. A single note altered anywhere would destroy it. Yet few would want to suggest that while he was composing it the composer was compelled to develop it as he did. It is only as we view it 'backwards' that its inherent necessity is conceived and understood. Does the development of New Testament Christology appear to the backward glance as analogous to a musical whole or a meaningless and discordant accumulation of notes? That is the issue between an interpretation like Dunn's, and one which stresses the chaotic diversity of the matter. Is there a logic in the development, or necessary contradiction? It has already been suggested that Knox sees incompatibility because of the dualistic assumptions which he brings to the study. We cannot predicate both humanity and divinity, historicity and eternity, because the two are necessarily incompatible. Involved in this matter of dualism are also assumptions about the way in which language works. What *is* logically primitive in the development of New Testament Christology?

The question brings us to our second consideration, and we approach it by quoting a splendid dictum cited by Michael Polanyi. 'The true artists of speech remain always conscious of the metaphorical character of language. They go on correcting and supplementing one metaphor by another, allowing their words to contradict each other and attending only to the unity and certainty of their thought' (Polanyi, 1962, p. 102). Here once again we should beware of a romanticism of contradiction; of suggesting that it does not matter what a writer says so long as he is profound enough in his basic direction. It is, rather, a matter of levels. If we remain on the verbal level alone when we read the New Testament, we shall be able to find apparently contradictory Christologies. But if we look to a deeper level, to that which is logically primitive, we can understand how the different writers 'go on correcting and supplementing one metaphor by another' in their effort to speak faithfully of the reality which is prior to all their language, Jesus Christ. The dictum that Polanyi quotes, by a German philosopher K. Vossler,

71

is not meant to provide excuses by which theologians may say what they like. It is true of any area of human discourse that the rationality of its subject-matter is not fully expressible in words, and so different metaphors and concepts must be summoned in an attempt to do justice to the reality. How much more must this be true of those who strove to express the reality of Jesus Christ. Are the many Christologies of the New Testament the final word? Or shall we say, rather, in Dunn's words: 'One Jesus: many Christologies'? Which, then, is logically primitive? The Jesus Christ they strain to portray, or the words by which they portray him? Here we reach another version of a question we have met before: Are the writers variously interpreting a reality other than themselves, or simply projecting on to poorly understood historical realities a pattern of experience? It can be agreed with the sceptics that the words are relative. But to what are they relative: to the reality they name Jesus Christ, or simply to their own culture and experience? If we take the one human and divine reality of Jesus Christ to be the logically primitive reality, then the diversities of expression can be understood as different attempts to express in words the richness of this reality which must necessarily transcend all its verbal expressions. The saying of von Campenhausen about the Christology of the Fourth Gospel can then apply to the Christology of the New Testament as a whole: 'This abundance of "names" is no doubt deliberate. Jesus himself in his uniqueness is the sole content of the Gospel. Each possible title is no more than a reference, and none can describe Jesus completely as he is in truth' (cited by Hengel, p. 58).

Considerations such as these relativize the way in which historical development must be construed, for they suggest that such development as there was took place against a background of belief, grounded in worship, in the risen and continuing reality of Jesus Christ. If, then, there is a major doubt about Dunn's thesis it is that he is overdominated by the question of whether and when the New Testament began to see Jesus as the incarnation of a pre-existent hypostasis or reality separate from God the Father. As a result he underplays the significance of such passages as 1 Corinthians 8.6, where Paul describes Christ as 'one Lord . . . through whom are all things and through whom we exist'. The phrase, especially when it is seen alongside the previous and parallel description of 'God, the Father from whom are all things and for whom we exist', ascribes to Jesus an equality of status with the Father alongside a difference of function. 1 Corinthians is a relatively early work, and suggests that belief in Jesus, if not explicitly as the incarnation of a pre-existent hypostasis, then certainly in terms of equality in eternity and divinity, developed very early. 'The circumstance that Paul mentions the cosmological work of Christ only incidentally in an ethical section, indicates that belief in the cosmic Christ was shared in common by Paul and the early Church, so much so that Paul could cite that belief without elaboration and expect its acceptance by the Corinthians as a matter of course' (Gibbs, p. 59). To view the development in that way, instead of from the point of view of a later formulation, suggests that it was not in every way even, and certainly was fairly rapid in one essential aspect, the ascription of equal divinity to Jesus.

In its turn, this more fluid way of viewing the development enables us to stress once again the occasional rather than the systematic way in which New Testament beliefs about Jesus Christ are expressed. The formula from 1 Corinthians was introduced to provide theological support for Paul's profound reflections on the ethical issues involved in eating food once offered to idols. Many of the dogmatic formulae of the New Testament perform similar functions, as for example the elevated Christology of Colossians, which appears to effect a contrast between the revelational and functional unity of God and Christ, on the one hand, and, on the other, the multiplicity of authorities the recipients of the Letter may have been in danger of worshipping. A slightly different approach is provided by the Fourth Gospel's Prologue and the opening verses of the Letter to the Hebrews, which set in the context of eternity the human story and its significance as they proceed to recount it in the body of their works.

In other places, where the writer is chiefly telling a story, the emphasis falls on those parts of the story which the writer sees to be the most significant. This does not mean that the Synoptic authors would not accept those things taught by John with his different intentions. Rather it is that, because they do not consciously distinguish between the human and divine aspects of the story, they do not need to worry over problems that concerned those living at a different stage of the Church's history. What they have in common is that all write of Jesus as inseparably bound up with God's saving activity, sometimes explicitly calling him divine, at others suggesting or implying by the course of the story as a whole that the agent of salvation is here in person. That is the human and divine reality with which all New Testament Christology is concerned, the theme on which the writers write complementary variations. Within all the diversity of expression there is a fundamental unity of direction and intent to be discerned.

This fundamental unity has been expressed by a number of recent writers on the New Testament, and it is with some of their words that this long section can conclude. 'All three [namely, the Synoptic] Evangelists record the intervention of the living God in the heart of Judaism at a particular period of history in the words and actions and death of Jesus of Nazareth . . . and all three regard these happenings as one great act of God by which his rule is inaugurated on earth, and as a result of which those who believe are enabled to do the will of God. . .' (Hoskyns and Davey, pp. 103f.). '. . . the evidence, as I read it, suggests that Jesus was, *from the beginning*, such a one as appropriately to be described in the ways in which . . . he did come to be described in the New Testament period – for instance, as "lord" and even, in some sense, as "God" ' (Moule, p. 4). '. . . the title "Son of God" connects the figure of Jesus with God. He is the beloved . . . and the first-born Son. . . This is meant to express that in Jesus, God himself comes to men, and that the risen Christ is fully bound up with God' (Hengel, p. 63).

THE PLACE OF HISTORICAL RESEARCH

It was stated above that counterbalancing the assertion that it is the one human and divine reality, Jesus Christ, who provides the logically primitive level of New Testament Christology, there must be another factor without which it cannot play its proper part. This is that, insist as we may on the unity of the New Testament's witness, we cannot deny the temporal and historical role of the reality, that it is *human* and divine, *temporal* and eternal. If it is human and temporal it must in principle be a possible object of historical research. If the beliefs of the New Testament are about Jesus of Nazareth, albeit about one risen and transformed, then they are about one who once walked this earth. Therefore some kind of 'quest' cannot be ruled out as impossible or illegitimate. But what form does it take and what uses does it have? If the biblical depictions of the *Christusbild* are inseparably entwined with the Church's later confessions, then a totally autonomous quest of the historical Jesus, by which an independent basis for belief is erected, seems to be excluded. But that does not rule out a quest of a different nature. Perhaps three functions for historical critical inquiry within the terms of the documents' character may be isolated. The first is that often associated with the name of Käsemann whereby the continuity between the historical ministry of Jesus and the Church's later confession of him is examined. While it is not *a priori* impossible that Jesus may have been God present to the world while being entirely unconscious of it, it would be disturbing if there could be found no continuity at all between the way in which Jesus spoke and behaved and the later beliefs about him. The significance of the resurrection was held to be in part a demonstration of the fact that God had acted for human salvation through this man and not another. Therefore the kind of life he lived and the kind of things he said are essential to our understanding of him *as God*. The second function for historical research follows from this, and is more relevant to the interests of a study of method in Christology. We saw in Chapter 3 that the danger of an òverphilosophical approach to Christology is that what we say about Christ will be divorced from Christology's historical grounding. The importance of the *Christusbild*, particularly that of the Gospels, lies in a theological concern to avoid a non-historical Christology. But, once again, any such historical inquiry will take place not in abstraction from, but in the context of, the theological nature of the documents. It will devote itself to testing whether the beliefs of faith and expressions of doctrine conform to what is written of the object of faith.

The third function is less germane to a study of Christology, unless it is thought that the main aim of that discipline is apologetic. It is also the most hazardous, in that it may, unless carefully pursued, involve the same abstraction from the texts as characterizes the quest of the historical Jesus. But, for all the dangers of misunderstanding, it is worth acknowledging the positive values of the historical quest even in its old form. By claiming that the object of its faith and the vehicle of its knowledge of God is a human, historical, figure, Christianity throws open its faith to the risk of secular inquiry. Theology is the science of the Christian gospel, that intellectual discipline which tests the beliefs of the Christian community, accepted as they are on the basis of preaching, experience, tradition, authority and all the other ways in which people happen to become believers. One of the ways in which tests are made – and it is only one, if a very important one – is critical investigation of the texts believed to be authoritative. That investigation cannot prove the truth of the gospel, for the reason already set out, that theological questions cannot be settled conclusively by historical inquiry alone. But it is conceivable that such inquiry could falsify or qualify it out of existence. If certain accounts were shown to be fabrications, the credibility of the gospel would suffer, for, to repeat, it is concerned with a human and divine, and therefore partly contingent, story. 'No one who is in earnest concerning the foundations of Christian belief can pretend that his belief would not be radically affected, if he became convinced that as a matter of historical fact Jesus had never prayed in the garden of Gethsemane that the hour might pass from him and then after agony of prayer freely accepted his Father's will. Whether or not he did so pray is a matter of historical fact to be settled by methods precisely akin to those which Roman historians use to determine whether or not Julius Caesar was aiming at Oriental despotism. . .' (MacKinnon, 1963, p. 20). Not everyone would accept that example as a good one, but it is clear that if it could be shown either that in general the Evangelists were knaves or fools in their reporting of historical events – as Reimarus and Strauss respectively appear to have suggested – or that certain central events of the gospel stories did not take place, then the credibility of Christianity in general would suffer. The possibility of falsification must always be acknowledged.

What kind of status the beliefs of Christianity can have in the light of the risk involved here must await another chapter. Clearly, to throw one's views open to the possibility of empirical falsification of itself entails that certain forms of certainty are excluded. But because to some readers the thesis being argued in this chapter will appear to be special pleading, we must now concentrate attention on giving further reasons why the historical features of New Testament Christology cannot be studied in abstraction from their theological content.

GOD AND HISTORY

The first reason is a repetition of the main thesis of this chapter that the documents say what they do on the basis of a view of history in which time and eternity are, so to speak, given together. History, the network of events that take place in space and time, is considered to be open to the action of God who is a reality transcending space and time. We may think that it is necessary to approach the texts in the light of a 'modern' view that the world is a totally closed and mechanistic system of cause and effect (so Bultmann, Harvey), but in that case we should not expect to understand them. If we are to do that – and in this respect the question of whether we believe them or not is a different one – then we must take them on the basis of what they say. And what, for example, the Fourth Gospel appears to say is that the divine Word 'became flesh', and that therefore there was a series of events taking place within the continuum of space and time which were also more than simply spatial and temporal.

How is it that the New Testament writers can in different ways so intermingle time and eternity? If we are not simply to dismiss their writing as a prescientific confusion of categories, we must understand that their writings have a background and that is, of course, the Old Testament tradition about the God of Israel (Hoskyns and Davey, especially pp. 32–4, 57f., 71ff.). In this respect it is surely significant that one conspicuous feature of much contemporary discussion of Christology is the absence of substantive use of the Old Testament. This may be partly and properly due to a wish to abstain from imposing a unity on a library whose diversity exceeds that of the New Testament. But it may also be due to the fact that the interpreter of New Testament Christology gains a certain freedom from constraint if he sits fairly loosely to this part of the canon. It is easier to interpret Jesus in terms of some Hegelian or other philosophy of immanence if the Old Testament's stubborn insistence on the concreteness of the divine presence is ignored or played down. In this respect suspicion must fall even on Pannenberg's putative orientation of Christology to the Old Testament. Is the conception of universal history with which he works an imposition of a general philosophical pattern on the essentially episodic Old Testament history – an overall scheme imposed upon a consistent but discrete series of divine acts? Of importance here is the fact that the elusive conception of the history of transmission of traditions (*Überlieferungsgeschichte*) is preferred to a more forthright reference to the history of God's relations with Israel. By the use of an essentially ambiguous conception attention is concentrated on the linguistic tradition rather than on the reality to which that language affects to refer, after the modern fashion of avoiding ontological commitment where possible. But ontological commitment is precisely what is required here. Does the Old Testament show us something of God that gives us a clue to the nature of what happened in Jesus? Perhaps, if the New Testament witness to Christ is not to be transmuted into a Gnosticism unrelated to the events of the first few decades of our era, the matter must be put more bluntly. The Old Testament, for all its diversity, is, like the New, concerned with a history in which the temporal and the eternal are interwoven. Its pervasive concern with real, concrete historical events in which God calls, redeems, disposes and judges his people Israel is precisely what must be kept in mind if the central object of New Testament witness is not to be etherealized by theologians into a reflection of their own images of human life.

And there is more to be said. It can be argued that the way in which God is pictured in relation to Israel provides the essential backdrop to a theological understanding of Jesus the Jew. Barth's statement that 'The angel of Yahweh in the Old Testament is obviously both identical and not identical with Yahweh himself' provides a suitable starting-point (Barth, *Church Dogmatics*, 1/1, p. 299). The God of Israel is the one who is conceived to be really present to his world without being any less himself. The story of Jacob's wrestling in Genesis 32 provides an interesting illustration. Is the nocturnal antagonist man, angel or God? The story as we have it, whatever may have been the case in its sources, makes no categorical assertion, though it seems to suggest that he is all and yet none of them. The same is true of the angelic visitor to Manoah in Judges 13. He is at first supposed to be a man, but at the last realization dawns: 'We shall surely die, for we have seen God' (verse 22).

The view that the Old Testament provides the groundwork or 'inner logic of incarnation' is developed in the pivotal chapter of that title in Ray S. Anderson's *Historical Transcendence and the Reality of God*:

At the heart of these narratives which testify to God's action in calling, redeeming and establishing a people for himself in the world, lies the reality of divine self-communication. It is God himself who appears to Abram (Genesis 17.1), who confronts Moses as Jahweh, the God of Abraham, Isaac and Jacob (Exodus 3.15), who speaks the law from Mt. Sinai in the wilderness (Exodus 19.3ff.), and it is God who will give himself the task of claiming the promised land (Exodus 34.10ff.) (Anderson, pp. 110f.).

Especially important is Exodus 3.13–15: 'This self-communication of God . . . marked Israel off from all others, but also served to place the reality of God *in* the world even as he was marked off *from* the world' (p. 112). Anderson proceeds to raise a question which is exactly that asked of proponents of a traditional Christology from above: 'But *how* does the infinite enter into the finite, or the Name into an act, without tearing the fabric of historical reality itself?' (p. 113). How can God become man without involving some docetic overwhelming of the humanity? In Anderson's words, 'the inner logic of the incarnation is organically connected to the relation of Jahweh to Israel' (p. 118), and the point cannot be dismissed by appeal to the 'anthropomorphic' modes of thought of the oriental mind. The Old Testament is saying something about *God*: 'God's self-communication is a unity of act and being. There is no Logos of God apart from the Logos of the flesh – this is not made explicit prior to the incarnation, but the inner logic is there in God's self-communication to Israel, in his humanity' (p. 118).

It must be made very clear what is being claimed here. It is not that the reality of the incarnation, or its implications for what is to be said of Jesus Christ as both God and man, is being established or proved, and certainly not by a literalistic appeal to the Old Testament. Rather, it is that the assertion or denial of traditional christological teaching is made on the basis of arguments that presuppose a certain understanding of the relation of God to the world. Reference to the Old Testament shows a theology not at variance with the kind of claims made in orthodox dogma. Where the Old Testament is ignored, or ceases to be constitutive, the danger is that some other framework will be provided. That framework may be the doctrine of the impassibility of God or of the rigid division of reality into phenomena and noumena. Both are contested by the Old Testament in many of the things it says about God, for it sees him in too close a relation to his creation even to admit their conceivability. Alternatively, a framework may be provided by one of the philosophies of immanence that have proliferated in the post-Kantian era. Christology becomes then a function of cosmology, for the life of Jesus is seen to emerge from a single cosmic process rather than being in that process and yet taking place by God's free initiative from 'outside' it.

A recent example of the latter danger is provided by J. A. T. Robinson's *The Human Face of God*, where the author speaks of 'two sets of language, man-language and God-language, in which it is possible to speak of the single cosmic process' (Robinson, p. 116). If this means that God is to be reduced to, or even identified as a part of, a single cosmic process, then it must be asked whether it is remotely credible that the story of Israel could be described in such terms. The repeated representations of God's contradicting his people through the mouths of the prophets, the element of judgement for apostasy and rank injustice, the difference in character of such events as exodus, exile and restoration all give the story an unevenness that does not submit lightly to the Whiteheadian eyes through which Robinson wishes to view the matter. What has been called a processive type of Christology (Rupp) must methodologically exclude the historical unevenness of the Bible's view of the divine relation to the world. So it is that a Christology from below which begins with certain philosophies of immanence produces a Christology that says something different from that of the Bible. As in the theology of Arius, and that of one side of Origen's thought, soteriology is subordinated to, even overcome by, cosmology.

To this the response may be: so much the worse for Christian belief if it is based on a no longer credible view of history. It may be necessary to choose between the modern world and ancient Christology. I do not myself believe that this is necessary, although discussion of this issue must await a later chapter. But the chief point here is this. If we are to *understand* New Testament Christology, we must see that its historical claims are also theological ones. A quest based upon a positivistic or immanentist view of the world may find many interesting things, but it will not understand what is being said. Thus the first defence against the charge of special pleading is that without the kind of interpretation suggested here we shall not understand what is being said. The second defence takes us into a discussion of time and eternity.

THE PRESENT AND THE PAST

Why is our theology so concerned with the Bible as a text from the past? Why does Pannenberg believe that Christology is the discipline concerned with what Jesus was? Why is Christology understood more by analogy with history than, say, with natural science, the discipline essentially concerned with the way things *are*, with the present? Part of the answer lies in the nature of the case: Christianity is related to past historical events. Part lies also in the nature of our culture, with its tendency to make absolute a division between the modern and the primitive. But a deeper reason may well lie in our view of the nature of time and its relation to eternity. Without doubt, we have, since the Enlightenment, tended to stress the importance of time, in reaction against the 'otherworldliness' of earlier eras. This reaction explains the preference for Christology from below, whether that Christology is cosmologically or historically rooted in certain immanent phenomena. But how far is it a reaction that operates within the same kind of framework of understanding as that of the past? Here we shall attempt to limit the discussion to the question under review, leaving the substantive question to later chapters.

As has been mentioned already (Chapter 2, p. 28), Dietrich Ritschl has argued that underlying the crisis of modern christological hermeneutics is a view of time and eternity derived from Augustine. By his combination of Platonic ideas of eternity with the Christian gospel, Augustine held together the historical elements of Christianity and the idea of God as timeless. It is this latter feature that generates difficulties, for in its train come 'the negative evaluation of "ordinary" world history, the idea that God's decisive actions lie in the past. . .' (Ritschl, pp. 6f.). It is this orientation to the past that concerns us, for it is what recurs in programmes of Christology from below despite their more positive evaluation of the temporal. The underlying rationale is something like this: that if

81

Jesus represents the presence of the timeless in time, then he is to be found only where the past event once happened or where it can be conceived to repeat itself. (In this respect it can be seen how essentially Augustinian is Kierkegaard's view of time and eternity.) In the light of some such view the investigation of the past becomes the prior and dominating task of Christology.

But suppose that we look at the problems of Christology in the light of a different conception of eternity: one more eschatologically oriented, to use a fashionable way of putting it. In it, the eternity of God is not an expression of his timelessness but of his overarching of past, present and future in such a way that in Jesus of Nazareth we see the anticipation of what will be. The relationship of the past figure to time is immediately inverted, and he is seen as one who *belongs to all time*. There is an orientation to the past as well, but it is held in polar tension with the eschatological reference such as that derived by Ritschl from the Pauline account of the Last Supper: 'in memory of him . . . until he comes' (1 Cor. 11.23ff. Hence the title of Ritschl's book). Christian existence is what takes place between past and future in relation to Christ. But which Christ? Not the Christ of the past, but the one of the present. Therefore we must see the problems of Christology in the light of a different time-scale:

> The real problem of Western Christology . . . does not lie at the point of concentration and focus in the present scholarly discussion. Exegetes and dogmaticians are presently in large measure preoccupied with modifications of Martin Kähler's problem of the historical Jesus and the post-Easter Christ, although in reality the problem lies in the relation between the 'historical-risen' Christ and the *Christus praesens* (pp. xif.).

There can only be serious Christology at all if there is a present Christ in the light of which the past Jesus can be considered: 'It is Christ's self-presentation in the present which opens the eyes to the understanding of what happened in the past' (p. 203).

The wider implications of such an alteration in perspective must await later discussion. But Ritschl's proposal enables some conclusions to be drawn about the interpretation of New Testament Christology. If the method of interpretation is to cohere with the content of what is said in the text, we may not operate with a simple distinction between Christology from below (a quest of the historical Jesus pursued with the techniques of secular historiography alone) and Christology from above (a purely dogmatic repetition of the theological formulae of the past). In so far as a Christology wishes to make use of the New Testament, it can only be as the intellectual quest of those who seek understanding of the faith in the present Christ which has been received in worship, biblical exploration, experience or some other means. This is because the New Testament knows of no other Jesus than the one who was past but has become present and will be in the future. It also knows of no other Jesus than the one whom it understands from the beginning as God's presence in time. The temporal ('below') is from the outset charged with the life of the eternal ('above'). And so we return to the point with which Chapter 2 ended. To seek the Jesus of the New Testament is to seek a human and earthly figure whose intrinsic meaning is to be expressed in expressions employing the word *God*.

How, precisely, the relation of time and eternity, man and God, is to be understood and expounded systematically is a matter for further inquiry. If we begin as we have done with faith's attempt to understand New Testament Christology, with its unselfconscious interweaving of time and eternity, we are not bound to begin with all the questions of Christology and its relation to the doctrine of God already settled, as Pannenberg suggests. The way in which Jesus can be conceived to be at once human and divine has still to be worked out. And so, there *is* a movement from below: from confession to systematic exposition, but it is not a movement that ignores either the past life of Jesus of Nazareth or the concerns of modernity. Quite the reverse: for the beginning of theology in the Christian present means that it will be an interpretation *from within* the modern world in which we are set.

CONCLUSION

The introduction here of problems of time and eternity was designed to show that there is no interpretation of New Testament Christology which avoids questions of ontology, of the way our world is. Beliefs about the nature of things are interwoven with what we regard as sayable. In this respect it has already been suggested that underlying John Knox's account of New Testament Christology is a dualism which makes the divine and the human, the eternal and the temporal, in some way mutually exclusive. Such a dualism makes it impossible to take seriously the kind of things said by the New Testament writers about Jesus. They become the mutually contradictory interpretations of a series of events to which they remain essentially external. If we are to understand the New Testament witness to Jesus as a serious attempt to speak theologically about him, we must avoid such presuppositions.

The same warning must be made about systematic Christology. Much modern as well as ancient Christology is vitiated by axioms that are best described as dualistic. The aim of Chapter 5 will be to show both the effect of dualism on Christology and the way in which ancient and modern Christology are similarly, though asymmetrically, affected by different forms of the same cosmological doctrine.

REFERENCES

Anderson, Ray S., *Historical Transcendence and the Reality of God: A Christological Critique.*

Baillie, D. M., *God Was In Christ: An Essay on Incarnation and Atonement.*

Barth, Karl, *Church Dogmatics*, Eng. trans. ed. G. W. Bromiley and T. F. Torrance.

Bultmann, Rudolf, 'New Testament and Mythology' in *Kerygma and Myth*, ed. Hans-Werner Bartsch, Eng. trans. Reginald H. Fuller, vols. i and ii, pp. 1–44.

Dunn, James D. G., 1974, 'Paul's Understanding of the Death of Jesus' in *Reconciliation and Hope: New Testament Essays on Atonement and Eschatology*, ed. Robert Banks, pp. 125–41.

Dunn, James D. G., 1977, *Unity and Diversity in the New Testament: An Inquiry into the Character of Earliest Christianity.*

Dunn, James D. G., 1980, *Christology in the Making: An Inquiry into the Origins of the Doctrine of the Incarnation.*

Elert, Werner, *Der Ausgang der altkirchlichen Christologie. Eine Untersuchung über Theodor von Pharan und seine Zeit als Einführung in die alte Dogmengeschichte.*

Frei, Hans, *The Eclipse of Biblical Narrative. A Study in Eighteenth- and Nineteenth-Century Hermeneutics.*

Gibbs, J. G., *Creation and Redemption: A Study in Pauline Theology.* Supplement to *Novum Testamentum xxvi.*

Grillmeier, Aloys, *Christ in Christian Tradition*, vol. i: *From the Apostolic Age to Chalcedon*, 2^e revised, Eng. trans. John Bowden.

The Form of New Testament Christology

Harvey, Van A., 1967, *The Historian and the Believer: The Morality of Historical Knowledge and Christian Belief*.

Hengel, Martin, *The Son of God: The Origin of Christology and the History of Jewish-Hellenistic Religion*. Eng. trans. John Bowden.

Hoskyns, Edwyn and Davey, Noel, *The Riddle of the New Testament*.

Kähler, Martin, *The So-Called Historical Jesus and the Historic Biblical Christ*, Eng. trans. Carl E. Braaten.

Kierkegaard, Søren, 1941b, *Training in Christianity*, Eng. trans. Walter Lowrie.

Knox, John, *The Humanity and Divinity of Christ: A Study of Pattern in Christology*.

MacKinnon, D. M., 1963, 'Moral Objections' in *Objections to Christian Belief*, pp. 11–34.

Moule, C. F. D., *The Origin of Christology*.

Nineham, Dennis E., 'Epilogue' in *The Myth of God Incarnate*, ed. John Hick, pp. 186–204.

Pannenberg, Wolfhart, 1968, *Jesus – God and Man*, Eng. trans. Lewis L. Wilkins and Duane A. Priebe.

Polanyi, Michael, 1962, *Personal Knowledge: Towards a Post-Critical Philosophy*.

Reimarus, H. S., *Reimarus: Fragments*, Eng. trans. Ralph S. Fraser.

Ritschl, Dietrich, *Memory and Hope: An Inquiry Concerning the Presence of Christ*.

Robinson, J. A. T., *The Human Face of God*.

Rupp, George, *Christologies and Cultures: Towards a Typology of Religious World Views*.

Schweitzer, Albert, *The Quest of the Historical Jesus: A Critical Study of its Progress from Reimarus to Wrede*, Eng. trans. W. Montgomery.

Strauss, David Friedrich, *The Life of Jesus Critically Examined*, Eng. trans. Marian Evans.

Weiss, Johannes, *Jesus's Proclamation of the Kingdom of God*, Eng. trans. R. H. Hiers and D. L. Holland.

5

CHRISTOLOGY AND DUALISM

DUALISM AND DUALITY

Chapter 4 was an attempt to show that there is in New Testament Christology, for all its diversity of expression, an orientation towards a single theme. In its different ways it portrays Christ as one in whom the work and presence of God are given through the medium of a human being. The different ways represent partly a development from the first utterances of faith in the significance of one raised from the dead to the more strictly incarnational theology of the Fourth Gospel; and partly an attempt to come to terms with the fundamental Christian claim that here both eternity and time, both the eternal God and his historical self-presentation, are given together.

Dualistic axioms make it more difficult to discern a unity in the different strands of New Testament Christology. In this context dualism does not refer to a metaphysic in which two different kinds of reality are supposed, but one which conceives two realities as either opposites or contradictions of each other. Mainstream Christianity has always held that God is other than the world but, because he is its Creator, has denied that the two are related in a negative way. Because the created order is dependent upon God, he can be conceived to interact with it. Dualism denies such an interaction, either explicitly or by conceiving the two in such a way that it becomes impossible consistently to relate them. In this sense, both adoptionism and docetism, the earliest and most logically primitive Christian heresies, arise from the same root. Because their assumptions are dualistic they are compelled to deny either that Jesus was fully God or that he was fully man. It is not difficult to understand, also, how attempts to abstract a merely historical Jesus from the

New Testament material about him operate with similar presuppositions.

In this chapter we proceed to examine the operation of dualism in systematic Christology. Here, the chief purpose is to close the gap between early Christology and our modern problems by showing that in both cases Christology is similarly affected by dualistic assumptions. This relates in important ways to our central preoccupation with form, content and method. It was suggested in the introductory chapter that to posit a radical discontinuity of tradition makes impossible a decision about whether a Christology is the same as one from the past. If completely different language has to be used, there is no way of telling whether the same enterprise is being adopted. If, then, it can be shown that the same kind of intellectual issues are at stake in modern as in ancient Christology, those who reject the latter in the name of modern experience or understanding will be challenged at the heart of their assumptions. To put it more concretely, we can say that the heirs of the Enlightenment, who claim that the conditions in which theology is being done are a whole world away from the conditions of the first five centuries of Christianity, will have one of their central doctrines undermined. For in many ways, it will be shown, post-Kantian dualism and the dualistic thinking of the Greeks that provided the background of much ancient Christology – as well as the foreground of ancient heresy – are one and the same intellectual phenomenon. This demonstration, if successful, will not solve our problems in Christology, nor of itself make New Testament talk of Jesus Christ any more self-evident. But it will change the way in which the problems are viewed.

But why should such a change be demanded? What is the point of an insistence on a non-dualistic understanding of Christology? Here we can only allude to a point which will later require separate treatment. The context of New Testament Christology is, as has already been suggested, the telling of a story in which events of saving significance are set forth. This story form was retained in the Apostles' Creed and to some extent in that of Nicaea. It is a history of salvation, linking God's purposes for human life to the life of Jesus of Nazareth. It is because the New Testament is more concerned with these aspects of its message than with systematic Christology that its doctrine of Christ takes the relatively occasional

87

form that we have noticed. But it was in order to preserve the biblical claim that in this historical figure salvation is to be found that the Fathers developed their systematic Christology. Even the abstract terminology of Chalcedon is concerned to preserve the soteriological integrity of the Christian gospel.

It is for this reason that the question of dualism is not simply a matter of loyalty to the tradition. The Christian tradition is concerned with the transmission of a gospel, not simply with solving intellectual puzzles about the person of Christ. The Fathers saw the content of Christianity as gospel to be intrinsically linked to the form of its Christology. And so in this chapter, devoted as it is to the philosophical and ontological assumptions at work in Christology, we are indirectly deciding matters of enormous import: of what it is to be human, and how the Christian gospel is conceived to bear upon our humanity. It is for this reason that our discussion will begin and end with modern treatments of Christology, using the Fathers as a sounding-board against which to test the purity of their tones.

SCHLEIERMACHER'S CRITIQUE OF THE TRADITION

Schleiermacher's critique of traditional Christology is important not simply because it represents the first major attempt to incorporate into Christian theology the Enlightenment's savage attack on orthodoxy, but because of the way in which it both criticizes and employs dualistic axioms. It rejects past forms of expression but shares the kind of assumptions that make traditional categories so problematic for contemporary understanding. Schleiermacher's pattern of thought appears most clearly when, at the beginning of his critique of traditional Christology (Schleiermacher, pp. 391–8), he rejects that aspect of it known as the 'two-nature doctrine'. He is without doubt justified in lighting upon this part of the tradition for the main thrust of his critique. The word *nature* has undergone marked changes of meaning since the time when the Greek οὐσία was translated into Latin *natura* for theological and philosophical usage, and now tends, as Schleiermacher observes, to denote this-worldly reality only. In earlier times, when *nature* embraced two worlds, the one of our direct experience and a transcendent realm (*nature* and *supernature*), interacting according to supposedly fixed patterns, its use in Christology posed few problems. But now it tends to bring Jesus too much down to a simply this-worldly level (p. 392).

Schleiermacher's first criticism of the tradition is, then, a linguistic one. The word *nature* is inappropriate to the dual reality of the Christ, and should be replaced by more appropriate language. But when he comes to elaborate his reasons for rejecting the language, Schleiermacher reveals that his own assumptions are dualistic. Why may we not use the same word of both the divine and the human in Christ? Chiefly because the meaning of the word *God* forbids it. 'Over against this divided and conditioned [namely, existence] we set God the unconditioned and absolutely simple' (p. 392). Schleiermacher's assumption is that because (by definition) God and the world are opposed types of reality ('unconditioned'/'conditioned') we cannot use the same language, even analogically, of both God and man. But on what grounds has he decided that God and the world are so different that they cannot, except by negation, share the same predicates? Without doubt we encounter here a modern form of the Augustinian dualism that has so plagued Western theology.

As always in this topic it is what is believed to be true about God that is at the heart of things. If it is assumed that God is absolutely simple and unconditioned, his relationship to time, and to historical particularity above all, becomes essentially problematic. And that it is not only a problem for the nineteenth-century Protestant is indicated by a recent statement by Edward Schillebeeckx: 'But (God's) so far transcendent activity cannot be described as his acting in history, as this absolute initiative of God could not be at the same time immanent in our history without losing its transcendence' (Schillebeeckx, p. 627). Why not, we may ask? Does it not depend on what we mean by *transcendence*, which can itself be construed dualistically or non-dualistically? Why should not the unconditioned (or transcendent) become conditioned (or immanent) without loss of its transcendent reality?

However, we have so far viewed only a part of Schleiermacher's argument. He continues by taking objection to the idea which he believes to be implicit in traditional Christology that 'one person is to share two quite different natures'. As a matter of fact, that is a very Nestorian way of putting the matter, but his reasons for so arguing are remarkably like John Knox's reasons for discerning contradiction in the different forms of New Testament Christology: 'How can the unity of life coexist with the duality of natures, unless the one gives way to the other, if the one exhibits a larger and the other a narrower range, or unless they melt into each other. . . ?' (p. 393). The question might have been asked by Apollinaris, and is for that reason of considerable moment for Christology. Just as in the previous argument all depended upon the way in which God and the world were understood and defined in relation to one another, so it is here with the definition of *nature* which is according to Schleiermacher 'a sum of ways of action or laws, according to which conditions of life vary and are included within a fixed range. . .' (p. 393). But who is to lay down in advance that God – or man for that matter – is such that his activity is definable in terms of 'laws' 'within a fixed range'? Dualistic assumptions are once more not far below the surface. There are two areas of being, each with fixed laws, neither of which can have any relation to the other.

What is striking about so many of Schleiermacher's arguments in this context is their apparent lack of awareness of the complexities of the debate before and after Chalcedon, Antiochene and Alexandrian alike. And even where his arguments seem to have greater weight, a strange naivety characterizes them. Thus in section 96 he rightly adverts to the tendency of christological expression 'to vacillate between the opposite errors of mixing the two natures to form a third which would be neither of them . . . or of keeping the two natures separate, but either neglecting the unity of the person in order to separate the two natures more distinctly, or, in order to keep hold of the unity of the person, disturbing the necessary balance, and making one nature less important than the other and limited by it' (p. 394). As a matter of fact, that is what christological debate has tended to do, often overemphasizing the one side of the matter in an attempt to correct earlier underemphasis. (So, for example, it is sometimes said that while Luther tends to be monophysite in Christology, Calvin leans in a Nestorian direction.) But was not the employment of the term *nature* of both aspects of Christ's reality an attempt to prevent such imbalance, by suggesting a completeness on both sides? Schleiermacher's argument here suggests not the necessary inadequacy of *nature* language, but the sheer difficulty of writing orthodox Christology, a different matter altogether.

Schleiermacher is equally unhappy in his choice of an example of bad orthodox Christology, instancing the monothelite controversy of the seventh century. Now it must be remembered that this was a controversy that took place after Chalcedon and within the limits set by the formula, at a time when the danger was thought to threaten that the truths there canonized would be lost. Without doubt, it does appear to be absurd to suggest that two wills were operative within the consciousness of Jesus of Nazareth, like the warring drives of a schizophrenic personality. But we must beware, if we are to understand the theological issues at stake, of treating the will as a kind of separate faculty within the mind, a thing-like entity lodged within the skull. Suppose the matter be put in a way that plainly avoids this kind of picture. Were only the divine will being done in the ministry of Jesus with God, so to speak, forcing Jesus into a pattern of behaviour against his will, not only would the gospel stories be falsified, but the real humanity of Jesus would disappear. Matters of real human importance are at stake, as Henry Chadwick observes. Speaking of the destruction by Maximus the Confessor of Monothelitism, he says that Maximus 'saw that the Monophysite doctrine implies a pessimistic estimate of human nature. Chalcedon, he urged with arguments of the most subtle refinement, safeguarded the autonomy of manhood and granted an independent status and positive value to the order of creation' (Chadwick, p. 211).

If, on the other hand, it were simply a matter of the achievements of a human willing and doing, a piece of moral titanism on Jesus's part, the character of the ministry and passion as God's act for and among men would be lost along with, once again, the biblical account of what happened. When the Fourth Gospel presents Jesus as saying 'I seek not my own will but the will of him who sent me' (5.30, cf. 4.34), we are given the picture of one who was willing to bring it about that his will was also the Father's so that in his freely accepted obedience both his will and the Father's are done. That seems to be a fair interpretation also of the Synoptic accounts of temptation and Gethsemane, as well as of the Fourth Gospel's interpretation of the relation of Jesus and the Father. Through the human will in gracious and willing dependence upon the Father the object of the divine willing is achieved: a life both of full human willing and in its entirety the will and work of God.

The conclusion to be drawn from this digression into discussion of the reality of Jesus's willing, is that the dyothelite doctrine, for all its apparent abstractness, was developed in order to preserve the reality of the gospel's claim that through the human career of a man the saving purposes of God were made real in time. It is therefore anti-dualistic in direction, excluding the conception of the human and divine in Jesus as alternatives. Schleiermacher, by taking it as an example of the errors of ancient Christology, succeeds only in revealing that he is himself operating with dualist axioms. Therefore he fails in his attempt to demonstrate that the chief problems of Christology are immanent in the tradition. The problem, rather, is the critique of the tradition from the transcendent perspective which Schleiermacher himself adopts. If the relation between God and the world is the relation of the unconditioned to the conditioned, as he supposes, then necessarily any Christology which teaches, as do both the New Testament and the two-nature doctrine, the co-presence in time of both God and man, will be excluded. It will be logically required not by the two-nature language, but by that through which Schleiermacher views the past.

DUALISM AND IMPASSIBILITY

The two-nature doctrine, then, can plausibly be understood in part as a weapon against those who would, for whatever reason, conceive the reality of Christ in such a way that either the human Christ was divided from the divine (classically, Nestorianism, whether or not the heresy is rightly attributed to Nestorius) or the divine word so overwhelmed the humanity that it became a mere cipher (classically, Apollinarianism and succeeding monophysite Christologies like those of Eutyches). That this is so is indicated by the fact that Leontius of Byzantium developed his conceptuality within the framework of Chalcedonian language in order to combat both types of heresy at once. As a preface to his attempt, in the *Three Books Against the Nestorians and Eutychians*, to show how one hypostasis in two natures may be conceived, he attacks the dualistic assumptions of his opponents (Leontius, 1267ff.). He does not quarrel with either Nestorians or Eutychians about the fact of the one Christ (1277a).

That is agreed between them. What he takes exception to is that the one side is docetic about the divinity, the other about the humanity (1276a). Why is this so? It is because both use the same argument and share the same presuppositions.[1] 'For they say: If you predicate two natures of the one Christ, there is no anhypostatic nature, for there would then also be two hypostases...' (1276d). Now we are not here concerned with the viability of Leontius's terminology so much as with what he is rejecting with its assistance. His point is that his opponents are simply refusing to allow the possibility of a duality in the unity of the person of Christ, just as Arians and Sabellians excluded *a priori* the possibility of God's being both three and one. A genuine hypostatic union, they are saying, is impossible. If divinity and humanity are predicated together, the former must overwhelm the latter, or there must be a division between the two that is only solvable by εὐδοκία and χάρις: that is to say by predicating a unity that is less than ontological, less than real.

Leontius's enemy is manifestly dualism, in this case the dualism that says that God and man or God and the world are entities so opposed ontologically that it is *in principle* impossible for them to come together in this unique way. That is the force of the word *must* in the final sentence of the previous paragraph. Certain things cannot be said to happen because our understanding of *God* and *humanity* preclude them (compare Schleiermacher's argument on pp. 89f.). By contrast it might be claimed that Leontius's peculiar technical vocabulary is devised in order that human language about God may be so stretched as to be able to express the reality of this unique historical phenomenon.

Leontius's arguments are similar in form to those of Athanasius in *Against the Arians*. Not all of Athanasius's arguments appear very convincing, taken simply as arguments. Without doubt he sometimes misrepresents the position of his opponents. But what gives the arguments their force is their employment against a background of anti-dualist axioms. Thus opposing at once those Jews who ask, 'How, being a man, can he be God?' and Arians who ask, 'How, if he were very God from God, could he become man?' Athanasius simply accuses his opponents of making count against his position

1 1276b, ταῖς αὐταῖς προτάσσειν and 1276d τῷ αὐτῷ κέχρηνται προβλήματι.

statements he refuses to concede. 'Both parties deny the eternity and Godhead of the Word in consequence of those human attributes, which the Saviour took on Him by reason of the flesh that he bore' (Athanasius, iii. 27). But because of what he believes *to have happened* in time and history Athanasius is unmoved by mere logical counters. The logic of words must give way before the logic of facts. Therefore although Athanasius may appear sometimes to be less careful than he might in guaranteeing the full historical humanity of the Saviour, he is completely aware of the issues at stake. Partly for soteriological reasons, he refuses to acknowledge his opponents' presuppositions. And so we find that of crucial importance here, as with Schleiermacher, are fundamental assumptions about the nature of God and his relations with the world.

It is here, too, that we can begin to discern what modern post-Kantian Christology has in common with that of the patristic period. In the previous section we saw the ontological axioms dominating Schleiermacher's critique of the tradition: as the world is 'divided and conditioned' God is 'the unconditioned and absolutely simple'. We may suspect, particularly in the light of Origen's cosmology (Chapter 3, pp. 35ff.), that this is very much a variation on the traditional theme of the opposition of the sensible and intelligible worlds. If so, we have further evidence of a fundamental continuity between the ancient and modern. Schleiermacher's characterization of God as the unconditioned gives the game away, for it is markedly similar to a dominating feature of early Christology, the doctrine of the impassibility of God. Just as the question of dualism in contemporary Christology centres on axioms like those of Schleiermacher, so in patristic times it centres on that almost ubiquitous concept.

It is easy to see why, in that Platonic world, the doctrine was philosophically so important. If the perfect is that which is in possession of a static totality of being, as Platonists tended to argue, then clearly any form of suffering or change would involve a lessening of that perfection. It is, likewise, easy to see why the doctrine, along with its concept of perfection, should be widely questioned in contemporary thought. There are, however, important aspects of the doctrine whose insights are worth preserving. If the suffering of Jesus is to be understood not simply as passively receptive but as such also the sovereign grace and power of God in time, it is reasonable to use the doctrine as a way of ensuring that God endures suffering willingly and not through incapacitating weakness. The very weakness and suffering of Jesus is the irresistible power and glory of God. Perhaps impassibility is not the best word to use of this divine indefectibility. But that it can be so taken, and indeed sometimes was, is shown by an example cited by Werner Elert. The Origenist Gregory Thaumatourgos held both that if God is free, he must be free to suffer, and that God endures suffering without suffering. Is this merely sophistry? asks Elert. Not entirely: 'God, through his freely willed suffering, becomes truly the Lord of suffering. Whereas, with Tertullian, the suffering was allowed to touch only a part of the person of Christ, in the case of Gregory 'the impassibility principle takes on a different, christological meaning . . . that God, even in his suffering, remained God, that his suffering of the blows inflicted upon him by man could not impair or damage his Godhead' (Elert, pp. 76f.).

The general thesis of Elert's book, however, is that for the most part the doctrine of impassibility played a baneful role in early Christology, taking hold as a result of Tertullian's struggle with patripassionism. It became an axiom of thought, sundering thought about God and thought about Christ. Here, if anywhere, should the legitimation of doctrine have been sought by reference to the biblical picture of Christ, but it was not. Instead, there was 'a judgement of Solomon: Divide the child in two' (pp. 73–5). Because impassibility was construed dualistically, suffering was centred on the human Jesus alone and the divine Christ became separated from him. Here we see the fountainhead of the christological schizophrenia of the West. In Christology, as we have already seen, the outcome has been such dualisms as those of the Jesus of history and the Christ of faith; in soteriology, the suffering Jesus has often been divorced from the forgiving God; and in political thought the power of God has been understood in abstraction from the cross of Jesus (see below, Chapter 9). So it is that contemporary problems are so often mirror images of those that so exercised the Fathers.

The most vivid illustration of the operation of the axiom of impassibility in early Christology is found by Elert in the thought of the Antiochene tradition. This may be surprising, in view of the fact that the Antiochenes are often thought to be the early theologians most devoted to the historical Jesus. But, according to Elert, it was their presupposition of the impassibility axiom that made them resist Cyril's insistence that Mary should be the bearer of the whole Christ. 'Human birth is a suffering (*Erleiden*), and therefore it cannot be predicated of the Logos – any more than any other suffering in general' (p. 93). That is to say, it was their assumption of a dogmatic opposition of the passible to the impassible that made it inevitable that the Antiochenes should divide the one Christ, making a dualism where there was a duality.

This is well illustrated by a work to which Dr Pittenger has referred his readers in support of his own neo-Nestorian Christology from below, Theodore of Mopsuestia's *On the Nicene Creed* (Pittenger, pp. 89f.). In it, Theodore asks the fundamental question of all Christology, that concerning the relation between the one who is eternal and another who was at one time non-existent and began his existence later (Theodore, p. 45). He makes it clear that he would not have accepted the doctrine of enhypostasia, for he holds that the destruction of the union would have left Jesus a mere man like ourselves (p. 64). Further, he claims that Philippians 2 makes a clear distinction between the divine and the human Jesus: human acts are only ascribed to God as a matter of convention because of the closeness of the union (pp. 66f.).

Theodore is rightly concerned to stress the reality of Christ's full humanity. But, precisely because of his philosophical presuppositions, he is at the same time unable to make the divinity any more than occasional. When it comes to the suffering of Jesus, God, by definition impassible, is absent; near, but absent, 'because it was impossible for Him to taste the trial of death if (the Godhead) were not cautiously remote from Him. . .' (p. 87). It is this 'cautious absence' of the Word that signals Theodore's dualistic assumptions. Yet this is not written to condemn him outright but, rather, to show how certain philosophical axioms were almost unavoidable. We are, today, perhaps excessively ready to condemn the Fathers for succumbing to Platonist presuppositions. The examples chosen in this chapter suggest again what has been said earlier in a similar context, that the line between overcoming and succumbing to the assumptions of an age is not clear or distinct. Theodore appears to have been slightly on the wrong side, though there are interpreters who would rank Cyril with him. It is, of course, easier to discover the presuppositions of other cultures than of our own. We have, however, already begun to search out those of Schleiermacher. We now return to the modern era, and begin a new section with a general-ization of what the times have in common.

PLUS ÇA CHANGE

Post-Kantian dualism is to our time what the axiom of impassibility was to that of the Fathers. Just as the world of the Fathers was the world of Platonism, in which the axiom of impassibility inevitably played a major role, ours is a culture in which we must face the sheer difficulty of any ontology which attempts to conceive a transcend-ence which is other than and yet apprehensible through the im-manent. Ours tends to be a dualism from below, seeing the world as a closed and self-sufficient system with no possibility for or need of reference beyond it. This dualism is always near to a collapse into a monism which makes the immanent the *only* real. In that sense Kant and Hegel represent the two poles of modern thought, the one positing a transcendent world about which nothing can be known; the other a transcendent world which can only be conceived within the immanent. Both are dualistic in that they deny the co-presence, without mixture and without confusion, of two ontologi-cally distinct realities; both therefore represent a radical version of Augustine's – and before that Parmenides's – dualism of time and eternity.

Christology must be done from within this world, just as it was once done from within the world that followed Plato and Aristotle. It will inevitably find itself using Kantian and Hegelian ways of expression. But if it accepts their dualism to the full, it will suffer the same kind of fate as Arius and Apollinaris, for it will no longer be able to conceive the human and divine reality that is Jesus Christ. The difference between a merely 'immanentist' Christology from below and one that escapes the full impact of the dualism is therefore likely to depend on the ways in which its linguistic expres-sion is transformed by the reality which it seeks to express. A successful transformation will involve coming to grips with ques-tions of space, time and deity, and an attempt to sketch the main issues will follow this chapter. But in this chapter we are concerned to sketch the methodological implications of dualism. We have seen already how it prevented Theodore of Mopsuestia from conceiving

Christ as a unity. We now move to an illustration of how it affected the Christology of the nineteenth century's greatest theologian.

Schleiermacher's theology was written against the background of the philosophy of Kant, who had effectively limited the exercise of rational thought to two areas. Theoretical thought was limited to the this-worldly; practical reason had implications for the transcendent, which could, however, be conceived not as it is in itself but only as the oblique implication of ethical reasoning. Realizing that this was to subordinate theology to ethics, Schleiermacher sought a third area in which theology could find a place. Theological statements derived neither from the theoretical nor from the ethical but were the expressions of feeling, of the affective side of human experience. For all its creativeness, this solution was to concede the ontological case to Kant. The dualism was transcended, but only in feeling, in an experience in which time and eternity were held together but without any intellectual resolution of their apparent contradictoriness. When it comes to Christology, Schleiermacher is unable to maintain the polarity of time and eternity, and inevitably does what he has accused earlier thinkers of doing, collapsing the one into the other.

We saw above that some kind of axiomatic dualism shaped Schleiermacher's critique of inherited patterns of Christology. One way of testing the claim that dualistic assumptions also shape the form of his own Christology will be to see whether it shares features that were characteristic of dualism in patristic times. It will then be seen that his account of the person and work of Christ reveals two features: its character as Christology from below and its Apollinarian and monophysite overtones. Schleiermacher is too great a theologian to reproduce crude versions of these doctrines, and in section 97 in particular is careful to show the positive points in favour of such doctrines as anhypostasia. But the drive of his logic is irresistible. Christ's uniqueness or 'dignity' is defined in terms of his God-consciousness, which can be crudely paraphrased as his spirituality or religiousness. It is essentially a human quality, and is understood from below as something that developed, as with anyone else. The God-consciousness 'in Him too, as in all, had to develop gradually in human fashion into a really manifest consciousness, and antecedently was only present as a germ, although in a certain sense always present as an active power' (Schleiermacher, p. 381).

Anything else would be docetic. Nevertheless, the development takes place in a unique way, with the result that, in the words of the summary heading of section 94, 'The Redeemer . . . is like all men in virtue of the identity of human nature, but distinguished from them all by the constant potency of His God-Consciousness, which was a veritable existence of God in Him' (p. 385). The divinity of Christ consists in this God-consciousness: 'To ascribe to Christ an absolutely powerful God-consciousness, and to attribute to Him an existence of God in Him, are exactly the same thing' (p. 387).

The objections to all this are essentially the same as those made against some versions of Christology from below in Chapter 2. If the saving uniqueness of Christ is grounded in a human character- istic rather than being discerned as a function of the human life taken as a whole, it is doubtful whether the full humanity of Jesus can be maintained. Conversely, Schleiermacher's account makes it impossible for the birth and childhood, in which the germ of God- consciousness was developing, to be seen as human events revela- tory of God in the self-emptying in which he comes among us, precisely because the God-consciousness is there incomplete. More important, it becomes impossible, if the God-consciousness is the means of salvation, for the cry of dereliction, which represents, if taken seriously, a loss of God-consciousness, to be an expression of God's oneness with humankind in its alienation from him. And this is not simply a literalistic appeal to the historicity of the words from the cross – though there seems no adequate reason for doubting either their authenticity or the authenticity of some such expression – but rather to the point that their ascription wants to make about the crucifixion. The point can be put another way. If it is the God-consciousness which saves, humanity is saved by a kind of christological triumphalism, by successful religiousness rather than by the 'failure' of the cross. If Jesus's baptism is seen as his iden- tification with Israel in her sin, then this 'baptism' ('made . . . to be sin who knew no sin, so that we might become the righteousness of God', 2 Cor. 5.21) represents the completion of the identification and its extension to all mankind.

The very 'ideality' (*Urbildlichkeit*) of the consciousness that Schleiermacher attributes to Jesus makes this identification with the depths of human alienation impossible or, if not, presents us with a dilemma. If, on the one hand, the God-consciousness is simply exemplary, it would mean, as Schleiermacher himself recognizes, the end of worship of Christ as redeemer (pp. 378–80), for he is not sufficiently 'other' to merit worship. But if, on the other hand, the ideality is understood from below as an attribute of the humanity, the danger threatens of a kind of neo-Apollinarianism or Eutychianism, of lifting Jesus from below to above in such a way that he no longer belongs truly below at all. His very ideality lifts him out of the realm of the genuinely human. In other words, Schleiermacher's dualism makes it impossible to sustain both the saving uniqueness of Jesus and his being of one substance with our humanity. Jesus's very religiousness takes him out of our class. And that is the same elevation to superhumanity which we saw to eventuate in the thought of those who would establish Jesus's significance only from below, simply on the basis of immanent characteristics. Because of its dualistic assumptions Christology from below in some of its forms generates the very docetic or monophysite Christology which it seeks to avoid.

CONCLUSION

What, then, is the point of these comparisons between ancient and modern dualism? The first lesson to be learned is the inescapability of ontology. The requirement that a Christology comes to terms with its assumptions about what is real cannot be evaded by appealing to experience or consciousness, as the heirs of Schleiermacher and Hegel sometimes do. As soon as such concepts are brought to employment in Christology, certainly where the word *God* is used, some understanding of the relation between God and the world is presupposed. Some early Christology failed because it could not face the theological implications involved in saying that in what happened in Jesus of Nazareth God the Word was sharing in pain and suffering. That is not likely to be our problem today: we are, if anything, over-anxious to proclaim the divine suffering. Our version of the syndrome is more likely to be a dualism from below, an inability to see the human events as any more than the outworking of a principle immanent within our universe.

As we have seen, the two-nature doctrine was developed in part to resist any reduction of time to eternity or eternity to time. If we are to be true to the duality of the New Testament's picture of Jesus, some such conceptual tool is still necessary. We return here to the moment of truth in the impassibility concept. According to the New Testament, Jesus Christ is not simply or even chiefly a man of superhuman powers. He is, as human, the saving, gracious and loving presence of the eternal God, who wills freely to be with and for his creation in what happens with Jesus of Nazareth. It is this freedom of the eternal to identify himself with us that is at the heart of the matter of Christology. At stake are not simply matters of irrelevant cosmology, but the ability of theology to bring to expression the love of God as it operates not only within the world but for it and, where necessary, against it. That is why the New Testament depicts Jesus as both human and divine, and why the Fathers fought more or less successfully those philosophical presuppositions which made the expression of both aspects within a personal unity logically impossible.

The argument of this chapter, then, is designed to reinforce the argument of Chapter 4 by showing that questions of meaning and truth similar to those which arise in New Testament interpretation emerge in both ancient and modern Christology. The reader may decide that, in that case, the heretics were right to deny the arguments of the orthodox. As a matter of fact, that is the conclusion being drawn by a number of contemporary theologians. What is more difficult for them to claim, however, is that it is a conclusion required by modernity. If it was not required of all the theologians of the patristic period by the exigencies of Greek philosophy, then neither is it required by the contemporary representatives of Hellenism. Our question, then, recurs. To be true to the content of Christology must we give it a form determined by the mainstream of contemporary culture; or is it possible that the content may be strong enough to create its own form from the materials available in contemporary thought? In order to explore that question we shall begin by sketching in bolder outline some of the continuities between ancient and modern culture.

REFERENCES

Athanasius, *Four Discourses Against the Arians: Nicene and Post-Nicene Fathers*, vol. iv.

Chadwick, Henry, *The Early Church*. Pelican History of the Church, vol. i.

Elert, Werner, *Der Ausgang der altkirchlichen Christologie. Eine Untersuchung über Theodore von Pharan und seine Zeit als Einführung in die alte Dogmengeschichte*.

Leontius of Byzantium, *Three Books against the Nestorians and Eutychians. Migne Patrologia Graeca* 86, 1, 1267–1394.

Pittenger, Norman, *The Word Incarnate: A Study of the Doctrine of the Person of Christ*.

Schillebeeckx, Edward, *Jesus: An Experiment in Christology*, Eng. trans. Hubert Hoskins.

Schleiermacher, F. D. E., *The Christian Faith*, Eng. trans. of 2ᵉ, H. R. Mackintosh and J. S. Stewart.

Theodore of Mopsuestia, *Commentary on the Nicene Creed*, Eng. trans. A. Mingana, Woodbrooke Studies v.

6

THE LOGIC OF THE DIVINE LOVE

PROBLEMS OF TIME AND ETERNITY

What, then, is the characteristic difference between the dualism that drove Apollinaris and Schleiermacher to such similar conclusions? We shall not go far wrong if we locate it in the different ways in which they conceived the relation of time and eternity. Because they both tended to be dualistic about the relations of the two orders, they came to similar conclusions. But while one operated cosmologically from above, the other operated from below. Their methodology, therefore, shares similar epistemological features within a different orientation. What, then, are those two conceptions of the relation of time and eternity which produce such similar problems for Christology?

Let us begin with a look at the characteristic features of ancient cosmology. Plato, as is well known, described time as the 'moving image of eternity'.[1] What lies behind this definition? At the least, it might seem, there is an element of discomfort with the temporal and this-worldly. Predecessors of Plato, and perhaps particularly Parmenides, had questioned the very reality of the temporal world presented to the senses. They appeared to mediate a realm in which change and decay were the all-pervading characteristics. How could one place one's reliance on a world halfway between being and non-being, a world whose very fleetingness apparently defied rational apprehension? That is the questionableness of time which underlies its definition as *moving*; it also underlies, of course, Plato's quest for a solution to the problem through the doctrine of the Forms and an approach to knowledge which transcends the fleetingness of our sense experience. But Plato was not concerned in all

1 Plato Timaeus 37d5, εἰκὼ . . . κινητόν τινα αἰῶνος.

this to underwrite an ultimate scepticism about the temporal world. His programme was to provide for it a metaphysical framework, in which the temporal was undergirded by the eternal.

On the face of it, such a framework provides an ideal basis for Christology. All that is said about Christ is rooted in the eternal goodness of God. But there are difficulties. Because of the way in which Plato and his successors formulated the problem and essayed its solution, they gave birth to a world which was inevitably more confident in dealing with eternity than with time. Added to this must be the fact that when they spoke of eternity they tended to conceive it in terms of timelessness, on the analogy of the timeless-less of a theorem of geometry. (This association of the eternal with the timeless has also brought in its train other difficulties, not just for theology but for all disciplines. For if simple mathematics of this type becomes the model for all knowledge, many of the things we want to say and believe become inherently suspect. It is this relation between ontology and epistemology that will later be seen to provide the link between this chapter and the next.) Together the priority of eternity over time and its being conceived as timelessness generated the philosophical background for the development of Christology. It was the general confidence about eternity which made it possible, as Cyril appears to have done according to Meijering's account (Chapter 3, p. 49), to treat the eternal Son in almost total abstraction from Jesus of Nazareth. In its turn, this generated the problems with which we have seen Dietrich Ritschl to be concerned, the eternalizing of Christ and his being effectively anchored in the past.

It is for reasons such as this that ancient Christology is often dismissed as being 'docetic' and that the formula of Chalcedon is rejected as being unable to do anything more than simply juxtapose, in a dualistic manner, the divine and the human in Christ (Pannenberg, 1968, p. 284; Mackintosh, p. 214). As a matter of fact, one might ask why, if they were so dualistic, the members of the Council of Chalcedon were *able* to juxtapose (if that is the correct word) the human and the divine in the 'one and the same Christ'. But if they were able to do no more than state a case without explaining it, it was surely partly because in their Platonic background there lay the conception of eternity derived from some such definition as Plato's. If time is the moving image, the implication appears to be that eternity is unmoving. And if eternity is by definition motionless, what is it doing in the very temporal figure of Jesus of Nazareth? It is no wonder that he tended sometimes to be crowded out. The wonder is, rather, that so often the Fathers were able to break through the axioms of their world to produce what, as orthodox Christology, came to assert the co-presence of both eternity and time in this one historical figure. Against this background it is possible to see orthodox Christology as not the slave but the critic of Hellenistic philosophy.

At the same time, however, the Fathers produced the Christology from above that causes such problems for the modern mind. The reason is not far to seek. While the Greeks were more confident in dealing with eternity than with time, we are happier with time than with eternity. When we think of the modern world we think of science, and when we think of science we think, whether rightly or wrongly, of the understanding and manipulation of temporal phenomena. Here we come upon the characteristic feature of Christology from below: its proper attempt to take this world seriously in its speaking about Christ. And yet we have seen that in Schleiermacher this starting-point in time produces no less docetic a doctrine of Christ, and the same might be said of many other modern Christologies. Some, of course, have abandoned the attempt to conceive a divine Christ at all, in logical loyalty to a purely this-worldly metaphysic. But the denial of eternity in the name of time is as dualistic as making it a simple projection or epiphenomenon of this-worldly realities. If there is to be Christology, and for that matter Christianity, that is recognizably continuous in form and content with that of the past, we have to question equally a dualism from below and a dualism from above. This can be achieved in part by showing that the modern conception of time and eternity which underlies much recent Christology is to be understood as the obverse of that which sometimes overcame the temporal content of ancient Christology.

On the reasonable hypothesis that Kant is for our intellectual world very much what Plato was for that of the Fathers, we shall begin with him. Kant sums up an era, as did Plato. The greatest mind of the Enlightenment, he encapsulates its tendency to make absolute the temporal, just as Plato represents Hellenism's tendency to be dominated by timeless eternity. In the paragraph introducing his discussion of the nature of space and time Kant states, in the form of questions, the possible ways in which the two basic cosmological concepts may be construed. The last of the questions is that expecting the answer Yes:

> What, then, are space and time? Are they real existences? Are they only determinations or relations of things, yet such as would belong to things even if they were not intuited? Or are space and time such that they belong only to the form of intuition, and therefore to the subjective constitution of our mind, apart from which they could not be ascribed to anything whatsoever? (Kant, p. 68).

Kant's answer is that time, like space, 'is not an empirical concept that has been derived from any experience' (p. 74). We cannot, he claims, perceive it directly by any of the senses. Whence, then, does the concept come? It must be supplied by the mind as a framework within which our sense experience comes to be understood. Negatively, it is that without which there could be no experience at all. It belongs 'to the subjective constitution of our mind' as it orders the manifoldness of the phenomena that are presented to it.

'Time is the formal *a priori* condition of all appearances whatsoever' (p. 77). This view of Kant that time is, so to speak, the conceptual spectacles with the aid of which we are able to order our experiences into before, after and simultaneous, either leads to or is a function of the characteristic modern tendency to make the temporal realm absolute. Time is the way we order appearances; therefore, by definition, it is limited to the world of appearances, that which presents itself to us through our senses. No other world can be known. Or, to take the matter a step further, if time is a projection upon phenomena by the mind, the same must be true *a fortiori* of eternity. We can come to understand what we mean by time, for there are empirical events which, so to speak, fill out the concept. But eternity, if it can be known at all – and in Kant it cannot, at least not by theoretical reason – is conceivable only as *a projection of what is already a projection*. So it is that in Christology from below that is strongly influenced by a Kantian view of time, the eternal features of Jesus's reality are explained as functions, epiphenomena or projections of his humanity.

An alternative approach from within the same framework is represented by Kierkegaard's sceptic, Johannis Climacus, who accepts the definition of eternity as the unknown, but turns it to the advantage of a more orthodox Christology by conceiving Christ as the absolutely paradoxical place where time and eternity are to be found in relation. An interesting question here, worth mentioning though rather tangential to the main discussion, is whether Kierkegaard should here be interpreted as breaking through the axioms of a Kantian philosophy or as succumbing to the familiar process by which Jesus is eternalized. Perhaps both happens: certainly in *Philosophical Fragments* the absolute paradox has some of the characteristics of a Platonic form, while in *Training in Christianity*, which is written by the presumably Christian 'Anti-Climacus', much more attention is paid to the Gospels' picture of the human Jesus. But we can certainly say that the Christology of paradox, very much preoccupied with eternity as the essentially unknown, belongs in the post-Kantian world along with Schleiermacher's Christology of Jesus as a divinized man, and not in the ancient world with its greater confidence that it can deal with matters of eternity more directly.

The great difference between Kantian and Platonic ontology lies, then, in the tendency of the former to make the temporal order absolute and to deny the possibility of a knowledge of eternity. *But it is a difference within a shared set of presuppositions.* Kant's view of time is still dominated by the old Greek pessimism about its fleetingness. According to his view of perception, the phenomenal world present to our senses is characterized essentially by its multiplicity or manifoldness. That this for Kant is effectively the equivalent of Hellenism's fleetingness is indicated by the fact that he believes that the multiplicity is essentially disorderly. (Shades of Origen, here!) Plato reduced the manifold to order by positing a framework of eternal forms; Kant achieved a similar end by positing the ordering power of the mind. Both programmes have as their background a despair of conceiving an order that belongs intrinsically *within* the phenomena of time. Plato went beyond time into a negative eternity; Kant beyond into a godlike mind. But Christology requires, if it is to be true to the New Testament, an order of time that inheres in reality, for it wishes to link time and eternity rationally at the place where a human being lived and died. Is Christology then impossible?

An answer to that question depends upon a number of others.

But it is important at this stage to be aware of the fact that Kant himself may be interpreting modern culture in a way that owes as much to the tradition within which he thought as to the essence of modern science. If we can open up a gap between Kant and the modern science which is so often thought to rule out a classical Christology by its adherence to a closed world order, we shall at least suggest that the gap between our culture and that of the Fathers is not as absolute as is sometimes supposed. In other words, may it not be suggested that axiomatic dualism is more important for Kant than it is for the world of which he is often taken to be the spokesman? Here we can begin by indicating the background to Kant in two of his important predecessors. The first is Descartes, a classical dualist who represents a link between Kant and the Greek world. Descartes's method takes its point of departure from a characteristically subjective form of the Greek doctrine of time's fleetingness. The programme of the *Meditations* bears considerable similarities to that of Plato's *Theaetetus*, denying as they both do the possibility of knowledge deriving from the (temporal) world of our sense experience. Reliable, eternal knowledge – once again, on the analogy of geometry – is possible for Descartes only by the pure concepts of the mind. Where Plato turned outward to eternity, Descartes turned inward to the mind. Only one more step was needed for Kant to deny the link Descartes made between the contents of his mind and the transcendent eternal world. The concepts are indeed to be sought in the mind, but *only* there, as the empty battles between rival metaphysical theories and Hume's devastating criticism were to teach him. Thus, we might say, Descartes taught Kant to look within.

But who taught Descartes? Here we make yet another link between chapters of this study. Is not the crucial figure of Augustine the one to whom we should look? To Augustine is often ascribed the form in which the conception of time and eternity as negatively related to each other took deep root in the West. Certainly, the old platonic dualism of the sensible (temporal) and intelligible (eternal) worlds is very pervasive in his writings. And it can scarcely be denied that the decisive forerunner of the *Meditations'* subjective style of philosophizing is to be found in Augustine's *Confessions*. All this, of course, is very speculative and tentative; or it would be but for one significant fact, that remarkable anticipations of Kant's conception of time are to be found in the famous reflections on that topic in the *Confessions*. Augustine's discussion is far more fertile than Kant's, for instead of dismissing all alternative views in favour of the only one supposed possible, it refuses to dismiss completely all the possibilities. It is in fact bewilderingly many-sided, like all of Augustine's theology. Although the major reductive analyses appear in Book xi of the *Confessions*, Augustine returns to time, almost as an aside, during the discussion of creation in the following book. He conceives the creation of the visible world to have been preceded by the creation of an 'invisible and formless earth, this utter formlessness'. From this God made 'all the things of which our changing world consists'. To what is already a combination of Platonism (the creation of the world from the *formless*) and Christian doctrine (the *creation* of the formless earth), Augustine adds the following striking and perplexing comment:

– though it is not right to speak of consistency in this world, because its susceptibility to change is obvious from the fact that we are aware of time and can measure its passage. For time is constituted by the changes, which take place in things as a result of variations and alterations in their form, and the matter of all these things is that invisible earth of which we have spoken (xii. 8).

Among the things said or implied in this passage are these: The first is that our awareness of time is the ground for our attributing to the world its essential fleetingness – 'its susceptibility to change'. The second is the fundamental unreliability, irrationality almost, of the world of our sense experience – 'it is not right to speak of consistency in this world'. Both of these features owe more to Platonic – or would it be better to say Presocratic and Neoplatonic? – pessimism than to the Christian doctrine of creation that Augustine is expounding, and are themselves understandable in the light of the third feature. This is that time owes its fundamental questionableness to 'that invisible earth': what Augustine has already called 'this utter formlessness'. To be in time is, for Augustine, despite his confidence in the good divine creation, to be in a sphere of existence *finally lacking in reality*. Here lies the ambiguity, the two-headedness, that was to fly apart so disastrously for Augustine's own Christian thought world some thousand years later.

And so when Augustine says that 'time is constituted by the changes which take place in things' he is not saying, as a modern might, that here is a guide to a positive account of time. Change is the *problem*, and it is in the light of this essential pessimism that the analysis of the previous book of the *Confessions* should be understood. Augustine there argues – and for reasons whose strength should not be denied even if the axiomatic pessimism should be – that time cannot be conceived as a function of the interrelationships of bodies, heavenly or otherwise. He therefore turns within, and the weight of his analysis falls upon his subjective experience of time rather than an observation of what takes place in the world. The analysis is widely known (Lucas, pp. 20ff.) and need not be repeated here. Of chief interest is the anticipation of Kant to which Augustine is led. 'It seems to me, then, that time is merely an extension, though of what it is an extension I do not know. *I begin to wonder whether it is an extension of the mind itself* (xi. 26, my emphasis). Kant did not begin to wonder, but was quite sure that time is, if not an extension, then a projection of the mind. Herein is to be found the strong though sometimes wavering line that joins Kant with Parmenides, Plato, Augustine and Descartes.

The conclusion of the inquiry is that modern culture's tendency to make time absolute, in the sense of believing that only the temporal is real and can be known, is a direct outcome of ancient philosophical culture's pessimistic understanding of time and of its dualism of eternity and time. One dualism is the obverse of another, and the argument so far makes possible the reiteration of the conclusion of Chapter 5. Just as there is a continuity of assumption and background between ancient theology and modern, so there is between the cultures out of which Christology has to be done. We need not, therefore, stress the chasm that divides us from patristic Christology and therefore the need for Christology to be done in total abstraction from the way it was in the early days of Christian theology, as if there were, as is sometimes suggested, a total difference of experience between the ages. We have far more in common with the Fathers than is sometimes claimed. The matrix, so to speak, of discussion is the same, consisting of an identification of time with the fleeting and unreliable: with change and decay.

And yet, by the time we come to Kant and the modern world he has helped to form, the emphasis in the discussion within the matrix is importantly different. The problem, of relating the temporal and the eternal, is the same problem, but must be approached in a different way. The moment of truth in the demand for a Christology from below is that, partly as a result of what Augustine did, we can no longer move so confidently in the world of eternity. We return once more to E. P. Meijering's unhappiness with Cyril's *a priori* philosophical Christology. 'Here the great gap between patristic thought and ours becomes clear: we try not to interpret historical contingencies from a preconceived system, but make an effort to let our theological thinking start with the historical man Jesus of Nazareth. This implies that our theology is much more vulnerable than patristic theology. . .' (Meijering, p. 126). Unfortunately, Meijering's programme is more a wish than a fact, as we have seen from the heavy philosophical freight carried by Christology that supposedly begins with the man Jesus of Nazareth. Much depends, as we have seen in Chapter 4, on what we mean by this historical figure. My contention, rather, is that there is not so much a gap as an alteration of the way in which the same difficulty asserts itself. The difference is of degree rather than of kind. The emphasis of the problem is now centred on time and its relations to eternity rather than on eternity in its relation to time. But it is the same problem.

CO-PRESENCE IN SPACE

The assumption of the argument so far is that problems with time are more central to Christology's concern than the matter of space. It is on the basis of some such assumption that it has been argued that underlying both the eras with which we are concerned is a similar and alienated view of time. But it is not an assumption that is widely shared. In many recent discussions matters of space bulk larger than those of time. Indeed, the very inadequacy of the description of different methods of Christology as from above and from below may derive from imprisonment to a spatial metaphor. Be that as it may, we need not go far to seek the origin of Pannenberg's association of a christological *method* from above with the *structure* of concepts which speak of 'the descent of the Son from the world above' (Pannenberg, 1968, p. 33). Pannenberg's source is surely

Bultmann's celebrated attribution to the New Testament writers of a belief in a 'three-decker universe' so different from our own cosmology. 'The cosmology of the New Testament is essentially mythical in character. The world is viewed as a three-storied structure, with the earth in the centre, the heaven above and the underworld beneath' (Bultmann, p. 1).

Bultmann's programme of demythologization is predicated upon the assumption that the content of the New Testament teaching about Jesus can be separated from the form in which it is presented in the texts. It also makes a number of other assumptions of method, of which two are worth mentioning here. The first is that there is a radical discontinuity between our culture and that of the writers of the New Testament and creeds; the second that the modern world is what it is by virtue of its view of the world as a closed system of cause and effect. The second assumption can be translated as follows: to be modern means to share the Kantian view of space and time as part of the unchanging mental equipment of every human being. Together these views of Bultmann provide the starting-point of the next stage of the inquiry, which intends to deny them and, it is hoped, to persuade at least a few readers of the propriety of doing so.

The first denial is of the claim that it is essential to the form of the New Testament teaching about Christ that the writers should believe naively and literally in a three-storey universe. Basic to Bultmann's thesis was the view that early Christology took its form from a Gnostic 'myth' of a divine redeemer coming to earth from above. This is now widely questioned, largely on the ground that the Gnostic myths developed after, not before, early Christology (Hengel, p. 31f.). Now, there is no wish here to deny the use of spatial 'below' and 'above' language in the New Testament. What is being denied is both that it is constitutive and that the writers were unaware of the metaphorical nature of the language. (Similar remarks could be made about the New Testament view of time. Why do the New Testament writers appear not to have been alarmed by the supposed failure of the parousia to materialize in the way that Jesus and the first disciples are held to have expected? Is it perhaps because their view of time and eternity was less naive than that of their interpreters?) That a naive view of the three-storey universe is not constitutive of the early Christology is suggested by the fact that many of the central statements do not contain a spatial reference at all. 'The word became flesh' (John 1.14); 'God sent his Son' (Gal. 4.4). It is well that Pannenberg says only that 'some concepts that point in this direction occur already in the New Testament' (p. 33); none of Pannenberg's texts (the one from Paul already cited, plus Phil. 2.5ff. and Rom. 8.3) employ spatial imagery in their description of the events that took place with the coming of Jesus! And so far as the other point is concerned, a glance at the dialogue between Jesus and Nicodemus reported in John 3 should remove any doubts about at least one writer's awareness of the metaphorical nature of spatial language. Is it not more likely that language like that of Romans 10.6ff. and Ephesians 4.8ff. derive from the natural human tendency to use language of spatial transcendence in connection with God who is *ontologically* above us as Creator? Some such awareness of the nature of the language without doubt underlies Luke's account of the ascension, with its clear consciousness of earlier traditions of religious imagery.

The truth would, rather, appear to be that the form of New Testament Christology is more bound up with temporal than with spatial expression. The words which speak of the past significance of Jesus – and we should not forget that there are many present tense expositions, especially in Paul, which are even further from spatial imagery – are words of action in time, and are, as we have already seen, problematic not in themselves but in the light of concepts of timeless eternity or an entirely closed order of time. In this respect, space is secondary – in what sense, we shall explore later. It is worth noting here that the creeds are in this sense more 'mythological' than the New Testament. The expression 'He came down from heaven' represents a more explicitly spatial account of the matter, far less 'horizontal' than many New Testament accounts which are in this respect more concerned to express in different ways a Christology of *co-presence in time*. Thus Paul's language of 'sending' and John's of 'becoming' becomes at Nicaea 'he came down'. But it is interesting that, to repeat D. M. MacKinnon's point, Nicaea's use of a technical term like *homoousios* already mitigates the crudity of the 'mythological' expression, showing an awareness that the metaphorical language requires ontological control if its meaning is to be understood (Chapter 1, pp. 6f.).

The debate centred on Bultmann's account has, then, served to obscure the true problem of space in Christology. This is that if the life of Jesus of Nazareth is correctly interpreted by the New Testament in theological terms, God is there being conceived to be located in space as well as in time. We cannot have time without space when we are centring our theological language on the life of a human being, using words that imply the presence of God in particular human action and passion. This is of course the problem that is known as that of transcendence. How can the transcendent, 'other', God be conceived to be located in this world? But the problem is not that of the three-storey universe, which is its symptom not its essence. *It is not a question of descent but of co-presence in space.* In the same piece of space there are held to be present both God and man, without loss of the deity of the one or the humanity of the other. Can it be so, or is it contradictory, with our being compelled to make a choice, either a docetic Christ or one who is a human being, very special indeed but differing only in degree from the rest of us? Once again, all depends upon how we conceive space, and once again the nature of the problem is revealed to us by a glance at the philosophy of Kant.

In the famous scholium to his *Principia Mathematica* Newton, whom Kant revered, expounded his doctrine of absolute space, which remains 'always similar and immovable' (Newton, pp. 17f.). Difficulties with the concept as applying objectively to the 'outside' world led Kant to do for space what he did also for time. 'It is . . . solely from the human standpoint that we can speak of space, of extended things, etc.' (Kant, p. 71). The outcome is similar to that of the discussion of time, that space is not something perceivable, for 'objects in themselves are quite unknown to us' (p. 74), but a conceptual structure we impose upon reality. If we cannot know the spatiality of things in themselves, then *a fortiori* we cannot begin, except as 'mythological projection', to conceive of a spatial and historical human life which is also the locus of something transcendent, from beyond space.

I have argued elsewhere (Gunton, 1980, pp. 505f.) that many difficulties with transcendence derive from the way in which visual patterns of perception dominate our understanding of space. The things we *see* are mutually exclusive. For example, a patch of blue in a painting excludes the presence of any other colour. This mutual exclusiveness encourages us to conceive space as absolute: a thing

114

is there, and cannot *also* be elsewhere. The notion of the universe as a totally closed order follows from this. Accordingly, the fundamental metaphor dominating the way we see reality is that of the machine, with the world as a series of atomic pieces interrelated with each other *only* in a mutually exclusive way. The notion dies hard in our culture, and is another aspect of the deistic and dualistic way in which we view things. Christologically, it means that the tradition's doctrine of the incarnation seems to take the form of an 'intervention' by God who is *outside* of the machine, a crude piece of messing around in the works with a celestial spanner.

But suppose that we turn away from the visual patterning of experience with its primary stress on the mutual exclusiveness of things. Hearing provides us with other aspects of our experience. Take the example of narrative, the form in which much, though by no means all, of New Testament talk of Jesus is presented. If we prescind from our instinctive tendency to think in terms of exclusion, there is nothing *a priori* incredible in narrating an event of which it is said: 'Jesus did that'; 'God did that'. One can, in hearing, juxtapose two accounts of an event in such a way that there is no logical requirement that the one preclude the other. However, this is not, in itself, any reason for our believing the narrative. The reader of this account may quite rightly object that the attribution of an event to both man and God is simply a projection, a naive imposition of the primitive mind. But that would be to miss the main point which is that hearing opens out dimensions of reality not available if we remain wedded to a visual patterning of experience.

But do the phenomena of hearing enable us to transcend the alienation of absolute space? When do we hear two or more different things taking place together in space? The answer, of course, is in music. When, for example, the notes of a major triad are played simultaneously, we hear in one and the same place three tones which retain their identity and create a new reality, the chord. That is in itself an interesting parallel to the statement that in Jesus Christ there are two co-present realities – what Chalcedon called the human and divine natures – which in their association, the 'hypostatic union', form a new reality which yet does not do away with the specific characteristics of the old: 'without confusion, without change'. But it is only a parallel, for music remains a this-worldly reality for all its anticipations of heaven, while the claim in classical Christology is that in Christ we have the spatial co-presence of the finite and the infinite.

What, then, is being claimed on the basis of the things we hear in music? In a remarkable book, *Sound and Symbol*, Victor Zuckerkandl argues that the fact of music has implications for our understanding of the way the world is. He demonstrates the inadequacy of both 'subjectivist' and 'objectivist' interpretations of the meaning of music, holding that the phenomena are saved neither by a view that locates music in the emotional responses or projections of the hearer nor in the mechancial matter of the instruments and the sound waves they produce. All those things are real enough in themselves, but they are not music, which is the product of tones in dynamic interrelationship with one another (Zuckerkandl, pp. 15ff.). But if music exists as part of our universe, *where* is it? Although music comes to us through the agency of instruments, it cannot be located *in* them. Tone does not come to us from one particular location in space, nor from all of them: it is simply pure motion towards (p. 289). The details of Zuckerkandl's argument cannot be rehearsed here. For our purposes, it is valuable in showing, if not the reality – as I believe to be the outcome of his argument – but at least the conceivability of a different conception of space from that typically derived from our experience of things in exclusive juxtaposition. Zuckerhandl is himself anxious to draw out the implications for our view of reality of this distinction between what we see and what we hear. 'The interpenetration of tones in auditory space corresponds to the juxtaposition of colours in visual space' (p. 299), but because the former teaches us something different from the latter, we must extend our conception of what reality is. It is much more various and open than our modern way of conceiving things, dominated as it is by a pattern of epistemology inherited from Plato (Rorty, pp. 38ff., and below, Chapter 7, pp. 143ff.), suggests.

> The current criterion, according to which a body is where I see it or touch it . . . becomes untenable; a body is also where I neither see it nor touch it nor can in any other way find it physically present. . . (I)ts limits do not coincide with the limits of its material form. . . (I)ts limits are those of its field; that is – since a dynamic field is theoretically limitless – it has no definite

limits at all. . . All bodies are in all places, everywhere. . . (Zuckerkandl, p. 304).

The implications of such a view for Christology scarcely require pointing, though it is certainly worth stressing that the views of an entirely closed, self-contained material order, which form the presupposition of much post-Kantian theology, begin to appear less than self-evident. We are at least beginning to see cracks in the view that holds the spatial co-presence of two different entities to be inconceivable.

We shall return to Zuckerkandl's musical ontology later, when we revert to the question of time, which is more central both to music and to Christology. But how far is this theory of music and its ontological implications a freak, totally irrelevant to the problems that face us in connection with Christology? The answer is, Not at all, for in connection with his account of space Zuckerkandl refers to one of the fathers of the 'modern scientific world view', appeal to which so often provides a ground for rejection of classical Christology. In 1844 Michael Faraday published a paper entitled 'A Speculation touching Electric Conduction and the Nature of Matter'. The paper begins with an exposition of the current theory that atoms were isolated items of reality located in absolute space. According to the received theory, 'Space will permeate all masses of matter in every direction like a net, except that in place of meshes it will form cells, isolating each atom from its neighbours, and *itself only being continuous*' (Faraday, p. 2, my emphasis). Yet Faraday finds that the properties of materials which do and do not conduct electricity provide a refutation of this theory. And so he is led to a view of atoms as fields of force rather than discrete substances and a theory of the 'mutual penetrability of the atoms' (p. 7) – the opposite of the view we have suggested to have derived from relying overmuch on visual patterns of perception. This in turn suggests a view that 'matter is not merely mutually penetrable, but each atom extends, so to say, throughout the whole of the solar system, yet always retaining its own centre of force' (p. 8). In other words, one of the great minds of modern science came, on the basis of discoveries that were later to be confirmed, to be of the opinion that there is a sense in which *everything is everywhere*.

In the context of such a view, according to which the universe is a system of fields of forces, interpenetrating and interacting, the claim of Professor T. F. Torrance (1969) that patristic conceptions of cosmology are nearer to ours than is often assumed, comes into focus. One patristic view is expressed in a familiar passage from the *De Incarnatione*:

> For he was not, as might be imagined, circumscribed in the body, nor, while present in the body was he absent elsewhere; nor, while he moved the body, was the universe left void of his working and providence; but, thing most marvellous, Word as he was, so far from being contained by everything, he rather contained all things himself; . . . thus even while present in a human body and himself quickening it he was, without inconsistency, quickening the universe as well. . . (Athanasius, 1954, pp. 70f.).

It is often noted that on occasions Athanasius appears to speak in a way that makes the Word's relation to the body an external one, as when he says that the Word wields the body. But in other places, and here in particular, the relation is an internal one, suggesting not juxtaposition but interpenetration: twice in the passage just cited he says that the Son was 'present in the body'. It is because of this that 'without inconsistency' (εἰκότως, 'accordingly', in Thompson's translation, Athanasius, 1971, p. 175), the Son can identify himself with the person of Jesus while being present elsewhere also.

It is the internality of the relation between God and the world that comes to expression when we set aside the ontologies dominated by the relationships discerned by sight, and that is the point of the citation of Athanasius here. We shall return to his ontology later in its implications for our understanding of space and time together. Suffice it to say here that his conception will be totally misunderstood if it is in any way construed psychologically, as if there is any suggestion that Jesus of Nazareth is somehow by an act of will upholding the universe. For all its difficulty, particularly to an era preoccupied with seeing things from below, the point must be seen to be essentially about God, and could be crudely translated as saying something like this. The world is what it is through the operation of the spatially omnipresent divine field of force. In Jesus Christ we see the outcome of the self-differentiation of the divine omni-spatiality. Without loss to his general presence, he takes form within his world and alongside other men as part of that world. That is where the field of force analogy breaks down, or, rather, is shown to be only an analogy. For when Athanasius speaks of the Word he does not mean an impersonal field of force, but refers to the reality of the personal God. And the repetition by modern theology of what Athanasius is saying depends upon whether it is a justifiable interpretation of the significance of Jesus of Nazareth and what happened to and with him. It involves a claim that when we repeat the story of the events of Jesus's life, death and resurrection we are telling not just a story of happenings immanent to the universe, but of those immanent events as also the place where God differentiates himself, becoming present within one piece of finite reality (he in whom 'the whole fullness of deity dwells bodily', Col. 2.9), but without either losing his general relationship to the whole or depriving that one part of its genuine humanity. In this one piece of space there are co-present two levels of reality, that which permeates everything by virtue of his creating power, and that which by virtue of that same power, he takes freely and graciously to himself, becoming what in himself he is not.

CO-PRESENCE IN TIME

The problem about the co-presence in time of the eternal and the temporal cannot, then, be treated in total abstraction from similar questions about space. Despite the apparent priority in the New Testament of time language, questions of spatiality are raised by the nature of the way time and eternity are claimed to come together, in the spatiality of a human body. The argument of the previous section was that here everything depends upon how we understand space. If, to take one extreme, space is absolute and so externally related to God, his co-presence with a particular spatial being becomes at best problematic. If, however, space is seen in terms not of exclusiveness but of interpenetration (perichoresis!), matters are conceived otherwise. It is then possible for a theologian like Athanasius to conceive of God at once as Creator of space and as able to relate himself internally to parts of it. This brings us close to yet another close parallel between the ancient and modern periods, for Athanasius's polemics might as well be directed against deism as against whatever opponent he had in mind in his early work. For deism is a modern expression of the absoluteness of space and the external relatedness of God to it.

Athanasius, then, attacked his era's version of absolute space with conceptual tools derived from his beliefs about the incarnation. We turn back to the question of time and eternity with a reference to a similar weapon forged by Origen in his attempt to conceive a relation between the historic basis of his faith and what he believed about the eternity of God. By speaking of the 'eternal begottenness' of the Son, Origen struck a blow, whose implications he never fully worked out, against views of eternity as timeless. Whatever difficulties we have with Origen's concept, its thrust is clear. The relationship of the eternal to time is not one of pure negation, as Hellenism often taught. There are positive analogies between what God eternally is and what happened in the history of salvation.

But, as we have seen, despite the continuities expressed in the link between the ancient absoluteness of eternity and the modern absoluteness of time, we are not faced with quite the same programme. Our programme is to speak of the reality of Christ from out of our culture's tendency to make absolute the temporal and the immanent. Origen's and Athanasius's programme was to speak of Christ from within a culture wedded to timeless eternity and motionless spatiality. Where, then, shall we begin? The best launching-point would seem to be with an axiom of the dualist position that we have already observed: that the temporal, because it is the place of 'fleetingness', cannot be the locus of rationality. This resistance of the temporal to rationality, the feeling that time is in itself meaningless, is a contributor to, if not the determinant of, both Augustine's doubts about the reality of time and Kant's view that because the manifold was in itself patternless, the mind must impose rationality upon it. Both see time as essentially fallen, the place where there can be no intrinsic meaning and rationality, for it is the place of plurality and change. Both the negation of time by eternity and the attempt, by reaction, to make it the whole, are attempts to evade the consequences of time's supposed formlessness and irrationality. Both entail conceptions of the world hostile to Christology, which is the place where an attempt is made to conceive eternity and time in a positive relation, the one losing its fallenness through the saving presence of the other. To assume either that time is essentially fallen or that it is, through the action of the human mind, constrained to rationality, is to forfeit the capacity to conceive it as the locus of intrinsic meaning and rationality.

Against this, we must ask whether fleetingness, the origin of the tendency to see the temporal order as intrinsically resistant to rationality, is the sole defining characteristic of temporality. We cannot deny that it is one of them. The contrast between 'the grass withers, the flower fades' and the eternity of God (Isaiah 40.7f.) is too deeply etched in human experience to be denied.

A thing then will suffer something at the hands of time, just as we are accustomed also to say that time wastes things away, and everything is aged by time, and oblivion comes with the passage of time; but not that knowledge, youth or beauty comes through the elapse of time. For time is by its nature the cause rather of decay (Aristotle, *Physics IV*, 221a, cited by Lucas, p. 54).

But is that the sole feature on which we should base a philosophy? If we examine other areas of our experience, different features become evident. One such area is that of music, and we turn now to Zuckerkandl's parallel treatment of time. Although we have treated it second, it is prior in his argument both in place and in logic. For while music can teach us about space – and certainly about the right we have to use spatial metaphors, as when we go 'up' the scale – it is primarily a temporal phenomenon. Not only does it take place in time but, claims Zuckerkandl, in contradiction of the philosophies of Augustine, Hume and Kant, it enables us to realize that we *do* perceive time.

'Music is temporal art in the special sense that in it time reveals itself to experience' (Zuckerkandl, p. 200). What does this mean? It is that when we hear music we are enabled to understand uniquely the true reality of time. According to Zuckerkandl this happens particularly when we look with the help of music at the choice with which the philosophical and theological traditions have faced us: a choice between the timeless and the transient. Music shows us that we are not faced with the alternatives of absolute eternity and absolute temporality.

Music . . . questions the basic validity of the entire conceptual complex. The hourglass concept of time, it declares, is incompatible with the simple facts with which music confronts us (p. 224).

And what are these simple facts? They can be explained by a contrast with the discoveries of Augustine, for whom, on analysis, the present *disappeared* as he tried to anchor it between past and future. In music the reverse is the case.

> This is a present from which not *I*, thanks to my particular powers, look backward into the past and forward into the future, but which *itself* thus looks backward and forward. . . (T)he present of musical experience is not the dividing point that eternally separates past and future; it is the stage upon which, for every ear, the drama of the being of time is played – the ceaseless storing of itself and anticipating itself which is never repeated, which is every instant new (p. 225).

And similarly:

> Every melody declares to us that the past can be there without being remembered, the future without being foreknown – that the past is not stored in memory but in time, and that it is not our consciousness which anticipates time but that time anticipates itself (p. 235).

Because of the nature of the dynamic interrelationships of tones, the present is not lost, but, quite the reverse, becomes the place where the past is directed to the future. This means that to find the real world we do not have to abstract from time, but find the order that is *inherent within it*. This leads Zuckerkandl to reject the dogma that haunts all Christology, both ancient and modern, as we shall see more directly in the next chapter: 'That order is possible only in the enduring, the immutably fixed, the substantial' (p. 241). By contrast with this deeply engrained dogma, 'music presents us with . . . the unprecedented spectacle of an order in what is wholly flux, of a building without matter. . . Order, liberated from all relation to things, *pure order* . . . it is to music that we owe our awareness that such a thing can exist' (pp. 241f.).

In this remarkable argument Zuckerkandl has done a number of things that are germane to our theme. First, he has broken down the one-dimensional conception of reality that so dominates modern culture, and in particular its dependence upon the eye for knowledge of what is there (pp. 260–2). In so doing, he has not done anything explicitly theological, but, as he himself says, has opened up debates sometimes thought to be closed. 'To think of the musical view of the universe as a bridge between the scientific and the religious views is not sheer nonsense' (pp. 374f.). Second, he has, without making time reversible, or depriving it of directionality, none the less questioned the universality of the link between directionality and decay. He has thus queried the way in which modern culture makes time absolute, and so has related past and future in a manner analogous to that in which Faraday conceived an interrelatedness of spaces. His is an argument for the openness of times to each other. Third, he has made conceivable and credible, the notion of an order and meaning that is found within time. To be understood, a temporal event has to be neither objectively nor subjectively eternalized, after the manner of, respectively, Augustinian and post-Kantian Christology. It can be seen in its rational significance *in terms of its relationships to its context and not by abstracting it from them.*

The example of music is highly instructive, but no more than in the case of space does it have to stand alone. An equally strong argument for the inherent and open-textured rationality of temporal phenomena is to be found in the development of modern science. We shall have to move carefully here, for the present discussions about the philosophy of science in relation to cosmology do not present any wide measure of agreement. The case is similar with the general matter of the nature of time (Whitrow). But what can surely be claimed is, first, that the related views of time as absolute (Newton) and imposed by the mind (Kant) do not gain any widespread adherence. Rather, some version of the view that time is relative to events – in some sense a function of the way events are interrelated – appears to obtain wide consensus. And yet, and here we reach the second point, this is not a *relativistic* doctrine in the sense that it makes it necessary to deny the objective reality of the temporal ordering of reality. On the contrary, the very success of modern science derives from a denial that rationality is only to be found in the timeless in favour of a view that it can be discerned *within* the temporal ordering of things. The very presupposition of contemporary science is that temporal phenomena are not inherently disordered but manifest an order that can be discovered. The point is that stressed by Professor T. F. Torrance when he speaks of the concept of contingent rationality (Torrance, 1981). Rationality is to be discovered *within* the contingencies of the temporal order, and not by abstracting from them to some order of timeless truths or by imposing upon them a uniform structure produced by the mind.

The point about contingent rationality will be expanded when we come to questions about the epistemological status of christological claims. But here we are concerned to draw out the significance for ontology of the twin theses of the relative nature of time and the view that rational order is to be found within it. If time is not absolute, we shall not be forced to concede that it is in principle patient of only a narrowly empiricist interpretation. It may be that other patterns of rationality than the narrowly observable or mechanistic may be discerned within it. Conversely, when writers like those of the New Testament claim to discern the eternal within the temporal, we shall not be required to interpret their language as simply projections upon their experience. Such 'mythological' interpretations presuppose a Kantian view of the temporal order whereby any order is the imposition of the mind. But if temporal frameworks are there, not imposed, why should not equally those eternal ones indicated by talk of God in relation to time and history?

This is not a claim that there can be direct argument or movement from scientific modes of interpretation to theological ones. The rational patterns discerned by natural science remain immanent ones, without reference beyond the world to anything other than it. This is not an argument to a God found within the gaps of scientific knowledge, but an argument against the necessity of a closed world order, closed in itself and to the mind. To say of a human life that it is also the presence of God involves a different kind of claim. It goes far beyond the kind of ontological claims made by disciplines that concern themselves with the temporal order as such. Yet it is in parallel with them in seeking to conceive the temporal as the locus of rationality, albeit of a transcendent rationality. The intention of this section is to remove supposed disqualifications from certain modes of theologizing by disputing the assumptions that underlie them. For a positive development of a christological theme we return to topics adumbrated in Chapter 4.

JESUS, TIME AND SPACE

It was argued there that when the New Testament speaks of Jesus Christ, in all the diversity of ways that it does so, there is a common direction of interpretation. All of the writers see him as in some way or other the presence of the eternal God in time. The discussion of the question of the historical Jesus was intended to show that it is impossible to see him as historical apart from his context, which is always theological. If we do not interpret him within his theological context, we do not see him at all. Thus the New Testament interweaves the temporal and eternal, seeing the one to be the locus of the other. There is, then, a logic to be discerned within the temporal events that make up the career of Jesus. It is not a logic with a single level. That is excluded by the richness of its content and the very fact that it is speaking of God. But it is overall a consistent attempt to depict the life, death and resurrection of Jesus as having an intrinsic patterning or logic: a theological logic.

By *logic* is meant here not only the relation of the words to each other – words like *Christ, Son, Word* – but their relation as a network of interrelated concepts to the one reality they wish to bring to speech. In their different ways these and other words attempt to express the reality of the spatio-temporal Jesus as the *logic of divine love*. In the 'below' that is the space-time continuum is to be discerned the presence of the eternal divine love. Jesus is God's love taking place in our time and history. In that sense, Pannenberg is surely right to see Christology as a movement from the historical Jesus to his full theological significance. The logic of the divine love is a logic that has to be allowed to unfold as different aspects of its reality are expanded and conceived in their full significance. Here Christology is like the other sciences, which advance their understanding of different areas of reality by allowing ever more of their being to come to mathematical and conceptual expression.

But that is not the same as saying that the same kind of logic is to be discerned in each case. The logic of a piece of music is the logic of a beauty that cannot be adequately expressed in words, and yet it is a logic in that it brings aspects of reality to expression. The logic of the atom is one that comes to expression – though never entirely adequately – through metaphor, concept and mathematical formula. The logic of the divine love is what comes to expression as the story of a man's life, death and resurrection is told in the many ways that it is told by the New Testament writers. But as soon as we respond to this kind of claim by asking What does it mean to say that here the love of the eternal God takes temporal form, then Christology 'proper' begins. It begins because those who speak of Jesus in that way are required to be responsible for the language that they employ, to use a favourite expression of Professor Jüngel. To be responsible means to give some public account of the nature of the claims that are being made; and that in turn requires the working out of the ontological implications of the language. It is for this reason that this section has been preceded by discussions of the kind of notions of time and space that must be at least conceivable if responsible Christology is to be done. For if we assert the co-presence in space and time of the divine and the human, we are required to give some account of how these things can be conceived to be.

If, then, the logic of the divine love is a love that is expressed in space and time, one possibility for its exposition is through the language of evolution. There is something of a fashion for evolutionary Christologies (e.g. Robinson, Teilhard de Chardin), and for very good reasons. If Jesus is to be fully part of space and time as a human being, then indeed he must be part of the genetic process that is human birth and life. But to say that his eternal significance is adequately expressed in such terms is a different matter altogether. There are a number of reasons for this. The first is that to regard Jesus as the crown of evolution, the supremely evolved human being, is to run all the risks of degree Christology and its associated 'docetism from below' that we have already discussed (Chapter 2, pp. 15–18 and Chapter 5, pp. 98–100). Second, it is to treat the cosmic process as itself divine or, if not, to treat it in an anthropomorphic manner as itself the origin of God's love. So it is that J. A. T. Robinson says that 'at the Incarnation . . . God, the power of nature and history, the Logos or principle of the evolutionary process, began to be represented in a new way' (Robinson, p. 217). The problem with this is that it is so to regard the temporal order as absolute that it becomes itself divine. In its turn, it becomes impossible to distinguish the order of salvation from the order of creation. For if we cannot, the latter becomes conceivable only in terms of a divinized evolution, and ceases to be the bearer of any other intrinsic rationality. We are then back to a prescientific view of the divinity of the cosmos. In other words, unless the logic of the eternal is in some way distinct from the logic of the temporal, we can understand on their own terms neither the one nor the other. It is here that the importance of the Old Testament once more reasserts itself. If it, and not some near-pantheism of evolution, is the theological framework within which New Testament Christology is understood, we are preserved from a divinizing or making absolute of time. The logic of divine love becoming present in Jesus is, indeed, continuous with the saving activity of God elsewhere. That should not, however, be identified with the cosmic process in general, but with the way in which in the past God has freely related himself to the created order. On this account, the logic is not that of a divine, and thus almost inevitably impersonal, process operating immanently but of a transcendent love which is love because it freely takes to itself part of our space and time, not overriding it but fulfilling its spatio-temporality from within. And yet, despite its transcendence, its coming spatially 'from outside', that pattern is to be discerned within our space and time, as an interpretation of the meaning of the historical Jesus of Nazareth.

So far, then, we have approached the logic of the divine love become spatio-temporally present in Jesus negatively, by denying the adequacy of views that in effect remain imprisoned in ideologies which make our space and time absolute. By contrast, if we are to achieve a positive Christology that does not fall prey to the absolutism of time or eternity, we must hold firmly to the bipolarity of the New Testament's approach: that this life is both fully temporal and yet is the place where the eternal is present. One way in which this is expressed is by those passages which speak of the subordination of Jesus to the Father. Thus the Synoptic Gospels depict a pattern of obedience, while the Fourth Gospel juxtaposes expressions of the subordination of Jesus to the Father ('the Father is greater than I', John 14.28) with assertions of their equality (John 10.30). In these depictions, as well as in passages like Philippians 2, the writers are not expressing an ontological subordination, as in Arianism – for the obedience, humiliation and death are the way by which Jesus works out his divine calling – but showing that what happens here takes its origin in the eternal. It is the divine love, that which exists to all eternity, that is here to be touched and heard. This is the point of the metaphor of sending in Paul and of the setting by both John and Hebrews of the life of Jesus in the context of eternity. What happens with Jesus of Nazareth is first of all to be understood as the good news of the movement into time of the eternal.

It is for this reason that we must reject the opposition of Christology from above and from below. In the unfolding of the meaning of the event, we come to see that the 'below' can only be understood as the 'above', the man Jesus as God present to his world. And that this is not simply a dogmatic imposition upon the data is shown by the fact that it enables us to transform our concepts of space and time. In particular, we are able to escape the dominance of our concepts of time by our experience of its fleetingness. In the light of what happens here we are compelled neither to escape time because it is fleeting nor to impose upon its fleetingness an absoluteness that it does not have (for example, by divinizing evolution). For in what happened to Jesus, we are presented with time that is established *through and beyond its decay*. The life and death of Jesus on this account are seen not as the means by which temporality is escaped – as, unfortunately, they have often been construed, particularly in Western Christianity – but as the way by which God re-establishes authentic temporal existence. That, of course, is the point of the resurrection as an eschatological event happening in the centre of time. It is not, as tends to be the case with Pannenberg, simply the means by which we come to recognize Jesus as in some sense identical with God, but rather the way by which God begins to release the created order from its 'bondage to decay' (Rom. 8.21). Hence Jesus is described by Paul as 'the firstborn from the dead' (Col. 1.18). The fleetingness of time is thus a characteristic not of time as such, but of fallen, alienated, time, and the life of Jesus is the way by which the eternal takes to himself our alienated time and re-creates it as that in which there is construction and not destruction. (In other words, we might say, the life of Jesus, seen as the vehicle of a view of time as construction and not destruction, is remarkably parallel to the view of time generated by music; and it is perhaps not surprising that more than a few thinkers have seen music as an anticipation of heaven.)

But how far is this simply a repetition of the patristic tendency to see the problem of human life as that of decay, in face of which the gospel offered 'divinization'? Clearly, the modern problem is not quite the same. Our tendency is to swing wildly between the extremes of a complete pessimism and an uncritical optimism about time. The existential relevance of the redemption of time therefore takes in our culture a related but different form. What our culture requires is a view of time from a transcendent or, perhaps better, an eschatological perspective, and hence an ability to see time in both its centrality and its fallenness. Time, as the positive creation of the eternal love – a conception to which Augustine could not quite attain, with dire consequences for the future – is the proper place for the living of life and the exercise of thought. But it has become the place where actual human patterns of existence have made rather for death and despair. It was for this reason that the temporal order attempted to reject the logic of the divine love (1 Cor. 2.8!), and indeed that the divine love took the temporal form that it did. In order to enable the time of human and universal life to be a time of fulfilment and not simply death and decay, the eternal love of God – God the eternal Son and Word – identified himself within our time and space with our alienation and death.

Here the link of Christology with soteriology requires not simply an automatically evolving process (Christology from below *simpliciter*) but an initiative from the side of eternity. The logic of the divine love that is discerned in the historical Jesus of Nazareth is a logic of initiative, overcoming – indeed, of judgement – and, through it, of restoration: the restoration of our existence to authentic temporality. If, then, the life of the historical Jesus is God's way of righting what is wrong with our temporality, what kind of Christology becomes possible? If we are right in arguing that the essential context in which the life of Jesus is to be understood is that of eternity, what is the relation of Jesus to eternity? Certainly not that of the temporal to the timeless, as is made clear by the tensed verbs in which Jesus is depicted in the New Testament. Let us look at aspects of these verbs. How is the positive relation of God to time which comes to conception through Jesus to be expounded?

It will be remembered that according to the argument of Dietrich Ritschl recent problems of New Testament interpretation derive largely from the false time-frame within which they are viewed. The West's obsession with the past makes it difficult for theologians to operate within a perspective provided by the present Christ.

Ritschl's view is supported by the widespread use of the present tense in New Testament accounts of the reality of Christ. What systematic significance do these present tenses have? Historically they derive from the resurrection of Jesus, as a result of which the first Christians believed themselves able to speak of him as a present reality: 'Jesus *is* Lord'. Such expressions refer to the continuing presence, albeit in a different mode of existence, of the one whom some of them had known as Jesus of Nazareth. But he is present as Lord, and that means in the mode of divinity as well as that of humanity.

But what kind of presence is it? It can best be described as at once a revelational and soteriological presence. He is the one through whom they know God and through whom they are saved by God. The double focus of revelation and salvation is present throughout the Fourth Gospel, but in other Christologies also. The two are interwoven, for example, in the 'great Christology' of Colossians 1, where the predominance of present tense verbs is marked, as is the interrelation of soteriological, ecclesiological and cosmological expressions of Christ's significance. One other example is worth mentioning, and that is the Letter to the Hebrews' depiction of Christ's present reality. In it spatial imagery is used to express Jesus's transcendence of temporal barriers. Because 'we have a high priest . . . who is seated at the right hand of the throne. . .' (Hebrews 8.1) we are *now* able to come to God through his ministry. What happened in the past with Jesus of Nazareth has implications for the way in which people are able to be related to God in the present.

In these and other such passages we have expressions of the logic of divine love in the present. Because the logic comes to speech through the human and divine reality that is the risen Jesus of Nazareth, we have what can be called a perichoresis, a simultaneous interaction, of the temporal and the eternal. The eternal is here conceived as a time-embracing and not a time-denying reality, and leads to an interesting speculation about what might have happened had Augustine analysed time on its basis rather than on the basis of a subjective experience of fleetingness. Such a speculation is suggested because it enables us to see more clearly the alienating effect of our current preoccupation with Jesus as a past figure. To moor him in the past is to make absolute our own experience of the pastness of time. But if Jesus is the mode of God's becoming present to the world, this alienation is brought into question. Surely some such concern as this underlies the Fourth Gospel's reflections in chapter 16 on the different modes of Jesus's presence to his community. After he 'goes away' the Spirit will 'take what is mine and declare it to you'. Paul is similar, seeing the Spirit as the way in which Jesus continues to be present. In all these various ways, then, eternity comes to be understood through, rather than away from, the temporal. The risen Jesus is the continuing presence in time of the eternal love of God: the logic of present love.

From the present we move to the future, and here our task becomes more difficult, largely because recent theological fashion has tended to bewilder its readers with abstract talk of the 'absolute future' and 'pure futurity', and with its use of the word 'eschatological' in every possible context, sometimes as a means of avoiding too direct a use of the word *God*. Besides, the future has not yet happened. Here, it will rightly be objected that in a sense it has. In the resurrection of Jesus, an event belonging to the future has taken place, by anticipation or proleptically as it is often put, in the centre of time. What is the relation between our 'ordinary' knowledge of the future, taking the form of knowledge that we do not in fact have knowledge, and the claims that are made christologically on the strength of the resurrection? Once again the bearing is both revelatory and soteriological. The former aspect has been well spelled out in the theology of Pannenberg, who has argued that it is through the resurrection that we come to recognize the significance of Jesus for our understanding of reality as a whole. We see in Jesus the clue to the way the world is. But Pannenberg's emphasis on knowledge runs the risk of generating a speculative cosmology which in its turn will ultimately deny the reality of the very time it wishes to guarantee. His very process of arguing from the part to the whole, idealistically, drives him in the direction of a timeless construction.

It would seem preferable to allow the relevational aspects to derive from the soteriological, and here we must learn from the fact that the New Testament is more interested in the ontological than the noetic significance of Jesus's futurity. According to Ephesians in particular, the whole temporal order is what it is in its directedness to Jesus. His revelatory significance is of ontological dimensions, revealing as it does the divine purpose 'to unite all things in him, things in heaven and things on earth' (Ephesians 1.10). The logic of the future divine love, becoming real in the eschatological presence of Jesus to judge and heal our alienated existence in time, is the reality of the eternal love as promise: that within and by means of the fleetingness of time and its inevitable production of decay and death, the meaningfulness of the created order will be completed and revealed. This future, eschatological, restoration of all things to the end for which they were created is depicted, in the Synoptic Gospels in particular, as beginning not just in the resurrection of Jesus but in his ministry. That, surely, is the main significance of the miracles, both those called 'nature' miracles and the miracles of healing – as if they are not to do with nature too. Sickness and hunger belong to the bad old order of decay. In the presence of the bearer of that time (*sic*) when 'there shall be no more tears', they already begin to lose their demonic authority. That is why Paul can say, in a passage that is strictly more the realm of pneumatology than of Christology, that 'the creation itself will be set free from its bondage to decay. . .' (Romans 8.21). The future that begins in the ministry continues in the present because Jesus is not simply a past historical figure, but one who, as at once human and divine, belongs to all times ('the same yesterday and today and for ever', Hebrews 13.8).

In the programme of this section, discussions of present and future have preceded that of the past because that is the way Christology naturally unfolds, both historically (as Dr Dunn's study has shown) and logically. There is another reason for the direction, and that is in order to place discussions of the past in a wider context. Treatments of Christology as past have dominated recent debate – indeed, all the Christology of the West – for reasons that have already been much rehearsed. Moreover, the greatest difficulties present themselves here, because the cosmological problems are at their most acute. It is not all that difficult to conceive that Christ, certainly if he is understood rather docetically as completely freed from the trappings of space and time, should be present (timelessly?) to present and future eras, as a Platonic form is present to them all. But that a particular human being should, in the past, have been a unique spatio-temporal instantiation of the divine, is the most intellectually offensive of all Christian claims. Yet that is the burden of both New Testament and orthodox patristic Christology in its various forms. It is also the burden of this book, which wishes to argue both that it is necessary to say this – and the meaning of *necessary* will be explored in the next chapter – and that we are able to say it in continuity with the ancients.

Past-tense statements about Jesus in the New Testament take two forms. There are those, on the one hand, that attribute pre-existence to him. It may be (Dunn, 1980) that only in the Fourth Gospel is this explicitly asserted; but there is no doubt that pre-existence in terms of agency in creation is widely ascribed, for example in 1 Corinthians 8.6, Colossians 1.16 and Hebrews 1.3. Whatever we are to make of these, it seems clear that they are meant to refer in some way or other to Jesus. On the other hand, there are those statements which refer to the past as it happened in Jesus of Nazareth. Once again, an explicit doctrine of the incarnation appears to be developed only in John. But there are many other statements which locate the action of God before and at the beginning of Jesus's story, at its earthly end and at various times during its course.

Let us now attempt a systematic account of the matter with a reassertion of the pivotal statement of this chapter: Jesus of Nazareth is the logic of divine love, logic in the sense of spelling out and making present in earthly actuality its eternal reality. If we take the predicate of that sentence, the second half of the equation, we are led to say that because it is divine love, then it is the love of the eternal God. What more natural, then, than that its reality should be seen to belong to past as well as present? This is surely a main point of the language of pre-existence. Jesus of Nazareth is not simply an unprecedented irruption or intervention of God upon the stage of history. The love of God which becomes actual in this truly human and historical life is continuous with the love that operates throughout it. As Athanasius says, 'the . . . Word of God comes to our realm, howbeit he was not far from us before' (Athanasius, 1954, p. 62). That is the reason for the movement of thought in which Christ was seen to be active in creation from the very beginning (1 Corinthians 8.6 again). The love of God which made the world is the same love as that which comes to it in person, albeit now for a different purpose. The past tense of pre-existence makes it possible to relate the divine movements of creation and reconciliation without identifying them.

We should, however, beware of speaking of this as a hypostatization of the divine Word or love, especially if this is interpreted crudely numerically (tritheistically) or anthropomorphically. The point is rather that we are concerned not merely with an idea in the mind of God which here becomes actual in time. That would be to break the link between eternity and time, by eternalizing Christ. We are much more concerned here with the language of action and relation. At the centre of things is the self-actualization of God in time, the self-differentiation through love of the eternal to become temporal for us. The link between eternal and temporal is not ideal but actual. Something happens in time which compels interpretation as the actuality of the eternal. God, as the Creator of the temporal order through his outgoing Word, not only gives temporal and spatial form to what is other than himself (creation), but takes it also. He becomes flesh. This means that the eternal love of God locates itself in time and space, and so becomes datable. The love of God has the shape and form – the *logic* – of what happened in the life of Jesus: the birth as God with us; the care for the sick and poor and outcast as the grace of God coming to us in our need; the temptation and death as the love of God meeting our hate and overcoming it; and all as one of us. That is why the logic of the story drives us, as it drove the writers of the New Testament and the theologians of the early Church to speak of the incarnation. The doctrine is not then presupposed in a confession of faith such as those first uttered under the impact of new-found trust in God. It is what comes to expression when the implications of that trust for our understanding of Jesus of Nazareth are worked out in different directions and dimensions. Or rather, it is not *logically* but *ontologically* presupposed by the confessions; and as their expressions of the meaning of the life, death and resurrection of Jesus are expanded and their reality penetrated, the logical outcome is the conviction that in the spatio-temporal life of a man God has become real among us.

It is for this reason that although confessions of Jesus of Nazareth's temporal-eternal significance do not presuppose the doctrine of the Trinity, they inevitably lead to it, for they presuppose the reality of a God who is able to become spatio-temporal without loss of his divinity, of an eternal who is able to differentiate himself to become other than he is. It is that which dualistic philosophies of all kinds disallow, for they demand that we choose between temporal and eternal, and between (spatially) finite and infinite. But the impact of the reality of Jesus compels us to say that God is not to be understood as the bare negation of our time and space – as utterly timeless and spaceless – but as being eternally in himself that relatedness to the other which actualizes itself in our history. And that is one of the things meant when we say that God is triune, one in three ways of being.

CONTINUITIES

The theology of the incarnation sketched in the previous section is an attempt to say the same kind of thing as was said by the great Fathers of Christian theology in the first centuries of our era. Its methodological assumption is that the difference between our time and theirs requires a shift of emphasis rather than of form in Christology. Our necessarily more temporal interests require greater attention to be paid to Jesus of Nazareth as the locus of the divine loving, the time where it takes place in person. The shift is from a preoccupation with the eternal-temporal to a greater engagement with the temporal-eternal. But because we are in Christology above all concerned with *God's* love, we cannot avoid working through to the same kind of conclusions to which the Fathers came. If we begin with the preoccupations of our times, we cannot remain there any more than they did. They were forced, by the logic of the reality they knew, to see Jesus of Nazareth as the place where the eternal was temporally and spatially located. We, by contrast, may come to see that in this temporal and spatial reality not only immanent phenomena but also the eternal God are to be found.

There are a number of reasons why it should be possible for us to reach the same kind of conclusions as our predecessors. In the first place, as has been argued, they faced difficulties similar to ours, and yet refused to capitulate to them. This means that we cannot adequately understand the nature of the problem without them. But it is not to suggest that they solved the problems; rather that any theology that is true to them will see as its primary task the taking further of the process they began. This brings us to our second point, concerning the nature of such an advance. *What* did they begin? Cochrane observes that Athanasius's doctrine of co-inherence (or perichoresis within the Trinity) was the basis for an understanding of reality which at once transcended and destroyed classical ontology. 'With the acceptance of a starting-point such as that just indicated, it becomes possible to envisage the divine principle as both transcendent and immanent, "prior" to nature, the world of time and space in which we live, and yet operative within it' (Cochrane, p. 367). With Athanasius, then, began the real assault on classicism's absolute dualism of time and eternity. And that Athanasius's preoccupations were precisely similar to those of this chapter is suggested by the sentence following: 'For, while the properties of matter are such that two bodies cannot occupy the same space at the same time, the special characteristic of spirit lies in its permeability.'

And yet, although this intellectual revolution of Athanasius was one of the forces making for modernity, and in particular for the rise of natural science – for it makes it possible to conceive of rationality subsisting *within*, not outside, temporal realities – the dominating feature of theology, particularly in the West, has been its dualism. We shall examine the political and social aspects of this dualism in a final chapter. Here its christological aspect can be mentioned, taking as it does the form of a dualism of Father and Son, and a consequent tendency to abstract hypostatization of the 'persons' of the Trinity. The pervasive feature of Western Christology is its separation between the Father – seen in terms of power and impassibility – and the Son, with his tears and suffering. It comes to light particularly in medieval preoccupations with the passion of Christ, abstracted as it often was from any close relation to the doctrine of God. But it is also evident in modern reactions against it, with their tendency to locate the whole of Christology's theological load on the this-worldly and temporal.

In both cases what has been lost is the trinitarian context of Christology, which has become a cipher or reduced to the background. But if we take seriously the implications of this doctrine for our understanding of God, we shall not so easily abstract our Christology from eternity or our God from involvement in space and time. If God is triune, and oriented from all eternity to what happened in Jesus of Nazareth, we shall not be tempted to conceive him or the world in terms that exclude the interrelationship of eternity and time. But is not that to move in a circle, from Jesus to God and back again? In a sense it is, for it is an understanding of theology in which the different areas of thought interpenetrate and support each other, a network rather than an ordered linear progression. But that takes us to questions of the status of Christian talk of Jesus, and for that another chapter is required.

REFERENCES

Athanasius, 1954, *On the Incarnation of the Word*, ed. Edward Rochie Hardy, *Christology of the Later Fathers*. Library of Christian Classics, vol. iii, pp. 55–110.

Athanasius, 1971, '*Contra Gentes*' and '*De Incarnatione*', ed. and Eng. trans. Robert W. Thompson.

Augustine of Hippo, *Confessions*, Eng. trans. R. S. Pine-Coffin.

Bultmann, Rudolf, 'New Testament and Mythology' in *Kerygma and Myth*, ed. Hans Werner Bartsch, Eng. trans. Reginald H. Fuller, vols. i and ii, pp. 1–44.

Cochrane, Charles Norris, *Christianity and Classical Culture: A Study of Thought and Action from Augustus to Augustine*.

Descartes, René, 'Meditations on the First Philosophy', in *The Philosophical Works of Descartes*, Eng. trans. Elizabeth Haldane and G. R. T. Ross, pp. 131–99.

Dunn, James D. G., 1980, *Christology in the Making: An Inquiry into the Origins of the Doctrine of the Incarnation*.

Faraday, Michael, 'A Speculation touching Electric Conduction and the Nature of Matter' in *On the Primary Forces of Electricity*, ed. Richard Laming.

Gunton, Colin E., 1980, 'Transcendence, Metaphor and the Knowability of God' in *Journal of Theological Studies*, 31, 501–16.

Hengel, Martin, *The Son of God: The Origin of Christology and the History of Jewish–Hellenistic Religion*, Eng. trans. John Bowden.

Kant, Immanuel, *Immanuel Kant's Critique of Pure Reason*, Eng. trans. Norman Kemp Smith.

Kierkegaard, Søren, 1941b, *Training in Christianity*, Eng. trans. Walter Lowrie.

Kierkegaard, Søren, 1962, *Philosophical Fragments*, Eng. trans. David F. Simenson and Howard V. Hong.

Lucas, J. R., *A Treatise on Time and Space*.

MacKinnon, D. M., 1982, 'Prolegomena to Christology' in *Journal of Theological Studies* 33, 146–60.

Mackintosh, H. R., *The Doctrine of the Person of Jesus Christ*.

Meijering, E. P., *God Being History: Studies in Patristic Philosophy*.

Newton, Isaac, *Newton's Philosophy of Nature: Selections from his Writings*, ed. H. S. Thayer.

Pannenberg, Wolfhart, 1968, *Jesus – God and Man*, Eng. trans. Lewis L. Wilkins and Duane A. Priebe.

Robinson, J. A. T., *The Human Face of God.*

Rorty, Richard, *Philosophy and the Mirror of Nature.*

Teilhard de Chardin, Pierre, *The Phenomenon of Man*, Eng. trans. Bernard Wall.

Torrance, T. F., 1969, *Space, Time and Incarnation.*

Torrance, T. F., 1981, *Divine and Contingent Order.*

Whitrow, G. J., *The Natural Philosophy of Time.*

Zuckerkandl, Victor, *Sound and Symbol: Music and the External World*, Eng. trans. Willard R. Trask.

7

THE STATUS OF CHRISTOLOGICAL
STATEMENTS

THE PROBLEM

The problem for this chapter is that set for Christology by the tradition in general and by G. E. Lessing in particular. Deeply engrained in Western thought is a distinction between two kinds of truth claim and the two kinds of statement in which they are made. The distinction derives from Plato, in whose famous analogy of the divided line the two main segments represent the worlds of thought and of sense experience. Corresponding to the dualistic division of the world into the sensible and the intelligible realms is an epistemological dualism of the contingent and the necessary. Contingent truths are the truths arrived at on the basis of sense experience; necessary truths derive from reason. The distinction lived on beyond Plato, and is, for example, central in the work of Aquinas. In the modern world it takes a characteristically linguistic form in the distinction between synthetic and analytic statements, a distinction which was attacked in a famous paper by Quine.

The Enlightenment generated a characteristically firm version of the dualistic epistemology, helped on its way by Descartes's repristination of a Platonic kind of epistemology. It was this that presented Lessing with his now famous impasse. His epistemological objection to forming 'all my metaphysical and moral ideas' on the basis of statements about the historical Christ depends upon a particular view of the duality of the kinds of things that can be said. On the one hand he is, unlike many of those who have followed in his footsteps, quite willing to take certain biblical claims at face value.

That the Christ, against whose resurrection I can raise no

important historical objection, therefore declared himself to be the Son of God; . . . this I gladly believe from my heart (Lessing, p. 54).

The question of whether Lessing, the editor of Reimarus's *Fragments*, is being disingenuous does not concern us here. The point is rather that, even given all this, it does not get him where Lessing believes it must if he is to base his faith upon it. For:

Accidental truths of history can never become the proof of necessary truths of reason. . . That . . . is the ugly, broad ditch which I cannot get across, however often and however earnestly I have tried to make the leap (Lessing, pp. 53, 55).

Lessing's ditch has often, in a manner true to the canons of the Enlightenment, been understood as a temporal one, and the question in large part deriving from him about our relation to past history has already demanded our attention. But the form of the ditch as he expresses it is epistemological. How can the kind of certainty we demand of our moral and metaphysical beliefs be derived from beliefs that are *in principle* uncertain, corrigible and only probable in status? This was the problem which exercised Ernst Troeltsch in particular among more recent theologians, and which is the constant spectre at that which one would hesitate to call the banquet of contemporary theology.

It would be wrong to attempt to evade this problem. But the way in which a problem is viewed makes a considerable difference to the way in which a solution is approached. We shall begin our approach through the thought of Kierkegaard, particularly that of the *Philosophical Fragments* and the *Concluding Unscientific Postscript*. In the latter work Kierkegaard states his admiration for Lessing, whose essay – that from which the above quotations were taken – 'attacks the direct transition from historical trustworthiness to the determination of an eternal happiness' (Kierkegaard, 1962, p. 88). Kierkegaard's *Postscript* was, as the title implies, the further exploration of matters considered in the *Philosophical Fragments*, and it is here that we see a thinker making positive use of the apparent gulf between historical or contingent statements and those appropriate for the expression of things eternal. Kierkegaard agrees with the epistemology of the contingent and the necessary which he has inherited from the tradition. He has no wish to question it, and is even willing to sharpen it in the interests of faith. For if faith is to be faith it cannot have the objective necessity of a theorem from Euclid. This for him is the advantage Jesus has over Socrates. In the case of the latter we can lose the essentially paradoxical form of all real – 'existential' – knowledge and take refuge in the doctrine of recollection. We can, that is to say, attempt to escape from the demand of the moment by entering an otherworldly realm of necessary truths. By contrast, Christianity, in which the teaching is indistinguishable from the teacher, allows no such escape route. The historical reality of the teacher prevents an evasion of the temporality of truth.

It is at this point that Kierkegaard brings his discussion of paradox to a head. For him, all serious discussion of human knowing and being issues in paradox, in the attempt to hold together time and eternity. It is, epistemologically, possible to have a non-paradoxical account of either time or eternity. But anything existentially interesting will attempt to have both. Christianity provides the most philosophically interesting case of all, by means of its absolute paradox of the God-man, of eternity being given by means of a historical figure. It is because Lessing faced up to this kind of challenge that Kierkegaard admires him. 'The paradoxical character of Christianity consists in its constant use of time and the historical in relation to the eternal. . .' (Kierkegaard, 1962, p. 88). Faith, for Kierkegaard, is therefore that which accepts the sheer contingency of things, and yet gambles upon it its eternal destiny.

In one sense, Kierkegaard is a true disciple of the Kant who wished to limit the claims of reason in order to make room for faith. But he did not in any sense echo the near-paganism of Kant's later tendency to identify God and human reason, a tendency which came to full flower in the Hegel against whom so many of Kierkegaard's polemics were directed. That is his greatness, and his permanent contribution to theology especially for an age in which the tendency is to reduce everything to a philosophy of immanence and to evade the demands of eternity upon our theories of knowledge. But as an assertion of the rights of faith it can become an enemy of knowledge. In that respect it can appear to be no more than a quixotic tilting at those modern theories which have derived from the Enlightenment. That movement, particularly as it is represented by John Locke (Polanyi, 1962, p. 266) tended to understand faith or belief as inferior forms of knowledge. Knowledge is of that of which we are certain; belief is of that of which we are less, or scarcely at all, certain. The object of the one is the necessary statement; of the other, the contingent or probable assertion. Kierkegaard accepts this basic epistemological position and, rather than attempting to overturn it, strongly reasserts the rights of faith. The question to be asked of him is whether he can do this without a collapse into subjectivism. Perhaps he can, but those who have followed him have for the most part not succeeded.

For our purposes, the matter can be put like this. If there is no knowledge at all, and if truth must be defined as 'an objective uncertainty held fast in an appropriation-process of the most passionate inwardness' (Kierkegaard, 1941a, p. 182), then it is difficult to say in which ways Christology – indeed, theology in general – is a discipline that says anything, or attempts to say anything, about the way it is with the world. If there is to be responsible talk of God in Christ, must not some further account be given than of God as the unknown who is met in paradoxical relation to the temporal? In other words, we cannot finally bridge the gap between the divine-human reality of New Testament Christology and our present experience with an appeal to a timeless paradox, for that way lies either the subjectivism we have already mentioned or Christendom's vice of eternalizing the historical reality of Christ. In some way or other we must attempt to relate more positively the temporal and the eternal, the contingent and the necessary.

Here a word might be said in favour of the much-maligned Hegel. Hegel realized that the challenge to Christianity was in part a scientific one. It was a question of knowledge of things as they were at present, and of knowing them both eternally and temporally. He sought, as this book is doing, to see the eternal within the temporal. But for all of his correct viewing of the problem, the word in his favour remains only a word, for, as we have seen, the end result of his enterprise is to override the historical particularity of the Christ. The contingent is swallowed up by the necessary in a final philosophical synthesis. Faith is swallowed up in knowledge, in philosophical sight. Where Kierkegaard lacks an eschatological dimension, Hegel, in Robert Jenson's words, 'confused himself with the last judge' (Jenson, p. 233). This point, however, gives us an important clue to the next stage of the argument. 'Necessity', the aim and measure of real, reliable, truth according to Lessing and the Enlightenment, is an eschatological concept, implying as it does the certainty of final judgement: the anticipation of that time when we shall know as we are known. Could it be that the polarity of the contingent and the necessary is a false one so far as the conditions of human knowledge are concerned, and that we should attempt to see the matter more radically even than Kierkegaard?

CONTINGENT RATIONALITY

It is to Michael Polanyi, a twentieth-century philosopher of science, that we owe the insight that all knowledge is contingent. That is not to say that all forms of knowledge can claim the same status, but rather that different forms belong in a spectrum rather than in one of two mutually exclusive groups (Polanyi, 1959, p. 83). Polanyi's primary aim is to heal the moral and social alienation that has resulted from the bifurcation in culture begun at the Enlightenment. Writing as a practitioner, observer and philosopher of science he claims that his aim is to encourage a particular frame of mind: 'in which I may hold firmly to what I believe to be true, even though I know that it might conceivably be false' (Polanyi, 1962, p. 214). His programme is thus to help Lessing over his ditch by challenging the epistemology underlying the formulation of the problem.

What is this epistemology? It is the view that there are two ways to know the world, one giving certain, indubitable knowledge expressed as necessity; the other producing corrigible and hence unreliable statements of belief. It is, in fact, the theory we have already seen Polanyi attributing to Locke, that faith or belief is a different kind of orientation on reality from knowledge, inferior because failing to uncover certainties. The ultimate origin of the distinction is probably Plato's theory of knowledge, and confirmation of Polanyi's negative thesis is provided by those philosophers who have recently charted its demise. The theory holds that language successfully describes reality when it *pictures* it. Necessary statements picture exhaustively and precisely; contingent ones partially and imprecisely. The theory depends on a visual metaphor, a metaphor whose application to epistemology has recently been criticized by a number of philosophers, most notably Wittgenstein. The critique has recently been renewed by Richard Rorty, who traces the old view to a metaphor employed by Plato in his conception of knowledge as a kind of mental *vision*.

> There was, we moderns may say with the ingratitude of hindsight, no particular reason why this ocular metaphor seized the imagination of the founders of Western thought. But it did. . . The notion of 'contemplation', of knowledge of universal concepts or truths as θεωρία, makes the Eye of the Mind the inescapable model for the better sort of knowledge (Rorty, pp. 38f.).

Rorty's own view is that the ocular metaphor has led philosophy, particularly since Descartes, into a blind alley, and that we should instead take a pragmatic approach to knowledge. Polanyi, however, takes more seriously the epistemological task. His objections to the old metaphor are part intellectual (it distorts) and part moral (it alienates). In particular, by viewing the mind as *external* to the world – contemplating it from without, as one might view a landscape from an aircraft – it also sees it as impersonal and with pretensions to omniscience. The 'critical' ideology resulting from the picture makes the mind claim too much for some forms of knowledge – those it can, supposedly, *contemplate* in a totally objective way: truths of reason and of basic sense experience – and too little for everything else, including matters of morality, politics and theology. It is, we might say, a 'God's-eye-view' of knowledge, detached, objective and with pretensions to infallibility for privileged areas of culture, while despising all other intellectual enterprises as inferior. In place of it, Polanyi offers a different metaphor: not contemplation, but indwelling. As one commentator at least has realized, this alternative is more than a mere metaphor, being in fact an analogy of immense scope (Kuhn, p. 118). Just as, as persons, we indwell our bodies, so we indwell the world, and in various ways. The most simple is the way in which we relate ourselves to the world through the instrumentality of our bodies and of the tools which we use as extensions of them. Our use of words is continuous with this. As a blind man indwells his stick in order to know his way around the world, so we indwell words and concepts in order to come to terms with the way our world is. Words are thus not mirrors of reality but *the means by which we participate in reality*. Language, along with its expression of supposed knowledge of the way things are, is not then discontinuous with other aspects of our experience, an arbitrary imposition of a conceptual structure on reality, but grows out of the human relationship with the world. The metaphor of indwelling has, accordingly, both ontological and epistemological implications. The metaphor of mirroring tends to see the relation of words and things as external but direct: some words directly fit, or are made by the mind to fit, the data of experience. By contrast, the metaphor of indwelling sees the relation as indirect (because mediated by our *personal* relationship to the world). According to such a theory, which Polanyi defends with illustrations of what has actually happened in the develop.nent of scientific and other culture, there is posited a relationship of mind and world in which the one is open to the other. The intrinsic rationality of the world comes, though not directly or exhaustively, to expression in the structures of rationality of the other. The metaphor of indwelling thus replaces images which suggest the relationship as the confrontation of two foreign structures of rationality.

The theory reflected in Lessing's famous dichotomy becomes untenable on this account because it presupposes a view according to which some types of statement, but not others, directly mirror reality. Similarly, positivism's development of the Enlightenment's epistemology into its doctrine that logical and empirical truths mirror reality, whereas everything else is but the reflection (!) of human experience or subjectivity, falls down, because a privileged place cannot be ascribed in such an *a priori* and abstract manner to two narrow areas of linguistic expression. There is no automatically safe area of human rationality. All human intellectual enterprises are necessarily fallible, but not for that matter necessarily mistaken. In fact, the reverse is the case. *Because we indwell the world knowledge can be contingent, fallible and partial without for that reason losing its claim to be knowledge.* That is the significance for our purposes of the epistemology of Polanyi.

INDWELLING AND THE STATUS OF CHRISTOLOGICAL LANGUAGE

It would be foolish to suggest that all our problems can be solved simply by appeal to Polanyi. What is, rather, being argued is that his philosophy, with its partial confirmation in the work of Rorty, demonstrates that we are not bound to view the problems of

christological language from the perspective provided by the Enlightenment. Polanyi's alternative epistemological proposals, illustrated as they are by a wealth of examples of what has actually
happened in the course of the progress of modern science, suggest
that the rather monochrome view of modern culture to be found in
the books of theologians should by no means be taken for granted.

In this section and the next the fruitfulness of Polanyi's restructur-
ing will be tested in the light of two theses. The first is that the
metaphor of indwelling enables us to express the nature of the
christological enterprise in a way that does not entail its radical
discontinuity with other forms of human culture. If what is being
done in the Christology of this book is not utterly unmodern, it will
undermine the arguments of those who hold that modernity entails
a radical discontinuity with our Christian past. Thus from a different angle there is being attempted here a strengthening of the thesis
of the book as a whole that it is not impossible for the modern
Christian to affirm, albeit critically, a large part of both the form
and the content of orthodox Christology. The second thesis, however, must be that if the language which comes to expression in
Christology is truly to indwell and so to bring to expression the
reality of which it speaks, a certain Kierkegaardian note is also
necessary. Christology, if it is to be true Christology, may be continuous with other cultural enterprises, but is not identical with
them.

We begin by attempting to explore further a feature of Polanyi's
work that was outlined towards the end of the previous section: that
the relation between words and the world is indirect and internal.
(1) All language is indirect, which is the reason why it cannot
perform its task without metaphor and other figures of speech. The
view that there can be a direct fit between abstract concept and
thing 'out there' is false. But that is not to deny that abstract
concepts succeed in bringing aspects of reality to verbal expression.
They clearly do, for the success of modern science derives from the
fact that our words and mathematical formulae have brought to
light one hidden strand of reality after another. (2) There is therefore an internality of relation between our words and the world.
When we use them successfully, we are enabled to indwell what is
really there. If, then, the claim of the New Testament writers is true
that Jesus Christ exists now as the object of present knowledge, it

146

may justifiably be claimed that by our personal indwelling of his reality our words may come to express, successfully but indirectly, something of the truth about him.

How can this be? It is surely significant that the metaphor of indwelling immediately recalls Pauline talk of the believer's being 'in Christ' and Johannine expressions of mutual indwelling. Indeed, the speculation suggests itself that Polanyi's own use of the word may *derive from* the Christian language. It is often said now that modern science took its decisive impetus from the Christian doctrine of creation. May it not be that Polanyi, in making this decisive shift from metaphors of mirroring to one of indwelling, is providing yet more indirect evidence for that claim? Be that as it may, we must now explore the implications of the suggestion that we in some sense indwell Christ. The theologies of both John and Paul would indicate that the relationship is one that becomes real in a community – another way in which Polanyi, with his central category of conviviality (Polanyi, 1962, pp. 203–45), echoes Christian language – by the agency of the Holy Spirit. Language about Christ becomes possible for those who are related to him by virtue of their being placed in a community of confession and worship. This is not to suggest that Christ is to be found only in the community, or that language about him may develop only there. There is also a presence of Christ to be discerned and experienced in the created order – the cosmic Christ at the heart of the life of the world; and in our moral experience – the Christ who, as we are often told, meets us in the persons of the poor and oppressed. Yet the biblical testimony would seem to be that the priority belongs in worship, for it is there that we first meet him whom we are then able to recognize in the sphere where his dominion is not acknowledged. This is a theme that has been prominent in the recent writings of Professor T. F. Torrance, and is important for us here in giving us a factual and historical starting-point for Christology. Although worship has often taken an Apollinarian direction (Torrance, 1975, p. 116), Torrance argues that it should not be so, and shows that Apollinarianism in the liturgy is a deviation from a more authentic view which conceives Christ as present in worship as both human and divine. In the 'worship and prayer of the man Christ Jesus . . . we have the gateway into his whole ministry in the form of a servant on our behalf, without which the whole saving economy in the flesh is

147

ultimately meaningless' (p. 117). The eucharistic presence in worship is 'not just the presence of his Spirit or Mind, but the presence of the actual Jesus Christ, crucified, risen, ascended, glorified, in his whole, living and active reality and in his identity as Gift and Giver' (p. 119). Here is to be found the present Christ of Dietrich Ritschl's concern, the place where we may indwell in order, among other things, to speak rationally on the subject and object of worship.

We are in a position, now, to create another link, with the views of those theologians of several traditions who have recently come to emphasize the origin of theological language in worship. Language is used to speak in praise to God before it is used of him (Schlink, cf. Wainwright, Pannenberg, 1970): 'Doxology is based on God's redeeming act. The believer glorifies God for his action towards mankind and the world' (Schlink, p. 43). In doxology the worshipper is related to and so through the Spirit *indwells* the reality of God whom he believes to be present to him in Christ. The language of praise expresses this more or less direct personal relationship. However, alongside this primary language is the more indirect language of confession and doctrine, the latter being, in Schlink's words, 'the conscious and methodical exposition of the knowledge which is received by faith' (p. 25). We should not overemphasize the difference between the two forms of language, for the language of confession, in which language to God and language about him are combined, provides a link between the two. There is thus not a radical discontinuity between language and reality, as epistemology based on the idea of language as a mirror supposes. The personal relation of worship gives rise to doxological language; and as this language is, in its turn, indwelt, a more systematic account becomes possible of the one through whom indwelling becomes actual. Thus it happens that the God whom we worship through Jesus Christ comes to appropriate linguistic expression, as the personal relationship gives rise to a considered rational and indirect expression.

Such an account of theological language is directly parallel to Polanyi's account of the development of science from the primitive indwelling of reality. In the latter the basic relationship is mediated not through worship but through the sense organs and their extensions in tools and other instruments. As the blind man indwells his stick, he is able to learn what is there. The tool of language is that which makes possible the enormous advantages of human beings over other animals, for its generalizing function enables us to indwell ever greater areas of our world (Polanyi, 1962, pp. 69ff.). But language is continuous with sensation, and so makes possible the indirect expression and understanding of the way the world is. Scientific forms of culture develop as we indwell the world in order better to understand it; and theology, as we are related in worship to God in such a way that we are better able to understand who it is that we worship. The language of rational Christology is, then, that which attempts to give a true though indirect account of what is the case if human beings are indeed brought to God through Jesus Christ.

In this way the language of indwelling enables us to conceive Christology as the same kind of enterprise as that engaged in by exponents of other disciplines. It also enables us to stress once again our continuity with the past. Language is not a tool that, as it were technocratically, we wield as we will, taking a transcendent perspective upon the tradition and criticizing it from without. The writers of the New Testament and the Fathers indwelt the same human and divine reality as we do. The words that resulted from their indwelling developed within a culture different from, but in many ways continuous with, ours. Unless we indwell these words, or, better, indwell the tradition in order to converse with it, it is unlikely that we shall understand it, and certainly not well enough to be 'critical' about it. If we are to find an authentically modern christological language it must be that which reality gives us as we orient ourselves *to* it *through* the language of worship and tradition. Just as the language of a successful science must to some extent be the gift of that reality of which the scientist asks questions, so, to an even greater extent, our language about Christ must be the gift of God the Spirit and he gives to us the capacity both to indwell the Christ and to speak authentically of him. To appeal to worship and tradition is not to exclude this insight, but to give it shape and form. Words for the present do not come out of the blue, but emerge only as the present converses with the past in the light of the faith they both share. Only in this way are we able to move from where we are instead of from some supposed historical reconstruction. As Lessing saw, there is no route from mere historical testimony to philosophical certainty, from a past under our control to present conviction. We can only move from where we are to an attempted expression of the truth of Christology. The only 'necessity', and that can be no more than the provisional necessity of one stage in a process, is that which appears to inhere in a more satisfactory understanding of what is first approached in faith and worship. Christology, like all processes of discovery, is a movement from faith to a measure of understanding.

MODELS, MAPS AND METAPHORS

No language is fully adequate to reality. That is the message of contemporary epistemology, and a condition theology shares with all other disciplines. Rather, and this is the eschatological dimension of all human culture, our language must struggle to become ever more adequate to that which it seeks to describe. Here we reach also the gulf between theology and all other disciplines, for in that it seeks to speak of the eternal, albeit, in Christology, the eternal in time, theology takes on a dimension that is absent elsewhere. Human language is here less adequate to reality, and even where it is successful must be seen to be less successful. In this context we must always remember the message of Søren Kierkegaard. We are not concerned simply to speak of immanent phenomena, nor indeed of eternal realities, but of the two together. If there is not paradox, then there is certainly offence, and offence both at the particularity of Jesus Christ and at the manner of his life: its lowliness and its outcome in rejection and death. That God should come to language through the man of Nazareth hanging on a cross is the ultimate mark of the distinctiveness, difficulty and offence, both intellectual and moral, of the christological enterprise. How, then, do we attempt to express the truth of this human and divine story in such a way that its particularity is not glossed over or explained away? What kind of language do we use to express both what is there and the limits of that language?

A recent attempt to examine the language of Christology is John McIntyre's *The Shape of Christology*. Drawing on the work of Ian Ramsey, he suggests that we use the word *model* in Christology in a manner analogous to the way in which it is used in science. Models are to do with the articulation and representation of reality, but in a manner that avoids the notion that they perform their function 'with the accuracy of a mirror' (McIntyre, p. 63). It is clear that McIntyre's concerns are here very similar to those of this chapter. A superficial view of the word *model*, for example that drawn from its use of a model boat or building, suggests very much a mirroring function. But that is not what is intended here: 'If we break with the equation of description with pictorial representation, then it becomes possible . . . to say that articulation by means of models is the form which description takes when we are dealing with certain parts or aspects of reality' (p. 64). McIntyre, too, is concerned with the truthful but indirect articulation in language of what is there. 'In the end of the day . . . our models are controlled and indeed authenticated by the reality, Christ, whom we have come to know albeit through them' (p. 68).

Although McIntyre's later discussion of three central models suffers from being rather too general in scope to come to terms with the question of how we may come to know Christ *through* the models, his use of the concept has pointed the direction in which we must now proceed. With the help of the tradition we must examine the question of the kind of concepts that are to be used in Christology. But why begin to speak of concepts rather than models? The reason is that one must be understood in the light of the other. Christology, even the most subjectivist or idealist, cannot be undertaken without the use of concepts of some kind. But the word *model* enables us to realize that there is no absolute dividing line between concept and metaphor, reason and imagination. The indirectness of all linguistic expression necessitates the calling into play of metaphors whenever a new insight or discovery is being articulated. As soon as a feature of reality is brought to understanding by means of a metaphor, it ceases to be a 'mere' metaphor and begins to receive systematic employment. As it is indwelt by its user, it becomes more conceptual. Reason, we might say, refines and orders what was at first imaginatively or intuitively grasped.

It is in this context that the word *model* is useful as expressing something of the breadth of the way reality comes to expression. It can refer to linguistic, conceptual or mathematical articulation by which aspects or features of reality are putatively represented. In science, according to Mario Bunge, it is inaccurate to confuse a model with a metaphor, for the former is at its most basic 'a schematic conceptual representation of a thing or situation assumed

151

to be actual or possible, (Bunge, p. 97). The testing of these 'model objects' is a very complex matter, involving the generation of (revisable) hypothetico-deductive schemes which are both mathematical and theory-laden. But the meaning of model is not so wide that anything goes: it, rather, enables us to avoid both the 'pictorial' overtones of the word *metaphor* and the view that there can be no real bridge between scientific interpretation and the real world.

We cannot pretend that such a concept of model can be directly transplanted into the soil of theology. We are not here concerned primarily with observation and experiment, and certainly not with mathematics. But we have every need, if theology is not to be considered wishful thinking – or mythologizing, however modern – to be concerned with concepts. For concepts enable us to express that which we believe to be true, so that a decision may be made about the rationality, and possibly also the truth, of that which is asserted or preached. Concepts are the means by which Christian claims about Jesus of Nazareth are given rational currency. They are the way by which we attempt to speak systematically about him and his relation to God and ourselves, but not, if they are to be true to him, the way in which he is subjected to a system. That, as we have already seen, is the outcome of some approaches to Christology from above and from below. Necessarily, such models will draw more than science appears to do on metaphors. Particularly in its exposition of soteriology, which is so closely related to Christology, theology has always been dependent upon metaphors, classic images by means of which attempts are made to express the reality of grace, judgement and forgiveness come down to earth. The systematic question here is whether and to what extent the metaphors succeed in expressing the reality of the divine–human relation that is in question. Unless the metaphors can be given some conceptual co-ordination, questions of reality and truth cannot be adequately raised. That, of course, is the element of validity in programmes of demythologization.

The relation between our words and the reality of Jesus Christ can also be expressed by another term from the philosophy of science, *mapping*. 'The map metaphor for science preserves us from a vulgar fallacy – the tendency to conflate scientific knowledge with the material reality it purports to describe. No sane person would suppose a map to be identical with the land that it represents'

(Ziman, p. 85). A map is the means by which selected features of reality are abstracted from the whole and used as a guide to the understanding of that whole – in this case an area of land. It is not the function of science 'to provide an explanation for everything that is thought to have happened in the world' (p. 147) but, rather, to enable us to understand particular features and aspects of reality. In order to do this, the theoretician abstracts and overemphasizes certain elements of reality. 'The surveyor deliberately collects *redundant* data, so that the locations of the main features of the map are *over-determined*' (p. 82). This notion of the necessity of the over-determination of certain features is very interesting for Christology. For example, it might be said that Ignatius and his successors over-determined the doctrine of the divinity of Jesus Christ. Finding it explicitly expressed only a few times, but believing it to be implicit in the whole tradition, they emphasized it as a salient point on the map of Christian doctrine. Similarly, the Chalcedonian confession carefully mapped a number of central features of what the members of the Council held to be the crucial truths about the person of Jesus Christ: his unity, his divinity, his humanity and the four ways in which these three were to be understood. Did they thus falsify the picture or sketch a guidemap for Christians and writers of Christology? Whatever the answer to that question, the intellectual propriety of what they were doing should not be denied. It was a quite proper attempt to map and model the truth as they saw it.

THE CONCEPTS OF CHRISTOLOGY

As we have seen, there was expressed in Schleiermacher a deep discontent with the traditional language of Christology. As a child of the Enlightenment, Schleiermacher was brought up with that movement's savage critique of orthodox Christianity. As a pious Christian, he believed that the traditional concepts distorted the reality of the Christ through whom he had been redeemed. Instead he developed, as we have seen, a Christology based upon the God-consciousness of Jesus, and must therefore be seen to be an originator of what McIntyre calls the 'psychological' model of Christology. However, simply to treat Schleiermacher's Christology as a specification of the generic *psychological* is at once to fail to do justice to Schleiermacher's thinking and to treat the matter too generally.

153

'Psychological' is a characterization of a general type of theory, and it is at this level that McIntyre directs some very telling criticisms. But as an exponent of a general approach Schleiermacher also employs particular concepts in an attempt to articulate systematically the reality of the Redeemer. By the deployment of these concepts he intended to model the reality of Jesus and hence provide a form of words by which the New Testament Jesus could be understood.

Central to Schleiermacher's Christology is the concept of the ideality (*Urbildlichkeit*) of Jesus (Schleiermacher, pp. 377ff.). One does not have to be aware of Schleiermacher's distinction as a scholar of Plato to realize the intellectual pedigree of this term. It is a means of linking the historical with the eternal, of expressing the universality of Jesus's significance and the uniqueness of his experience of God. Against those who would avoid the use of the term, Schleiermacher protests its necessity if we are to see in Jesus not simply an example but the source of a like relation to God for later generations. He thus uses the model of ideality to interpret various strands of New Testament witness to Jesus, in particular its seeing him as the temporal locus of eternal salvation. In addition, we can observe the origins of his picture in aspects of Jesus's experience as it is depicted by the Gospels, and perhaps particularly the Fourth Gospel. Jesus is depicted there as uniquely dependent upon the Father at all stages of his life.

The question to Schleiermacher is not whether this is a useful model, as it clearly is, but whether it is asked to do more than it can bear. Does it enable us to understand the whole, or does it, rather, conform the whole to what is only a part? The critique of Schleiermacher's Christology from below in Chapter 5 suggests the latter. To hang a whole Christology upon the ideality of Jesus's God-consciousness leads to a kind of docetism. The great weight of ideality is centred on the historical Jesus – that is, the Jesus of his historical ministry – at the expense of those aspects of the tradition which conceive him in relation also to past and future eternity. The man Jesus is eternalized (Platonized) because the historical is made to bear too great a load. Yet as a depiction of the human Jesus in relation to the Father, the model is a very useful one. The Gospels and Epistles do see the outcome of Jesus's life as authentically and paradigmatically human as a result of his obedience to and dependence upon God.

But that is not all that they have to say. They also conceive the ministry as originating in the eternal love of God. Because the tradition which Schleiermacher rejects so harshly distinguished between 'of one substance with the Father' and 'of one substance with us', it was able, though only more or less successfully, to conceive at once the humanity of Jesus, as obedient and yet supremely free, and his divinity. Because the humanity was not the locus of divinity in itself but depended *for its humanity* upon the eternal Word, it was able to remain a genuine humanity. Here we may note in passing the function of the much despised concept-models of *anhypostasia* and *enhypostasia*. The former, often mistranslated with the help of the Latin as *impersonality*, is a model by which an attempt is made to locate the origin of *this* human reality not in itself but in eternity; the latter, to locate its *genuine* human reality in eternity. By locating it in itself, Schleiermacher loses the humanity altogether, and so commits the error he himself believes the tradition to embody.

Anhypostasia and *enhypostasia* are difficult and technical models, but are relatively subordinate. They were designed to make more precise, and so preserve from misunderstanding, concepts which found their classical expression in the Definition of Chalcedon. Central among those is that which we have recently met, *homoousios* or 'of one substance'. The term first came into widespread (though not yet universal) official usage at the Council of Nicaea more than a century before Chalcedon. It was designed, in face of theologies thought to endanger it, to guarantee a point of trinitarian theology, that the eternal Son is of the same οὐσία, or being, as the Father. It was also, of course, of christological importance, for it *identifies* Jesus Christ with the eternal Son and proceeds, in the spatial language we have already met, to confess that he 'came down and was made flesh, and became man. . .' (Bettenson, p. 25), so tracing a path from the eternal to the temporal.

What, then, of this word οὐσία or *substance* as it has since come to be translated? Is it now obsolete as a model for modern Christology? Certainly it has a strange ring in modern ears, particularly when we think of the everyday use of the word. It has also been described as 'static', and therefore inappropriate to the dynamic reality of the God who encounters us in the movement of temporal

155

reality. The criticisms have a measure of truth about them, but we cannot understand how far they are justified until we are more aware of what this particular model was designed to do. In this respect, a general point voiced by Professor D. M. MacKinnon should not be forgotten, that the category of substance was used by Aristotle as a means of indicating something that is really there: 'It is through the use of ontological categories that we are enabled to see precisely what it is that . . . confronts us in the person of Jesus' (MacKinnon, 1972, p. 294). Ontology, we may say, drawing on a previous section, enables theology to *indwell* or, in MacKinnon's words, operates 'to tie it tightly to the concrete' (p. 297). But the general point in favour of ontology does not solve the question of whether we are well advised to continue to employ this particular ontological model.

To see something of how the model was used, we turn to Professor Christopher Stead's detailed investigation of *Divine Substance*. The first lesson to be learned from him is the wide range and complexity of uses of the word both in classical and Christian employment. It does not necessarily have to be understood 'statically'. Second, however, its use did tend to be linked to 'the Platonic distinction between "intelligible" and "sensible" substances, or reality' (Stead, 1977, p. 158), and hence the early Christian opinion 'that it is characteristic of God that he can assume any form he wishes . . . lost ground before the Platonic doctrine of God's changelessness' (p. 171). Together the two lessons of the history of the concept teach the usefulness and flexibility of words alongside their inadequacy, as they stand, to perform a function as theological models. They have to be employed appropriately to the nature of what they model. *Substance* could have developed a meaning with associations hostile to the static and unchanging, expressing the dynamism of a God who becomes temporal without loss of eternity, human by means of his ever-rich divinity. As a philosopher used to say, it all depends upon what you mean by the word. And that is the third thing we learn from Stead, that this particular model was employed in a way specific to the subject-matter with which early Christian theology concerned itself. At Nicaea, he argues, the model *homoousios* was used only indirectly as an ontological characterization, for it was primarily concerned to see the Son as coming from the Father. Athanasius, whose uses of the term 'are almost without exception geared to the actual clause of the Nicene Creed', never departs completely from Nicaea's meaning, for he always uses it asymmetrically, never, for example, saying that the Father is *homoousios* with the Son: 'the Father initiates, the Son responds' even though 'the Father communicates to the Son all that he has and is, the Son receives the fullness of divine being' (p. 266).

Stead's account suggests that, at least in its use up to the time of Athanasius, the way in which the word was employed succeeded in modelling features of the biblical Christology, which does locate the origin of what happened in God and does see the relationship between Jesus and the Father in asymmetrical – though not ontologically subordinationist – terms; Jesus is, as God incarnate, dependent upon the Father. In that respect it is more comprehensive than Schleiermacher's use of *ideality*. And Stead himself adds two considerations in favour of the use of the term. First, '(t)o characterize God as a substance is to stake a claim against reductionist theories which in effect represent God as dependent on the human experience which he is invoked to explain' (p. 273). Second, the use of the language of substance does not necessarily imply a 'static ontology' (Stead's inverted commas): 'God can be, and has been, represented as changing substance, and indeed as one that is ever-changing and infinitely adaptable. . . (T)he description of God in terms of substance does not of itself prejudge the question whether God is, or is not, involved in change' (pp. 274, 275). Thus we might say that despite all the tendencies of Platonic or Aristotelian ontology to eternalize Christian language about Jesus, in the tradition there is made an attempt to use the language in a way appropriate to the divine-human reality that was at the heart of their gospel. And in this manner the language was itself adapted to that which it wished to portray.

But we have not yet explored as fully as we might the relation between the static and the dynamic. There is a sense in which that language which attempts to model divine – and therefore *eternal* realities – must have an element of, if not overtones of the static, then certainly of the continuous about it. If Jesus Christ is a human and divine reality, the same yesterday, today and for ever, then models evoking the reality of this continuity will be proper ones. To say that Jesus Christ is 'of one substance' with the Father and with us says something about what *he always is*, so that we may understand that he is a present and future as well as a past reality. Whether it is 'static' or not depends in large measure upon what is understood by the terms *God* and *man*. In any case, the discussion often evades the prior question, which is not whether God is eternal or not, but whether his eternity precludes dynamic interrelationship with the temporal. We are back with the matter of dualism: 'of one substance' can be understood dualistically or non-dualistically. In the latter case, it may still be understood successfully to model aspects of Jesus's reality, to map the way in which he is one with God and one with us.

Uses of 'substance' and its cognates demonstrate the tradition's development of words from Greek philosophical sources to express that which Greek philosophy would not easily say, the co-presence of time and eternity in a historical life. At the same time a model was developed which sat even less easily in philosophical company, and was a more directly Christian coining. When early Christian theology spoke of the incarnation, it was using very 'dynamic' language indeed. It was saying that the (eternal) Word became (temporal) flesh without being any the less the Word, Jesus of Nazareth any less a full human being. Here we have not so much the employment of old language in a new sense to describe eternal realities as a complex of terms attempting to model something which happened. What happened, at a particular time, was that the eternal Word became flesh. The form this took, a form which began with the conception of a child, was described by the terms 'hypostatic union', wherein was represented the new and unique historical reality which resulted from what happened in the incarnation. 'Hypostatic union' is a model which provides a conceptual link between historical event and eternal reality. When the eternal love of God takes to itself this human reality, there is created a being at once divine and human, the person Jesus Christ.

This very brief summary is not presented to suggest that things can, in twentieth-century theology, be put in precisely the same way – they cannot – but to attempt to show that by means of these models different features of Christology were brought to expression. *Hypostasis* and its cognates model primarily the historic reality of Jesus Christ; *ousia* and its cognates the (eternal and temporal) orders of being; *incarnation* the event in which the two orders are brought together in the historical reality that was and is Jesus Christ. The words, like all models, did not at once attain a fixed and static meaning, but changed and grew as centuries of debate made more precise the way in which they modelled reality. The notion of the incarnation would seem to be in many ways the central model, arising as it does directly from the New Testament. The other clusters of concepts are attempts to spell out what is true if the incarnation took place as Scripture, through the Fourth Gospel in particular, claims that it did. They are an attempt *to map the implications for ontology of the life in which the divine love took human form.* It is in that respect that they are properly described as 'second order' language, language, that is, which is used as a control on the more basic models of Christology. It is sometimes suggested that statements like those of Chalcedon should be understood as 'language about language' (Norris, p. 78; Butterworth, p. 115), but that is not the same thing as saying that language is second order. It supposes a neat classification of levels of language: the lower levels speak of 'things'; the higher ones of 'words about things'. But language is not like that, certainly if the Polanyian epistemology is correct, seeing, as it does, the levels interpenetrating each other, as reality is indwelt by the tools and concepts of a lower stage in order to make possible a process of discovery of higher and more complex levels of reality. Words like *homoousios* are still concerned with what is there – with ontology – but at a higher level of abstraction even than statements of doctrine like that of the incarnation.

Models, then, are the words and concepts by which the tradition, and we, in so far as we can indwell the tradition in order to speak in our own words, attempt to articulate the reality of Jesus Christ. The most (*logically*) primitive are those in which the New Testament writers express in a variety of ways the meaning of the life, death and resurrection of Jesus of Nazareth. As they develop their insights, they come to believe that this life and its outcome represent the movement of the love of God into time. In the Fourth Gospel, along with anticipations and parallels in other writers, this movement comes explicitly to expression in a statement of the incarnation, that in this human being God has himself become present in time. The early Christian theologians developed this model, and out of their own cultural heritage hammered a number of central concepts with which to express its various aspects: its uniqueness and novelty; its continuity with other movements of God into relation with creation and history; the way in which the human Jesus is related to the eternal reality of God.

This section, then, is intended to demonstrate two things. The first is that we can understand the kind of things that were attempted in early Christology. If the nature of human knowing indicates a real link between our rationality and that of the world, we should not succumb easily to culturally conditioned doctrines of cultural relativism. Cultures do change, but within a fundamental continuity of human rationality and tradition. The second is that contemporary theology should be able gladly to affirm the relative validity of the great christological creeds of the first few centuries. The validity is relative because no human statement made in the centre of time can claim absolute validity, certainly if it is of any scope and importance. Lessing's neoclassical dualism of the necessary and the contingent at once exaggerates the certainty of one supposed form of statement and underestimates the possibility of the truth of contingent assertions. If the normal form of human rationality is a contingent rationality, then we may say that, although relative, the traditional statements are valid and true. They express not absolute truths but truths none the less that the contemporary Christian may appropriate for himself, for they represent early theology's attempt to ensure that what we say about Jesus of Nazareth remains true to what he *was* and *is*: the temporal locus of God's love for his creation.

CONSISTENCY AND UNIQUENESS

But, that said, we reach a more radical critique of the language of Christology, one that has been with it from the beginning. It takes two forms: the first is that it is a logical contradiction to assert at once the humanity and divinity of Jesus; the second that it is in any case impossible to assert the uniqueness of this particular *hypostasis*. Both objections have ramifications in many directions, and some of them will be pursued in the two final chapters. At this stage we shall concentrate on a brief discussion of the logical problems involved, true to the programme of this chapter to consider matters concerning the status of christological claims.

1   'It is contradictory to say that Jesus of Nazareth is both God and man.' This objection to classical Christology takes a num-

ber of forms, many of which, in particular those centring on dualistic assumptions about the incompatibility of the eternal and the temporal, we have already considered. In the patristic period, the objection tended to be associated with beliefs about the impassibility of God, which apparently contradicted both the doctrine of the incarnation and the suffering of God the Word on the cross. In the modern period the objection derives from typical beliefs about the closedness of time and space, both in itself and in relation to the human mind. But here we reach a more radical statement of the objection, that the words *God* and *man* have meanings that make the christological statement that Jesus of Nazareth was and is both wholly God and wholly man an internally inconsistent one. *God*, it is said, means a being with certain characteristics like omnipotence, invisibility, omniscience – if not impassibility! – and therefore cannot be consistently claimed to be wholly present in Jesus of Nazareth, who is limited in power, visible and apparently – though the tradition has wrongly sometimes tried to prove that he is not – limited in knowledge and even fallible.

The objection to classical Christology with which we are concerned itself depends upon a number of assumptions, both about God and about what it means to be a human being. In particular, it assumes that the so-called divine attributes of omnipotence and the rest are static possessions which do not admit of exercise except in a purely external relationship to the world. Take, for example, the idea of omnipotence. Jesus, despite his apparent exercise of divine authority and power in relation to sin, sickness and nature, could not be said to have been omnipotent in the abstract sense often assumed in philosophical discussions of the topic. But in claiming the divinity of Jesus we are not claiming that Jesus of Nazareth was omnipotent. That is not the way in which the predicate should operate in this context. Rather, the whole human life and suffering of Jesus should be conceived as the exercise of divine omnipotence. If the predicate is understood from above in this way and not from below, the very humanity of Jesus is construed as the way in which God's power operates. We thus come to conceive omnipotence in a new way as the result of our engagement with what it means to say that this human being is God incarnate. To be God omnipotent does not mean an arbitrary throwing of the weight around, but of the exercise of power in this thoroughly human and gracious way. The power is not the less for its self-limitation. Quite the contrary is true, for the concrete channelling of its operation enables it to operate truly effectively, from within the circumstances of history and humanity.

The same kind of conceptual reconstruction enables us to see something of what is meant by the omniscience of God. Omniscience is, like omnipotence, often approached in an abstract way, as in the classical claim that God knows all events timelessly and the neoclassical revision that he knows the past timelessly and the future only by anticipation. Both of these conceptions accord ill with a view of omniscience centred on the life of Jesus understood as God's knowledge in action. Jesus Christ is both 'the power of God and the wisdom of God' according to Paul (1 Corinthians 1.24), especially in his crucifixion. Knowledge, then, means in this instance a divine attribute or perfection as it operates in the interests of human well-being. The life of Jesus of Nazareth is the all-seeing love and compassion of God operating under the conditions of temporality. In this instance, too, it makes a great deal of difference whether we try to demonstrate, abstractly and from below, that Jesus of Nazareth was omniscient, or whether we see the human life as a whole as God's omniscience in operation. The former patently contradicts the evidence, while the latter enables us to come to terms with the kind of God with whom we are concerned in Christology.

By making conceptual revisions of this kind we shall not achieve complete solutions of logical problems. But we shall see that the question of contradiction depends upon the meaning of the words in the statements we make. It also depends upon what we expect to find in the life of Jesus of Nazareth. If we expect to be able to discover the 'historical Jesus' as being himself omnipotent and omniscient in abstraction from his particular human calling, we shall dualistically divorce the Son from the Father and generate a docetic Christology. Necessarily, the historical Jesus was not omniscient. But if his (enhypostatic) humanity is understood as the Father's historical giving of form through the incarnate Word to his providential and eternal concern for the integrity of human life, we shall avoid both dualism and docetism. The very power and knowledge of the love of God is expressed in the humanity of his approach to us in Jesus, who must therefore be understood as the living expression of God's power and knowledge. It may therefore strain all our

162

powers of language and thought to say that Jesus is both God and man, but it is certainly not necessarily a contradiction. It is only a contradiction if we assume that the kind of self-differentiation here being supposed is logically impossible for God.

2   The logical problem supposed to inhere in claims that Jesus is uniquely God brings us to a different, though related, set of problems. It is very difficult for a theologian writing in the modern West to achieve a balanced discussion of the issues involved. For very sound moral reasons, we have come to suspect that the way in which the uniqueness of Jesus has been asserted in our past has assisted the development of political authoritarianism in our internal affairs and an association of Christianity with colonialist attitudes in our relations to other cultures and religions. Some of the moral aspects will be dealt with in later chapters, but it is important to understand here the intentions behind assertions such as the one that Jesus is in some sense functionally rather than ontologically unique, and, more recently, that he has a 'uniqueness of the pattern-setting or criteriological kind transcending the "exclusive/ inclusive" or "culture-bound/imperialist" alternatives' (Wainwright, p. 69). Unfortunately, such proposals do not transcend but rather evade the moral questions, since by their evasion of ontology they also make it difficult to discuss the way in which the uniqueness is understood to subsist. And if this cannot be discussed, we cannot raise either the question of by what right Jesus is claimed to exercise divine functions or to present pattern or criterion for anything else.

We must therefore face the problem in its full and traditional form: what does it mean to claim that here, in what happened with Jesus of Nazareth, we are presented with the reality of God in a way that we are presented with it nowhere else? At this stage, the form in which the question is asked must be made more precise. No suggestion is being made that God is met with nowhere else than in Jesus of Nazareth. The very eternity of the latter's significance means, according to the New Testament's 'cosmic Christologies', that God can also be met in the created order, in history, and in other political and religious movements than the Christian Church. What is being claimed in continuity with the New Testament and the mainstream Christian tradition is that we are here presented with the reality of God in a manner that is unique.

But how is this uniqueness to be understood? Once again, it

should not be sought in some abstract achievement of Jesus, such as his experience, moral teaching or moral superiority. They should rather be understood as functions of the life as a whole. For this reason the uniqueness should be seen as the perfection of a pattern of the divine loving, which can be found elsewhere but is only here to be found as present in person. This love can be found especially in the ways of God towards Israel, for it is the Old Testament which enables us to understand both the concreteness of the divine love and the anticipatory form which it took in relation to Israel. If we are able to conceive Jesus as uniquely the presence of God, it is because in this essential context we have a preparatory conception of his presentness which is both corrected and transcended by what happens here. The Old Testament theologies, then, provide what can be called the formal basis for the ascription of uniqueness to Jesus.

But that is simply, from the systematic point of view, a clarification, not an answer to the question. That can only be answered by an indication of what in the *content* of the divine presence marks it out as being in principle unique. Here we must point to the ubiquitous linking by the New Testament of Christology and soteriology. Jesus is unique because he is the way by which God restores his human creation – and, along with it, his whole creation – to a wholeness of relationship with him. That is the final reason why he is identified with God and why all the devices associated with orthodox Christology have been developed. From the human point of view we must say that only here is authentic humanity understood and given. More theologically, we are led to the further specification of the logic of the divine love that is Jesus of Nazareth. In this logic we come to learn that the logic of love and the logic of morality are not finally in conflict. God as love and God as judge – as upholder of the moral order – are not ultimately distinct, for the one who judges does so only by means of the love that is his Son. It is only when we appreciate that it is in and through Jesus of Nazareth that God meets humanity where it is, in its alienation and fallenness, and so liberates it for an imitation of that love, that we shall begin to understand that the assertion of Jesus's uniqueness, far from being immoral or illogical, is the presupposition for an understanding of the love of God for all of his creation. It is, to borrow

164

P. T. Forsyth's much-used expression, love only as holy love, which loves only while taking seriously our failure to love.

It is for reasons such as these that we must conclude that difficulties about the divinity and uniqueness of Jesus are not simply logical problems. The logical problems arise for two reasons. The first is intellectual, and arises from the fact that any attempt to express the truth about God must fall far short of that which it seeks to portray. Here we cannot escape Kierkegaard's formulation of the problem, even though we shall not concede the necessity of ultimate paradoxicality. Of course God cannot be encompassed in our logic, but that is not to say that all expressions of his reality are illogical. The very fact of Jesus of Nazareth means the reverse: that, despite the inadequacy and indirectness of all our language, it can still speak a measure of logical truth. The second reason is moral, for the nature of Jesus's life, and particularly its outcome on the cross, is offensive to us human beings who would evade the challenge it makes to our own self-understanding. That our lives should be measured and healed by this lonely and suffering figure is the real reason why the ascription of uniqueness is difficult. But it is also the reason why it should be made. Christological statements obtain their claim to truth and rationality from the prior ontological and soteriological claim that Jesus of Nazareth is the logic of the holy love of God.

CONCLUSION

This chapter has argued that Lessing's formulation of the problem of the nature of Christian talk about Jesus is mistaken. By setting up false criteria for the reliability and credibility of statements of faith, it has misunderstood the way in which our language is related to reality. By contrast, a view of the human intellectual enterprise which aims not at disembodied objectivity but at personal engagement with the material at hand makes possible a number of revisions of contemporary assumptions. We are required neither to contemplate the reality of Christ from afar nor to stand loose to the Christian tradition, as if Christology since the Enlightenment had become an entirely different intellectual enterprise. On the contrary, by indwelling the tradition's language about Christ we may become truly critical of our own understanding of our relation to his human and divine reality. Our language may come to be only with the assistance of our great predecessors.

This means that our christological language is justified if it says what is true about Jesus Christ. Whether it is true or not depends upon whether it is a fact that Jesus of Nazareth was and is God's holy love for his world. Whether, in turn, we can know that to be true, is in large measure an eschatological question. But we have provisional aids by which we can test our statements: the Bible, the creeds and the worship and experience of the Christian Church. Some of the concerns of the latter will occupy the remaining chapters of the book. But this chapter must end by repeating a saying of Polanyi, for it has attempted to do for the doctrine of the person of Christ what he achieved in his own work: to show 'that I may hold firmly to what I believe to be true, even though I know that it might conceivably be false' (Polanyi, 1962, p. 214). The status of christological statements is that they attempt to express how and in which ways this is possible for those who believe in God through Jesus Christ.

REFERENCES

Bettenson, Henry (ed)., *Documents of the Christian Church.*

Bunge, Mario, *Method, Model and Matter.*

Butterworth, Robert, 'Has Chalcedon a Future?', *The Month*, ccxxxviii, 111–17.

Jenson, Robert W., *The Knowledge of Things Hoped For: The Sense of Theological Discourse.*

Kierkegaard, Søren, 1941a, *Concluding Unscientific Postscript*, Eng. trans. David F. Swenson and Walter Lowrie.

Kierkegaard, Søren, 1962, *Philosophical Fragments*, Eng. trans. David F. Swenson and Howard V. Hong.

Kuhn, Helmut, 'Personal Knowledge and the Crisis of the Philosophical Tradition' in *Intellect and Hope: Essays in the Thought of Michael Polanyi*, eds. Thomas A. Langford and William H. Poteat, pp. 111–35.

Lessing, G. E., *Lessing's Theological Writings: Selections in Translation*, Eng. trans. Henry Chadwick.

McIntyre, John, *The Shape of Christology.*

MacKinnon, D. M., 1972, ' "Substance" in Christology – a Cross-bench View' in *Christ, Faith and History*, eds. S. W. Sykes and J. P. Clayton, pp. 279–300.

Norris, R. A., Jnr., 'Towards a Contemporary Interpretation of the Chalcedonian *Definition*' in *Lux in Lumine: Essays to Honour W. Norman Pittenger*, ed. R. A. Norris, pp. 62–79.

The Status of Christological Statements

Pannenberg, Wolfhart, 1970, 'Analogy and Doxology' in *Basic Questions in Theology I*, Eng. trans. George H. Kehm, pp. 211–38.

Polanyi, Michael, 1959, *The Study of Man*.

Polanyi, Michael, 1962, *Personal Knowledge: Towards a Post-Critical Philosophy*.

Quine, W. V. O., 'Two Dogmas of Empiricism' in *Clarity is not Enough*, ed. H. D. Lewis, pp. 110–32.

Rorty, Richard, *Philosophy and the Mirror of Nature*.

Schleiermacher, F. D. E., *The Christian Faith*, Eng. trans. H. R. Mackintosh and J. S. Stewart.

Schlink, Edmund, *The Coming Christ and the Coming Church*, Eng. trans. G. Overlach, D. B. Simmonds *et al.*

Stead, G. C., *Divine Substance*.

Torrance, T. F., 1975, *Theology in Reconciliation: Essays towards Evangelical and Catholic Unity in East and West*.

Wainwright, Geoffrey, *Doxology: The Praise of God in Worship, Doctrine and Life. A Systematic Theology*.

Wittgenstein, Ludwig, *Philosophical Investigations*, Eng. trans. G. E. M. Anscombe.

Ziman, John, *Reliable Knowledge: An Exploration of the Grounds for Belief in Science*.

8

THE LOGIC OF THE SAVING LOVE OF GOD

THE NEED FOR ONTOLOGY

The transition from the previous chapter to the two chapters with which the book closes can be put as follows. Suppose that some success has been achieved in showing the way in which our statements can 'map' the way things are, is there any point in doing it? At one level the question should be dismissed as philistine. If a matter, particularly one that has been so seriously debated for centuries, is concerned with the truth, then its rehearsal needs no justifying. But Christian theology has always, at its best, refused to abstract questions of truth from questions of relevance. And if Jesus of Nazareth is the historical reality of God's holy loving, then the impact of this love, the way in which God's relating of himself to us makes a measure of difference to our human reality, is very much the heart of the matter. In this chapter, then, we shall ask about the impact of Christology on that closely related topic of soteriology. But it will be done in continuity with what went before, in the hope of demonstrating further that Christology is not a matter of how we prove that a man is God, but of how the love of God becomes real in the world.

In the last few centuries there has been a tendency to reject ontological Christologies on the ground that they are simply abstract theorizing, and it has become fashionable to reject the most technical of the confessions, that of Chalcedon, as intellectually bankrupt. But, whatever one's views on Chalcedon as a piece of theologizing, views of its bankruptcy usually reflect a poor understanding of its historical place. Patristic and conciliar Christology can only be understood against a background of a fierce, often too fierce, concern to defend the Christian understanding of salvation.

The same is true of biblical Christology, with its constant linking with the history of salvation. Christology and soteriology are always in the closest relationship, for good or ill, because they concern the way in which the reality of Jesus is understood to bear upon our present human condition.

How, then, are we to understand the relation between an orthodox Christology – one that remains true to the tradition's insistence that Jesus Christ is both fully man and fully God – and the Christian doctrine of salvation? It is widely taught and believed that modern moral theory has rendered obsolete the kind of atonement theory underlying ancient Christology. And even those who have strongly reasserted the necessity for our continuing to uphold the sacrificial and even penal aspects of the tradition have sometimes held that they can be retained independently of the Christology. For example, Peter Taylor Forsyth, though an advocate of a theology dominated by the historical redemption achieved by the cross of Christ, remained hostile to ontological Christologies, especially that of Chalcedon. How could this be? Was it that here if not elsewhere his head remained in the nineteenth century even though his heart was pulling him to the sort of position later to be associated with the theology of Barth?

Forsyth's objections, as they are set out in a chapter significantly entitled 'The Moralising of Dogma' in *The Person and Place of Jesus Christ*, are two. First, he holds that the inadequacies of the ancient formulae have been exposed by modern criticism, psychology and theology. It has been shown that 'The truths were not really and inwardly adjusted, but only placed together; and they are thus the more easily shaken apart' (Forsyth, p. 217). There is thus a theologically contingent connection between the cross and what was achieved by the Council of AD 451. Second, Forsyth contrasts the modern ethical approach to religion, learned at the Reformation, with rationalism, ancient and modern. He rejects Hegelianism, which he believes to have been an attempt to 'scholasticise Christianity anew' *pari passu* with Chalcedonian metaphysics (p. 218), appealing to the evangelical spirit to be found in Schleiermacher, Ritschl and others:

The incarnation, being for a moral and not a metaphysical purpose, must be in its nature moral. Its metaphysic should therefore

be a metaphysic of ethics, and not of thought as pure being. . .
The Godhead that became incarnate in Jesus Christ did so not
to convince but to save (p. 219).

Thus Forsyth's objection to ontological expressions of Christology
is that they are rationalistic at the expense of a stress on the saving
reality of the Christ event:

> Now concerning the union of the two natures in Christ the old
> dogma thought in a far too natural and non-moral way. Its
> categories were too elemental and physical. . . (The) incarnation
> takes place not by spiritual power but by natural power, however
> vastly magnified and deified, by a fiat rather than a moral act
> (pp. 223f.).

> The formula of the union of two natures in one person is essen-
> tially a metaphysical formula, and the formula of a Hellenic
> metaphysic, and it is more or less archaic for the modern mind
> (p. 229).

This summary of Forsyth's position reveals the nisus of his objections. Ontology calls attention away from the moral realities to the
metaphysical. A similar point is made by H. R. Mackintosh against
the 'two-nature' theory: 'the term "nature" . . . is not an ethical
word at all. Now non-ethical realities admit of no true unity. . .'
(Mackintosh, p. 214).

It has been argued in previous chapters that the unity of God
and man in Jesus can be expressed in ontological terms. Unless we
conceive the relation of time and eternity in dualistic terms, it is
possible to argue from Jesus of Nazareth to a view of things in
which God's love takes form within the conditions of time and
space. But Forsyth's and Mackintosh's objections also go deeper.
Why bother with ontology, when we not only do not need it (for we
are concerned with moral, not metaphysical realities) but are also
prevented by it from conceiving clearly the moral realities involved?
It has, however, already been suggested in the course of the argument that those who have no explicit ontology will almost certainly
employ an implicit one unconsciously. That this is so here also, and
that Forsyth in particular cannot escape ontological questions, soon
becomes evident from his writing.

'Soteriology is the way of access to Christology' (Forsyth, p. 220).

Now Forsyth is not, after the manner of some of his successors in this tradition of interpretation, claiming that Christology is to be reduced to moral or experiential categories. He is insistent that the intellectual work must be done. He also rejects 'a bland version of salvation': the person of Christ becomes intelligible only when viewed through the prism of the momentous work of salvation. For this reason, he argues,

> Some metaphysic is involved . . . but it is a metaphysic of the conscience. It starts from the conviction that for life and history the moral is the real. . . The spiritual world is not the world of noetic process or cosmic force, but of holy, i.e. moral, order, act and power (pp. 221f.).

Forsyth's demand for a metaphysic of conscience is to be understood in the light of his positive assessment of the work of Schleiermacher and his successors. He sees the great nineteenth-century theologians as critics of the tendency to treat Christology scholastically, with the result that for him the formulas of the tradition become not the vehicles of a saving experience but simply intellectual counters.[1]

And yet Forsyth's greatness is that he partially breaks out of the nineteenth-century mould, and produces a Christology that goes beyond a simply ethical framework. His kenotic theory of the incarnation is more than 'a metaphysic of conscience', for it is essentially an attempt to make logical sense of the incarnation conceived as something that really happened in human history. It thus belies his proclaimed lack of interest in metaphysical theories. It is, in fact, largely concerned with considerations of *a priori* metaphysics, asking how traditional attributes like omnipotence and omniscience can be reconciled with the manifest humanity of Jesus. Thus, of omniscience: 'When the Eternal enters time it becomes a discursive and successive knowledge, with the power to know all things only potential, and enlarging to become actual under the moral conditions that govern human growth and the extension of human knowledge' (pp. 307f.). Forsyth describes what happens as a 'retraction of their [the attributes'] mode of being from actual to potential. . . The self-reduction, or self-retraction, of God might be a better

---

1 We may also suspect that Forsyth's formulation owes a no doubt unconscious debt to Kant's movement to reduce talk of God to the oblique presupposition of the language of morals.

phrase than the self-emptying' (p. 308). As kenotic theories go, Forsyth's is interesting, particularly in view of the remarks that accompany it and weaken the force of its logic, if not actually destroy it. But it serves to illustrate that those who attempt to avoid ontology run the risk of doing ontology badly. Claiming to eschew any attempt exhaustively to explain how the incarnation takes place, Forsyth does very nearly that in his kenotic theory.

But there is an even greater objection to be made against Forsyth's procedure. It is that kenotic theories, far from replacing two-nature doctrine, in fact *presuppose* the latter and then proceed to say that they cannot go so far as Chalcedon but must in some way qualify the assertion of unity so that it is not quite so bald. They are therefore essentially dualistic. Unlike Chalcedon, which says that in the one Christ there are, simply given, the two realities, make of them what you will, they say, 'Chalcedon gives us two realities in one. We know (or believe) that this is impossible. Let us therefore qualify this full-blooded assertion and hold that the divine Son is not present in his fullness, but only almost so.' It is the kenotic theorist who rationalizes Christology, not the Chalcedonian Definition. He also in effect divides the Son from the Father, by saying that God cannot empty himself and still remain God. Eugene R. Fairweather, in a note on kenotic Christologies appended to F. W. Beare's *Commentary on Philippians*, quotes what is for him the key objection to them: 'God is always God even in his humiliation. . . The deity of Christ is the one unaltered because unalterable deity of God. Any subtraction or weakening of it would at once throw doubt upon the atonement made in him. He humbled himself, but he did not do it by ceasing to be who he is' (Fairweather, p. 173, citing Barth, *Church Dogmatics* iv/1, pp. 179f.). It seems thus not inappropriate to speak of a self-emptying of God, but only if it is understood in such a way as to be an *expression* rather than a 'retraction' of his deity. The self-emptying is part of God's fullness, for the heart of what it means to be God is that he is able to empty himself on behalf of that which is not himself. In other words, it is part of his love, through which he comes among us in our time and history to transform our existence from within.

Of course, Forsyth very nearly said that. His insistence on the fact that what happened on the cross is the work of God means that he cannot finally avoid talking in terms very similar to those of the tradition. As he turned from his central preoccupation with soteriology to a consideration of Christology, he found himself wrestling with the language of the incarnation in such a way that he came to speak also of the presence of the eternal in the cross of Jesus Christ. And is that not precisely what the traditional models of 'nature' and 'homoousios' were designed to ensure? For all his talk of a 'metaphysic of conscience', Forsyth was too good a theologian not to realize that unless soteriology is grounded on what is *really there*, then it ceases to be Christian soteriology.

AN OLD ARGUMENT REVIVED

What, then, are the problems that face us as we attempt to relate Christology to soteriology? There seem to be two in particular. The first concerns the degree to which we can share the affirmation of the Fathers that the defence of the Christian understanding of salvation requires the teaching that Jesus Christ is both very God and very man; and the second is the matter of the universality of Christ. We shall approach the first question by means of a discussion of the second. The matter of universality is best discussed through an examination of a famous passage in which Gregory of Nazianzus, following others of the Fathers, attacked the theology of Apollinaris.

> For that which is not assumed he has not healed; but that which is united to his Godhead is also saved. If only half Adam fell, then that which Christ assumes and saves may be half also; but if the whole of his nature fell, it must be united to the whole nature of Him that was begotten, and so be saved as a whole (Gregory, pp. 218f.).

The doctrine that Gregory is defending is that of the full humanity of Jesus Christ, against arguments that the human mind was replaced in the incarnate one by the divine Word. Like so many of the arguments examined in this book, it has to do with dualism: the dualistic assumption, on Apollinaris's part, that full humanity and divinity are incompatible. But other issues are at stake here. Gregory's fundamental argument is that if, in the historical event of the incarnation, God did not assume full humanity, then our full humanity is not taken up into his saving work. That is the argument.

173

Its assumptions are numerous. One would appear to be that a historical Adam fell; another that in some sense or other all men are affected (to put it at its weakest) by that fall and by the incarnation. Do these assumptions disqualify it as an argument now? The first assumption is easily translatable into terms more easily digestible by those with difficulties about the existence of a historical Adam. While the tradition, following Paul, has interpreted its theological anthropology largely in terms of Adam, a theology of the Fall need not be so limited in its biblical roots. Paul's understanding of sin in Romans 1ff., for example, sees it as very much a social and corporate phenomenon and is developed without reference to the Adam typology. Similar things could be said about the views of man to be found in Hosea, Jeremiah, the Fourth Gospel and the Apocalypse. Gregory wishes to argue that the universal human condition is not healed at its roots if the Church's Lord is not fully human, and his argument does not depend upon the form in which it expresses the reality of that condition.

But is it meaningful to speak of 'the universal human condition' with or without an Adam typlogy? In 'The Unassumed is the Unhealed', a paper discussing the same kind of question as this chapter, though coming to an opposite conclusion, Maurice Wiles sees that some kind of corporate or Platonic conception of humanity is presupposed. 'But I doubt if many people today can really visualize or express that which is common to mankind as a whole as strongly as our principle seems to require if it is to retain its verisimilitude' (Wiles, p. 117). That is a matter for debate: it might be argued, to the contrary, that ours is an age in which collectivist theories of man are rampant, providing at least an example of what might be meant. But what Wiles has on his side are the overwhelmingly nominalist tendencies of much modern thought, seeing in a class name no more than a convenient grouping, for the purposes of communication, of a number of individuals, with no other rationale than linguistic convenience. Surely such a view cannot plausibly be maintained. Something is called *cat* rather than *horse* because it is one rather than the other. Men are delimited from other entities because of real shared characteristics: language, laughter, physical shape, and so on. There is nothing *a priori* absurd in saying that one of the class should, while being *a* 'proper man' be also *the* 'proper man' on whom the well-being of the rest of the class should depend. 'It is important to acknowledge the universality of Christ's human nature, so that all men may share in the benefits of his atonement; but it is equally important to do justice to the particularity of the human nature of Christ, in order to secure its reality' (McIntyre, pp. 105f.).

But is it plausible to attempt to hold these aspects of traditional Christology in balance? It could be argued that, even for the nominalist, the problem could be solved, as indeed it sometimes has been, by theological fiat: it is God's will, simply and arbitrarily, to class all individual men together, and save them by their response to Jesus Christ conceived as a divine-human particular. However theologically objectionable such a procedure may be, it shows that Gregory's argument, even though he may be as a matter of fact a Platonist in his understanding of general terms, can be made to work independently of his philosophical position. And a moment's reflection will show that there is nothing absurd or implausible about a realism that posits a corporate interrelationship of humankind. It is becoming more evident, not less, that the human inhabitants of earth stand or fall together. The survival of humanity during the next decades depends, as we are often being reminded, upon the way in which we accept our mutual responsibilities and control our exploitation of the earth. While this does not demonstrate the correctness of, say, Paul's analysis of the human condition, it shows what kind of considerations can be brought to its defence. There is something that can be called human nature, not necessarily the *a priori* concept so obnoxious to individualistic existentialists anxious to establish their moral independence, but that which makes us 'a peece of the continent, a part of the maine' as one great Christian has put it.

Thus there is a case for arguing that all human beings form a corporate whole, even though the conception we develop falls short of a pure Platonism. As a matter of fact, it can be claimed, we are bound together in the kind of way that Reinhold Niebuhr has shown. Human beings do express their strengths and weaknesses most effectively in corporate form. But that only leads us to the second, and far more difficult aspect of Gregory's argument. There may be a corporate humanity. But, as we experience it, it contains not only Christians, but Jews, Marxists, Muslims and atheists, to mention but a few of the manifold overlapping and competing

175

allegiances of different groups of human beings. In the face of this massive plurality of human experience, can we continue to centre our understanding of ourselves as corporate in one questionable historical figure in our past? Is it not simply another aspect of Western imperialism that we wish to impose this pattern of humanity rather than another?

It is at this place that we realize the real difficulty that the modern mind has with Gregory's Platonism. It appears to begin with a conception 'from above' of Jesus as a representative or corporate human being, and then to impose the conception upon the whole of humanity. But if we are to appreciate the point of Gregory's argument, we should attempt to understand it apart from later associations of institutional exclusiveness and repression. He, and even more the Bible from which the notion of the universal significance of Jesus draws its origin, are not speaking primarily of a massive institution imposing its will on an unwilling world. When Paul uses the language of 'the body of Christ' in the different ways in which he does, and when he speaks of our being 'in Christ', he is speaking of small groups of people who have heard and accepted the Christian message. His theology begins not 'from above' in Platonism, though he may as a matter of fact be influenced by the language of Platonism, but concretely with those who are drawn together because they are drawn to Christ.

Therefore, if we are to understand the notion of the corporate universality of Christ, it must be first of all from below. The Church is the concrete place where certain human beings accept a call to associate themselves with the reality of him who is the logic of the divine love. They do it not in order to exercise institutional authority over others, but on behalf of the rest of humanity. In that sense the universality is construed not Platonically but factually. One aspect of this factual basis of the universality of Christ is expounded in the opening sections of Bonhoeffer's *Ethics*. In this book Bonhoeffer attempts to avoid the emptiness of 'Christian programmes and of the thoughtless and superficial slogan of what is called "practical Christianity". . .' (Bonhoeffer, p. 17). His concern is none the less firmly practical and ethical, and comes to expression with an original use of the word 'formation', which, he says, 'means in the first place Jesus's taking form in His Church. What takes form here is the form of Jesus Christ himself. The New Testament states the

176

case profoundly and clearly when it calls the Church the Body of Christ' (p. 20).

Notice that Bonhoeffer's central concern in this passage is with the present reality of Jesus Christ, and with how that reality takes concrete form in the lives and behaviour of a particular group of human beings. The universality of Jesus Christ's significance can only be understood in the light of its fundamental basis in practice. 'The concept of formation acquires its significance, indirectly, for all mankind only if what takes place in the Church does in truth take place for all men' (p. 21). We might say that the Church is the place where the logic of the divine love that is Jesus takes form in the present, and in so far as it does, it becomes real also for the rest of humanity. It is when the community is taken up into the love of God that it becomes that love for and on behalf of mankind.

How does this bear upon the problem of the universality of Christ? Put simply, it is that as the love of the eternal, Jesus is also universal in his significance. Because God's love embraces those who have been called into association with Jesus, then, by implication, it embraces *all* mankind. This would not be so were Jesus not the love of God in act. But it must also be understood as embracing all *mankind*. Bonhoeffer could not have said what he did unless he had viewed the Church in the light of the divinity and humanity of Jesus Christ. The Christ who takes form is both divine and human: otherwise he could not take universal and human *form*. 'Christ was not essentially a teacher and legislator, but a man, a real man like ourselves' (p. 22). Thus Bonhoeffer enables us to produce a version of 'the unassumed is the unhealed' from a more this-worldly and contemporary standpoint. Because Jesus Christ takes form in the here and now, in part of mankind and on behalf of others, we are able to bring to expression the universality of his significance. Underlying that universality is the Church's confession that his reality is at once human and divine, a presence whose basis is in eternity.

JESUS, GOD AND MAN

The excursion into Bonhoeffer took us away from soteriology strictly understood. 'Formation' belongs to ethics because it is a model by which we may understand the way in which salvation both becomes real in present behaviour and is based on the reality of Jesus Christ. In order, therefore, to complete this brief glance at the way in which Christology underlies matters churchly and anthropological, we move now to a look at what are among the three greatest theological treatises to bring together the two areas of our inquiry. The first is from the pen of one of Christianity's first great systematic theologians:

> In revealing the Father the Son nevertheless preserves the Father's invisibility, lest man should despise God, and in order that man should constantly have something to strive for; on the other hand the Son, by revelations in many different ways makes the Father visible, lest man should, losing God altogether, cease to live. For the glory of God is the living man. . . (*Adv. Haer.* 4.34.7).

The chief outlines of Irenaeus's theology are well known: its theory, sometimes fancifully elaborated, of recapitulation, according to which Christ is seen to restore the authenticity of humanity by repeating its stages; its comprehensive view of salvation, embracing not only sin but the more physical aspects of human flourishing; its development of a doctrine of God according to which the eternal is able to take the temporal to itself and restore its integrity. These are all important, and indeed play essential roles in the development of Christology. But what is of interest here is the reason Irenaeus gives for the revelational unity of Father and Son. Things being what they are, human life requires the redemption God provides in Christ. Further, God acts in the way he does for the sake of mankind. Irenaeus's much-quoted dictum, 'the glory of God is the living man', reveals the anthropological thrust of his theology. His defence of orthodox Christology against those opponents who would deny it is necessary for the sake of mankind. The teaching that Jesus Christ is both God and man is not simply orthodox for its own sake, but is serviceable in defence of the claim that we human beings both require and have received healing for the ill that distorts our humanity.

In an age when human beings are treated as never before as the disposable creatures of greater and lesser world powers, Irenaeus's stress on the importance of the doctrine of the incarnation and its associated Christology that Jesus is both God and man is no less valid than it was against Gnostic distortions of Christianity. Those in our time who would abandon the doctrine of the incarnation must realize that a heavy price has to be paid for the change. It may be necessary; I believe not. But once again the question of form and content cannot be evaded. Is it any longer authentic Christianity which wishes to say different things, or even to attempt to say the same things, on a different intellectual basis? Loss of the concrete history of God with man has always entailed a collapse into a kind of Gnosticism – salvation by knowledge – and thus the transmogrification of Christianity into its opposite.

If Irenaeus teaches us of the importance of authentic Christian anthropology, Anselm reminds us of the sombre background against which that humanity is reclaimed. In his great christological treatise, which is more reminiscent of Athanasius's *On the Incarnation* than is often acknowledged, Anselm argues for the necessity of the Saviour's being at once God and man if the thraldom into which we have fallen is to be destroyed. In interpreting Anselm, it will be necessary to concede that some features of his exposition have a rather dated air. His preoccupation with atonement in terms chiefly of satisfaction – a preoccupation introduced into Western thought by Tertullian and Cyprian (Harnack, pp. 310f.) – is seriously one-sided, as is his predominantly otherworldly view of salvation. But Anselm's famous objection to the suggestion that sin might simply be blotted out in response to human repentance takes us to the heart of the matter. 'You have not yet considered what a heavy weight sin is' (Anselm, p. 138).[2] In common with Irenaeus and Athanasius, Anselm considers that the presupposition of the incarnation is the moral and cosmic disorder brought about by human sin. Something has gone so badly awry that only God can set it right. And yet, if God, as the one responsible for the ordering of things, were simply to set human transgression aside, his behaviour would be manifestly unjust, condoning wickedness. His justice appears to require that there be no mercy (pp. 141–4).

It is against the background of this hypothetical dilemma that Anselm considers the rationality of the fact that God became man. Like Paul, he holds that here God demonstrates both that he is just (that is, behaves in a morally responsible manner) and justifies (sets human life, by forgiveness, in proper relationship with him) (Rom.

2 *Nondum considerasti quanti ponderis sit peccatum.*

3.26). Man is the one who is responsible for the moral catastrophe, and so it is as man that Jesus Christ makes satisfaction. God, however, is the only one able to perform such a transformation of the human condition, and so it is as God that the relationship is restored. The compatibility of mercy with justice is shown in the fact that mankind is not left to wallow in its state of alienation but is restored to relationship with God from within by the incarnation. It is this fundamental theme of Anselm's work that maintains its perennial validity despite the battering it has received from critics in recent centuries. Human sin is such that only God is able to deal with it, and the doctrine of the incarnation is good news because it teaches that he does deal with sin in a way that respects human freedom and responsibility. A strong argument in defence of the doctrine, therefore, is that it enables theology to assert the fallenness, indeed radical fallenness, of humankind without in any way denying that it was created good and destined for fellowship with its creator. Theology can thus be true to moral realities, falling neither into a life-denying pessimism nor a naive and counter-intuitive optimism.

The weaknesses of Anselm's formulation have often been rehearsed. The two that concern us here are related to each other. The first is that he conceives salvation too narrowly in terms of the remission of penalty. But, it is asked, in what sense does such a transaction transform the moral agent? Is it not merely an external transaction? The second weakness is one which Anselm shares with much of the Western tradition as a result of what Elert calls (see Chapter 5, p. 95) the judgement of Solomon in which Christ was divided in two. In Anselm, what Christ does as man and what he does as God *tend* to be two different things, despite the author's attempt to avoid such an outcome. The direction is Nestorian, with Christ suffering as man what God's justice demands. The result is again that salvation tends to be rather external to the recipient, with God conceived to operate from outside.

It is not so with Karl Barth, whose whole stress is on salvation as something achieved by Jesus Christ as the Son of God in his total self-giving to our condition. In the words of the title of a central part of his exposition, the incarnation and cross together take the form of a history in which 'the judge is judged in our place' (*Church Dogmatics* iv/1, pp. 211–83). In face of the (otherwise) incurable human tendency to stand in judgement upon other human beings – a major expression of our alienation – God himself refuses to act as judge: or rather, judges by identifying himself entirely with us in our feeble attempts at self-deification. It is this total identification of God with us that is at the centre of Barth's soteriology. 'The Son of God exists with man and as man in this fallen and perishing state' (p. 215). This action is not performed simply to free us from false self-images, though that is part of it (p. 233). Its chief function is to renew the human condition from within, by taking human life up into the very life of God (Barth's equivalent of the patristic teaching on deification). But – and this is where the Christology underpins the soteriology – for this to happen, God must first share the life of the world. '(T)his participation of the world in the being of God implies necessarily his participating in the being of the world' (p. 215).

But because the life of the world is life under threat, God in Christ must share it in a particular manner. 'Jesus Christ was and is for us in that he suffered and was crucified and died' (p. 223). He shares our life as man, but without any loss to his reality as God; in fact, the reverse: 'It is the eternal God himself who has given himself in his Son to be man, and as man to take upon himself this human passion' (p. 246). Here we see emerging something that has occurred before in the argument of this book. Jesus is what he is not by virtue of his self-assertion or obvious religious success, but because his suffering is God's suffering, that by which God acts in the humanity of Jesus to save the world. Once again, a presupposition of the argument is that there is real reconciliation of man to God because Jesus Christ is both fully man and fully God.

And so from three major thinkers of the Christian tradition we learn the same basic lesson. The kind of bearing that Christian teaching has on human life depends upon what it is able to say in its Christology. If Jesus Christ is not fully man, the human condition is not restored *from within* – 'the unassumed is the unhealed'; if he is not also God, we are not healed, for only God can, by reconciling us to himself, restore to authenticity our deeply alienated lives. Irenaeus, Anselm and Barth understand the healing in various ways, but all are agreed that, without orthodox Christology, what they must say about human life cannot be said. The logic of the divine love must be shown to be the logic of the *saving* love of God.

CONCLUSION

The chief lessons of this chapter are two. The first is a repetition of the matter of form and content. The content of Christianity as a gospel about human forgiveness, reconciliation and flourishing is bound up with its Christology. Soteriology cannot be divorced from Christology, and if there is to be genuine continuity with the past in the former area, the kind of ontological questions asked in the latter cannot be evaded. As in the dispute between Athanasius and the Arians, ontology and soteriology mutually condition one another. This is not a request for an uncritical appropriation of the tradition. The dominance of Western discussions of atonement by notions of legal satisfaction has been gravely distorting. But the fundamental assertion that human ill is radical, and yet is revealed and healed by God in Christ, is not endangered by the correction of the place where stress is laid in the doctrine of the atonement (see, in particular, Aulén and Whale).

The second lesson is that orthodox Christology enables theology to say interesting and penetrating things about God and man, especially as they are seen to come into relation. Here the assertion of an earlier section will stand repetition, that a positive evaluation of the importance of human life without blindness to its need of healing is made possible by the doctrine of the incarnation. That the Word became flesh speaks volumes for the value to God, and therefore the eternal value and importance, of human life in its temporality. It forbids the mistreatment of any member of the human family or any attempt to escape from human relationships in the various ways that have been, and are always being, invented by our fertility in evil.

In this respect, Christianity's record in practice has not always been a good one. Heretics have been tortured, Jews persecuted and members of other faiths met with military violence. These atrocities are sometimes attributed to the orthodox Christology, although it should be evident from what it says that they are its denial. What has gone wrong? A reasonable hypothesis is not that orthodox Christology has led to the abuse of human beings, but that it has, in theory and practice, been ignored. This is the hypothesis to be defended in the final chapter.

REFERENCES

Anselm of Canterbury, *Why God Became Man*, Eng. trans. Eugene R. Fairweather, *A Scholastic Miscellany: From Anselm to Ockham*. Library of Christian Classics, vol. x, pp. 100–83.

Aulén, Gustaf, *Christus Victor: An Historical Study of the Three Main Types of the Idea of the Atonement*, Eng. trans. A. G. Hebert.

Barth, Karl, *Church Dogmatics*, Eng. trans. eds. G. W. Bromiley and T. F. Torrance.

Bonhoeffer, Dietrich, *Ethics*, ed. Eberhard Bethge, Eng. trans. Neville Horton Smith.

Fairweather, Eugene R., 'The "Kenotic" Christology' in *A Commentary on the Epistle to the Philippians* by F. W. Beare, pp. 159–74.

Forsyth, P. T., *The Person and Place of Jesus Christ*.

Gregory of Nazianzus, 'Letters on the Apollinarian Controversy' in *Christology of the Later Fathers*, ed. Edward Rochie Hardie, Library of Christian Classics, vol. iii.

Harnack, Adolf von, *History of Dogma*, vol. iii, Eng. trans. N. Buchanan from 3ᵉ German.

Irenaeus of Lyons, *Irenaeus Against Heresies*, Ante-Nicene Library.

McIntyre, John, *The Shape of Christology*.

Mackintosh, H. R., *The Doctrine of the Person of Jesus Christ*.

Niebuhr, Reinhold, *The Nature and Destiny of Man*, vol. 1: *Human Nature*; vol. 2: *Human Destiny*.

Whale, J. S., *Victor and Victim: The Christian Doctrine of Redemption*.

Wiles, M. F., 'The Unassumed is the Unhealed' in *Working Papers in Doctrine*, pp. 122–31.

9

CHRIST AND CHRISTENDOM

THE PROBLEM

From one point of view, the whole of this book is about Christology and culture. It began with a reference to the view of Charles Norris Cochrane that Christianity's intellectual achievement in the early centuries was to out-think a classical culture that was unable to form a scientific basis for culture. It continued with an extended dialogue with one feature of culture: the philosophical tradition in the context of which Christology, both biblical and systematic, is inevitably done. In only one chapter, Chapter 8, has it concerned itself with specifically churchly matters, and even there it is possible to argue that the way the Church understands, lives and teaches its view of salvation has important implications for its relation to the culture in which it is set. Culture, too, is concerned with authentic human living.

But when we come to questions of Christology and politics, we reach an area of theology's relations with culture that is, partly because it is a fashionable concern, fraught with difficulty. In particular, those should beware who would argue too directly from either politics or theology to the other. As with the matter of Christology and philosophy, it is a region where there is an intermingling of thought, language and influence. This is a book about Christology, and is not therefore concerned to spell out detailed programmes so much as to indicate what kind of bearing Christian thinking may have on matters political. It is a general, though none the less important matter, as is indicated by the allusion at the end of Chapter 8 to the matters of persecution and inquisition. What bearing does our thinking about the love of God become temporal in Jesus of Nazareth have on questions of political attitude and behaviour? In order to set the problem in its historical perspective, we hear again from Cochrane: 'Athanasius had declared persecution to be the weapon of the Devil; but Ambrose was prepared to use the Devil's weapons as a means of realizing the kingdom of God' (Cochrane, p. 350). Ambrose became Bishop of Milan in AD 374; Athanasius had died in May of the previous year, probably in his late seventies. There is thus a difference in time of about a generation. What had happened during that time? The practical men of this world, those who ascribe the development of modern science to the invention of the stirrup and/or gunpowder, will find an obvious explanation. Ambrose was an Italian, built on the model of the Roman bureaucrat. That is enough to account for any tendency to authoritarianism.

But there are reasons why the obvious explanation may not be the correct one. After all, Ambrose's willingness to use persecution as part of his pastoral armoury was not an isolated phenomenon. The reader of Peter Brown's *Augustine of Hippo* will be struck by the fact that there happened in North Africa in embryo all the things that were to stain the history of Christendom and are still to be found at the centre of the more naive kind of anti-Christian polemic: in particular, the violent persecution of heretics and the use of the civil police in matters with far-reaching social and political implications. Norman H. Baynes, a relatively uncomplaining chronicler of the movement from Christianity to Christendom, rather uncomfortably recounts the development of thought of Ambrose's greatest pupil. 'At the last he [Augustine] came to think that it was not so much the State which had a right to persecute the Donatists as that the Church had a right to demand this service of the State.' Clearly Augustine did not find it easy coming to this view, but, Baynes continues, 'It is not pleasant to think of Augustine as the spiritual father of the Inquisition' (Baynes, p. 304).

It is not enough, in a topic of this magnitude, simply to appeal to personalities. Not only were there great historical forces at work, the justification of whose developments was partly after the event, but also profound theological changes and developments were taking place. And the appeal to personalities accounts even less for Athanasius than for Ambrose and Augustine. Athanasius himself does not appear to have behaved always in the most scrupulous manner. But he was above all a theologian. May he not, then, have meant what he said when he ascribed persecution to the Devil? And may not Ambrose's theoretical willingness to use the Devil's weapons be at least in part attributable to a shift in theological emphasis, if not to something greater?

After all, these were momentous days. Contemporary with Athanasius had come the events which set the direction for both Church and society for centuries. Constantine had become a Christian, or had at least entered into a positive relation with the Christian Church. This need not have been a matter for dismay, but it either precipitated or allowed to develop a view of Christianity's relation to political culture which has been, to say the least, regrettable. Something did go wrong, as was realized by one of the greatest representatives of the culture Constantine's politics and Augustine's theology helped to form:

Ah Constantine! what ills were gendered there –
No, not from thy conversion, but the dower
The first rich pope received from thee as heir (Dante, p. 191).

The beginnings of the trend that was to put so many popes into Dante's *Inferno* are chronicled by Cochrane: the identification of God with the maintenance of human institutions (p. 336), the arrogation of divine authority by the priesthood (p. 348), the granting and extension of financial and other social privileges to the clergy (p. 325). That this went alongside more worthy developments is not here to the point. A natural reaction is rather one of astonishment that it should have happened so. Even the most superficial reading of the life of Jesus and its interpretation by the writers of the New Testament should, the modern with benefit of hindsight feels, have given grounds for suspicion, even allowing for what are supposed to be the weaknesses of natural men. There seems to be a contradiction, of life if not of logic, of the kind so mercilessly exposed by Kierkegaard (1944). What is there in common between the kind of teaching about leadership and ministry gathered by the Synoptists and John around the time of the Passion ('It shall not be so among you') and the active acceptance of power and social privilege by a small class of Christians? Of course, the anxiety of twentieth-century Christianity to achieve social and political respectability on the left suggests that the age of Constantine was not necessarily unique. But, once again, it is the theological question underlying it all that is of interest: what view of God licensed the kind of behaviour of which we are now ashamed? But before it can be faced, a prior question has to be asked. Did all this happen in the teeth of theological wisdom, or were there intellectual trends accompanying and encouraging the process? The answer, as we shall see, is, 'Both'.

A RECENT ACCOUNT OF THE DEVELOPMENT

In a recent paper, Don Cupitt raises the question of the relation between Christology and politics, and argues that the chief culprit was the development of what has come to be known as orthodox Christology. 'Early Christianity had repudiated the Emperor-cult, but now conciliar Christianity came increasingly to be modelled on the Emperor-cult' (p. 139). Cupitt's paper is an attack on the doctrine of the divinity of Christ. What he is saying is that to describe Jesus as divine is to lay oneself open to a Constantinian version of Christianity, with all that implies. The heart of his theological case lies in the charge that 'the doctrine of the incarnation unified things which Jesus had kept in ironic contrast with each other. . . A world-view which expressed disjunction and free choice was exchanged for a world-view which stressed continuity, hierarchy and due obedience. . . Christ crowned the Emperor, one a step higher in the scale of being merely stooping slightly to bestow authority upon one a step lower' (p. 140).

Now it is clear that Cupitt has been reading his Eusebius, whose almost sickeningly fulsome meanderings about the Emperor Constantine reveal the kind of theology that underlies his deferential attitude. There are two key passages to be found in the *Oration in Praise of Constantine*. The first is that in which the reign of Constantine is compared with the monarchy of God. Monarchy far transcends every other constitution and form of government, for it is at the opposite end of the scale from democracy, the constitution of anarchy and disorder, as Plato had once taught (*Republic* VIII). We are not here concerned with Eusebius's dislike of democracy as such, for no political constitution is in itself sacred. Crucial, rather, is the correlation between the concept of God and the theory of human society. Monarchy is good on this account because it is a

187

reflection of monotheism. 'Hence there is one God. . . There is one sovereign. . .' (Eusebius, *Oration* III.5f.). The other significant passages come later in the work, and reflect a marked christological subordinationism. There, in passages which smack strongly of Origen's more questionable christological utterances, Eusebius conceives Christ as a mediator figure in the chain of being. Eusebius's cosmology is highly dualistic. Because God could not 'unite himself to corruptible and corporeal matter' he must do it through one who is 'as it were an intermediate power' between the two realms of being (XI.12). The Word is intermediate in the sense that he 'looks upward to the Father and governs this lower creation, *inferior to and consequent upon himself.* . .' (XII.6, my emphasis). Thus the Word teaches us of God who is essentially, in himself, unknown. (In passing, it is worth observing that Don Cupitt's Christology, too, has a similar subordinationist tendency. It is not Jesus as the revealer of the Father in whom he is interested, but Jesus as teaching us about a God who is essentially other than himself. But more of the coincidences between Cupitt and Constantinian theologians later.)

We are not here concerned with the adequacy of Eusebius's Christology as such, but with the fact that it appears to have been the fountainhead of a particular way of understanding the relationship between God and the earthly ruler. One God, one ruler is the battle cry, and it links us directly with the question with which this chapter began: How did the once persecuted community come to believe – or behave as if it believed – that one should, in matters political, pay back wrong for wrong? – and with the further question, which is similar, of the justification of authoritarian, hierarchical societies in the name of the crucified. The references to Eusebius suggest that it is partly a matter of monotheism, and the relations between monotheism and authoritarian political theory have been explored this century by such theologians as Erik Peterson and Jürgen Moltmann. The natural correlation of a strong monotheism is a subordinationist Christology, or none at all, as has already been suggested. But it had also, in the period with which we are concerned, a rather different correlate. After all, the logical outcome of a rigid dualism is *either* subordinationism, in which the Son is not as fully God as the Father, because it is logically impossible that anything should be; *or* a wholesale identification of Christ with God, with his exclusion from the sphere of the earthly. It is with this latter outcome that we shall first of all concern ourselves.

An entry to this aspect of the inquiry is provided by Werner Elert's discussion of 'the political Christ' by which he means 'the Christ in whose name politics is done', whether this takes the form of the Church involving itself in state politics or the State involving itself in church politics (Elert, p. 26). Beginning his discussion with the seventh-century war of Byzantium against the Persians, Elert points out that 'the whole Persian war was prosecuted from both sides as *Religionskrieg*: Christ against the Zoroastrian firecult. . . This Christ, who is humiliated by the overthrow of the imperial forces and exacts requital through the war of the imperial arms, is the political Christ' (p. 28). When Elert comes to look at some of the personalities involved, a strange inconsistency comes to light. The very patriarchs who supported the Emperor's war effort in the name of Christ were those who had been involved in the monothelite and monoergist controversies. Figuring prominently in those controversies was the prayer of Jesus in Gethsemane (Matthew 26.39). Why was not the same consideration operative in the matter of the political Christ? 'How is it that the Christ of Gethsemane renounced the support of a legion of angels . . . while the political Christ needed the Byzantine legions . . . in order to ward off his enemies, the Zoroastrian Persians?' (p. 29).

Part of Elert's answer confirms Don Cupitt's analysis. The development has to do with the doctrine of the divinity of Christ. Alluding to the contemporary attempts to provide theological justification for the Emperor Justinian's theory of government, Elert locates the key in the process whereby the Emperor came to be seen as the one who represented God on earth. A conspicuous feature of the literature is that in it the terms *God* and *Christ* are virtually interchangeable. 'The God . . . in whose name Justinian rules the world is the God Christ. And this means . . . the *Lord* (*Herrscher*) Christ' (p. 168). And how is this lordship construed? 'The lordship of Christ is in content and method identical with the lordship of the Emperor' (p. 169). By the time of Justinian, then, a twofold development had reached some kind of completion. The authoritarian powers of the emperors had received an ideological justification in the development of a particular conception of Christ and of his relation – one of virtually unrelieved identity – with God. And, in its turn, the lordship of Christ had become modelled on secular, or non-Christian, ideas of imperial power. That development began some centuries before in Constantine's revolution and is illustrated by Elert, as by Cupitt, by appeal to Christian representative art. The shepherd modelled on the parables of Luke 15 is progressively replaced by a shepherd who no longer rules his own sheep by his word, but the world by imperial power (p. 170). Four revolutions in the social, political and theological spheres accompany this development: the suppression of pagan thought, culminating in the closing of the school at Athens by Justinian and the emigration of the philosophers to Persia; the conversion of the power of the heavenly Christ from something apprehended by faith to the object of earthly political experience; the bringing into the present of the eschatological, future, judgement of the quick and the dead: *die Weltgeschichte ist das Weltgericht*; and the imposition of the legislature of Christ on those outside the Church (pp. 172f.). The development in East and West is different only in the way the power was conferred. In the East, the emperor arrogated to himself the priestly function; in the West, the priest received the imperial regalia and functions (p. 174).

Whether or not all the details of this analysis are to be accepted – and they are confirmed by other historians (e.g. Cochrane, pp. 336f.; Johnson, pp. 80–264) – they appear to provide an important confirmation and expansion of Don Cupitt's thesis. The tragic political developments that followed the conversion of Constantine do bear a close relation to the teaching that Jesus is the heavenly Lord. Christology did have a bearing on politics, and politics upon Christology. But what are the theological issues at stake? Further analysis will require considerable qualification of the view that it was, simply, the doctrine of the divinity of Christ that caused all the problems.

A RETURN TO THE HISTORICAL JESUS?

Don Cupitt's argument is that the only solution to the problem of the political Christ is a replacement of the divine Christ by 'the historical Jesus': 'a "deabsolutized" Jesus can be recognized as revealing God to us in much more complex ways than the Christ of Chalcedon' (Cupitt, p. 141). A necessary distinction must therefore be drawn between Jesus and the God whom he reveals. 'For it is the divine *transcendence* which alone judges, delivers and restores, as Jesus, in his teaching and in his person, communicates the power of transcendence (the Holy Spirit) to his disciples' (p. 146). Cupitt thus appears to be advocating an approach similar to that associated with the name of Harnack: Jesus is the one who teaches about God, without being divine in the sense taught by Paul and the Fathers. Cupitt, that is to say, the anti-Constantinian, stands firmly in the tradition of one of the greatest of Constantinian Christians. This supreme irony must give us pause. How can so different a rabbit be produced from the same hat? Can it be that a different liberal Protestant face is gazing lovingly down the same well? Further inquiry is demanded, and will take us into the roots of modern Christology in the nineteenth century, and in particular in G. W. F. Hegel.

Here, as with everything to do with Hegel, the matter is highly complicated. The first thing we must note is a difference between Cupitt and Hegel. The latter's 'the divine nature is the same as the human is' (Hegel, 1949, p. 760) is a far cry from Cupitt's neo-Nestorianism. Indeed, the words with which Cupitt attacks the Christology of Chalcedon might appear more appropriately directed against the nineteenth-century philosopher. 'The assertion that deity itself and humanity are permanently united in the one person of the incarnate Lord suggests an ultimate synthesis, a conjunction and continuity between things divine and things of this world' (Cupitt, p. 140). Cupitt asserts disjunction between man and God in the teaching of Jesus. Hegel and, according to him, Chalcedon, teach or tend to a synthesis. In one respect Cupitt is right. To teach an ultimate synthesis of man and God does smell of the teachings of Christendom. A brief glance at some of Hegel's doctrines will confirm this side of his thesis.

In his *Philosophy of History* Hegel traces the process by which Christendom came to its fullest flower in the Protestantism of modern Europe, and especially that of his own Germany. It is the setting out at length and in detail of Schiller's *die Weltgeschichte ist das Weltgericht*. The process inaugurated by Constantine was but a preliminary anticipation of good things to come: 'In ancient Rome itself, Christianity cannot find a ground on which it may become actual, and develop an empire.' That, Hegel believed, was

Germany's destiny (Hegel, 1956, pp. 335f.). Rome merely gave birth to the process whereby the emperor was closely associated, if not identified, with the deity, as we have seen. Hegel wishes to take the process a stage further. For him, the doctrine of the Trinity, – and the same could be said of the orthodox Christology – properly demythologized, teaches that 'Man himself . . . is comprehended in the idea of God . . . Man . . . is God only in so far as he annuls the merely Natural and Limited in his Spirit and elevates himself to God' (p. 324). It is not the emperor who is divine, but man himself, so long as he adverts to his true nature as *Geist*: that is, realizes the identity of his spirit with universal spirit. The means of this realization is culture, and specifically the culture of Western Protestantism. Christianity is the means by which man's self-induced apotheosis is realized in secular culture (Crites, ch. 2). Thus there can be discerned by those who follow the Hegelian analysis the dialectical development which began with the adoption and use of the Christian religion as the cement of a culture, and ended with its final flowering contemporary with Hegel – he hoped – in nineteenth-century bourgeois culture. For Hegel, as for the Christian emperors, Christianity is the means by which society is held together: 'Religion is an integrating factor in the state, implanting a sense of unity in the depths of men's minds. . .' (Hegel, 1942, p. 168). Thus far Cupitt is justified: Christian teaching about Christ has been used in furthering authoritarian political institutions.

But here there enters on the scene a discordant and contentious voice, that of Hegel's great intellectual opponent, Søren Kierkegaard. He, too, believed in the divinity of Christ, sharpening the paradox of orthodox Christology into a knife-edge. But he did so as part of an attack at once on Hegel's philosophy and on the idea of Christendom. This is Stephen Crites's judgement: '. . . the heart of the Hegelianism he attacked was its interpretation of Christianity, its celebration of a worldly incarnation in the ethos of Protestant civilization' (Crites, p. 58). This is not to deny that in his role as a chronicler of what had happened Hegel had been right:

> Faith in the divine transcendence, faith in the 'absolute paradox' of the transcendent God-become-man, had steadily evaporated, not simply as a matter of doctrine but as it is reflected in the sense of self-identity . . . of these professed Christians, until it had

vaporized at last into a mere participation in bourgeois Protestant culture. . . . Not Hegel, but Christendom, Protestantism, had domesticated Christian commitment until it entailed little more than a well-upholstered family life, solid citizenship, and what is nowadays identified as the Protestant work ethic (p. 59).

But Hegel was more than simply a chronicler. 'Hegelianism is the spirit of the age become conscious of itself. . . So Kierkegaard's urbane polemics against Hegelianism were the first faint thunder of his stormy denunciation of the "lie" of Protestant Christendom' (p. 59).

However, our chief concern here is christological, and it is not sufficient simply to contrast the paradoxicality of Kierkegaard's Christology with the Hegelian synthesis. Rather, we have to ask what is the heart of the difference between the two Christologies as they bear on the question of the political Christ. Quite clearly, much will hang on the way in which Kierkegaard regards Christ as being related to society. In *Training in Christianity*, which provides a somewhat cooler analysis than the feverish journalism of the final *Attack on Christendom*, he presents the matter largely in terms of offence. For him, the heart of the offence is not the divinity of Jesus, but the fact that the divinity is given through and with 'this lowly, poor, impotent man' (Kierkegaard, 1941b, p. 105). It is this which Christendom cannot face, for such a Christology offends both the individual and the established order. Christendom, in fact, abolishes fear and trembling (p. 91) and so is a pagan denial of Christianity. Both Constantine and Hegel invert Christianity, deifying mankind rather than recognizing God in the lowly Jesus of Nazareth.

Kierkegaard's position, however, is not that of this book, which is concerned to defend the theological propriety of holding that because Jesus of Nazareth is the logic of the divine love, he is both fully man and fully God. Kierkegaard, partly because of Hegel, is suspicious of such dogmatic exposition, fearing that to formulate the matter as direct teaching is to evade the offence. 'All the talk about offence in relation to Christianity as a doctrine is a misunderstanding, it is a device to mitigate the shock of offence at the scandal. . . No, the offence is related either to Christ or to the fact of being oneself a Christian' (pp. 108f.). But, at the risk of the kind of distortion that always results from writing about Kierkegaard, and certainly in trying to use him, could it not be said that his opposition to Hegel lies in doctrines that are everywhere implicit and sometimes appear explicitly? Hegel was wrong about Christianity not because he attempted at all to give an account of its nature, but because of the particular interpretation that he gave it. Kierkegaard's own account, and particularly his Christology, cannot be spelled out formally but can be seen to presuppose a view of what is essential to a correct Christology. Against the generality and universality of Hegel's interpretation Kierkegaard sets the particularity and historical nature of the object of belief. 'By force of lecturing they have transformed the God-Man into that speculative unity of God and man *sub specie aeterni* . . . whereas in truth the God-Man is the unity of God and an individual man in an actual historical situation. . .' (p. 123). 'That the human race is or should be akin to God is ancient paganism; but that an individual man is God is Christianity, and this individual man is the God-Man' (p. 84). The difference between Christianity and Christendom lies in this simple distinction, but it is all the difference between the real thing and paganism. That *this* man, the lowly, crucified, impotent Jesus of Nazareth is God is true and offensive. That he reveals or teaches the divinity of mankind as a whole is false but attractive, particularly, as we have seen, to some exponents of Christology from below.

Thus there are, as can be seen from the nineteenth- and twentieth-century version of the matter, two very different ways of conceiving the divinity of Christ. The divine Christ is not necessarily the Christ of hierarchy, repression and authoritarianism. But the dispute between Hegel and Kierkegaard sets the contrast in its most striking form, and Kierkegaard's own account may be judged to be overdetermined by the form of that which it seeks to controvert. Therefore, in order to do justice to Don Cupitt's thesis, a further historical question must be asked. Is it also true that the Christ of Eusebius is, in important respects, different from that of orthodoxy? After a brief glance at this, we shall be ready to approach the central systematic question with which this chapter is concerned: Are there different ways of conceiving the divinity of Christ, such that a difference is made in the way we conceive his relation to political reality? Can we, that is to say, have a divine Christ who is not prey to the distortions that have been the fate of the Christ of Christendom?

POLITICAL AND DOGMATIC CHRISTOLOGY

Our quest must begin with another aspect of Elert's account of the development of political Christology. His crucial claim is that what he calls the *politische Christusbild* is not an integral part of the development of christological dogma in the early Church but is, rather, a piece of political idealization (*Wunschbild*, Elert, p. 175). This can be shown by two facts: first, that the conception of the political Christ was never given the kind of assessment and clarification that other dogmatic developments received (p. 176); and, second, that the conception developed independently of other dogmatic Christology. Evidence for the first claim is provided by the way in which a conception of lordship derived from a rural and pastoral milieu, with its personal overtones and biblical background, was allowed to develop with the help of urban notions of the possession of things (pp. 179f.). Thus the biblical picture of Christ was falsified with the employment of positive notions of despotism, and the end result was the conceiving of both Christ and the Emperor (Justinian) in the pattern of the oriental despot (pp. 181f.). The second feature is illustrated by the fact that while all this stress was being laid on the divine lordship of Christ, other fish were being fried by the dogmaticians. Developments from Nicaea to Chalcedon, and from Chalcedon to John of Damascus, were largely concerned with the humanity of Christ rather than his divinity (p. 171). How was it that the concentration on the humanity did not spill over into the political sphere? Elert's answer is that it was because the conception of Christ developed virtually independently of the dogma accepted by Chalcedon and clarified by post-Chalcedonian discussion (pp. 31f., 169ff.).

Partly as a result of writings generated by the German church crisis between the wars, this area of inquiry has become controversial, and there is no doubt that some of the details of Elert's account would be disputed (Beskow). But his historical account is supported by features of christological discussion that take us to the centre of the matter of the divinity of Christ. We saw earlier that an apparent inconsistency between the dogmatic and political use of Christology lay in the fact that the Christ who renounced the use of legions of angels was thought to sanctify the use of mortal legions in wars of religion. How could this be? 'This question seems to be answered easily so long as one draws boundaries between the earthly Christ of whom the Evangelists report and the exalted heavenly Christ' (Elert, p. 29). The political theorists ignored the disputes over the humanity of Christ because they had no interest in the earthly figure. The parting of the ways began about the time of Nicaea, and is illustrated in the work of Eusebius. 'This heavenly Christ is the one meant by Eusebius when he opines that the Son of God became the fellow-combatant of Constantine in his victorious battle against Licinius' (p. 31).

Here we are on firm ground. But the systematic implications of Eusebius's use of the person of the exalted are perhaps wider than Elert's mainly historical analysis suggests. Here our evidence is provided by Eusebius's description of the labarum, the standard Constantine constructed and used after his famous and fateful vision. First, there is its nature: 'A long spear, overlaid with gold. . . On top of the whole was fixed a wreath of gold and precious stones. . .' (Eusebius, *Life*, I.31). Second, there is its use. The standard not only appears to guarantee victory in war, but to save its bearer from injury, 'like some triumphant charm' (II.7; cf. 6–9 and IV.5). The standard bears no real relation to the historical cross, rough-hewn, offensive and the sign of defeat before it can become a sign of victory. The cross has been taken out of history and made into a timeless symbol. In this sign conquer: conquer in the sign of his death who refused precisely to conquer with the help of legions of angels or even Peter's sword. Thus the distortion is caused not merely by concentration on the figure of Christ in glory, but on that taken out of its context. It is equally possible to do the same with other parts of the story. Make absolute those aspects of the accounts alleged to depict Jesus the zealot, or Jesus the social reformer, and there, too, open possibilities for a whole new realm of political theology: for the taking up of arms in the name of Christ in a more acceptable cause – the liberation of the oppressed – but not necessarily by more justifiable means.

This development takes us to the heart of the matter of previous chapters, and shows us that orthodox Christology, if taken according to its basic logic, is the enemy of the authoritarian Christ of political theology after Constantine. If Jesus of Nazareth in his totality is the logic of the divine presence in time – and therefore at the heart of human life in society – it means that when we are speaking of the divine Christ we are confronted not with a timeless symbol, or a set of timeless symbols, to be abstracted according to taste to justify some pre-formed political programme, but with the account of a human life, with a narrative whose figure is indeed conceived to reign in glory, but only as the humiliated. The Christ seated in glory is the same as the human figure who is reported to have rejected the temptation of a ministry dedicated to political domination. That is not to say that he is an apolitical figure; quite the reverse. But his political significance is revealed only in terms of his accepting the cost to himself of the attitudes he took up to Israel's social and religious realities. In more traditional language, we may say that because Jesus is divine only as being of one substance with ourselves, we may not conceive his glory apart from his humanity and humiliation.

A second conclusion can be drawn by looking at the matter from another direction. Don Cupitt rightly emphasized the necessity of a stress on the humanity of Jesus and on ensuring a disjunction between him and God (or better, between him and the Father). But if the disjunction is made absolute, as he makes it, the result is either that our concept of God is formed in abstraction from the human story or that the person of Christ is reduced to a harmless triviality. The former happens when there is a Christology from above of the kind exemplified by Eusebius and those, like Hegel, who have followed him. The concepts of Christology are predetermined by some monistic theological scheme. The latter outcome is the achievement of Don Cupitt and the liberal Protestants he has succeeded. Both positions – along with both monophysite and Nestorian Christologies – share the dualistic assumption that the whole human life of Jesus of Nazareth cannot also be the presence of God in time. To look at the matter once more with the help of traditional language, we can see that we are in the area of Chalcedon's 'without separation'. Political distortions are of a piece with other heresies that attempt to evade the hypostatic unity of eternal Word and human Jesus.

Suppose, then, that we take the 'without separation' at its face value, and see in the humanity of Jesus the activity of God taking place at the heart of human political reality. It certainly represents a critique of many political institutions, but one that continues to respect the humanity of the opposition. It also represents, to use Cupitt's expression, a 'deabsolutizing' of Christology. But it is not one that is open to the relativizing tendencies of the liberal Protestant or Marxist Catholic face at the bottom of the ever shallower well. For it says that God's involvement in the political world is absolute – absolutely on the side of the humanity of the world and absolutely against its sin and corruption – but in a gracious and non-coercive way. The absoluteness of God is expressed in the contingency, relativity and vulnerability of a human career. It is an absoluteness which at the same time relativizes and exposes the absurd way in which men are tempted to ascribe finality or ultimate status to any human political theory or system, for that is to make absolute what belongs to the realm of the temporary and fallible.

Thus it can be argued that, in this context, the 'without separation' is, in systematic terms, the most important part of the linguistic armoury we have inherited from the tradition, and the doctrine of the divine-human Christ one of the weapons against the divinization of any human political system. The imperial Christ was a product of dogmatic divinity abstracted from the gospel accounts of the human Jesus. When the divinity was separated from the humanity it became possible to adapt the doctrine of the divinity of Christ to the political needs of the day, but only by ignoring the demand made by the very Christology that was being hammered out at the same time. In terms of the doctrine of God, this overlooking of contemporary dogmatic thinking made for a naked monotheism, with all its possibilities for absolutism. From monotheism came Hegel's monism. Here, it is the particularity of classical Christology, its grounding in the unique historical, human, figure that came to be transcended in a general teaching of the divinity of man – and *therefore* of the political institutions of modern Western culture. Kierkegaard saw the point of orthodox Christology in a way that is now often missed. Far from teaching a general synthesis of the divine and the human – the bringing of God down to earth or the elevation of man to divinity in the triumphalism of Christendom – its teaching implies that there has happened here what cannot happen otherwise. That is both the offence of orthodox Christology and its teaching that no political power can be identified with the Kingdom of God.

THE POLITICAL CHRIST

There is no doubt that Elert is too narrow in his definition of the political Christ as the one in whose name power politics is done. It suggests that to see Christ as political in any sense is to see him as a tool of some power politician or political ecclesiastic. Perhaps his is the Lutheran temptation to refuse to relate Christ to political reality at all. But may not the political Christ be distinguished from a politicized Christ? There is a political Christ: not only the one depicted in the Gospels as coming to grief in the political-religious cauldron of first-century Judaea, but also the one crucified by 'the rulers of this age' (1 Corinthians 2.8), however those ambiguous entities be conceived. The key conception, perhaps, is that thrice-repeated refrain of the Apocalypse: 'He shall rule the nations with a rod of iron' (Revelation 2.27; 12.5; 19.15). G. B. Caird rightly sees the importance of this, and its interpretation with the help of Jeremiah. The rod of iron is the Word: 'I have set you this day over nations and over kingdoms, to pluck up and break down. . .' (Jeremiah 1.10). 'Is not my word like a fire, says the Lord, and like a hammer that breaks the rock in pieces?' (Jeremiah 23.29) (Caird, pp. 8, 46, 245). Jeremiah makes a strange model for a politician. Yet did he not play a part in the downfall of Jerusalem, as Jesus was to do later? And what kind of models do these suffering yet intransigent figures provide for the involvement of Christians in the ambiguities of power? Scarcely those filled out by Cardinal Wolsey or Camillo Torres. Vague optimism about Jesus's teaching about God is not proof against this kind of distortion, which becomes theologically intolerable only when the human figure is also the divine Word. The paradox must remain: that the absolute claim of God is exercised through the contingency and vulnerability of the human. And this means that the function of a doctrine of the political Christ, or, better, the lordship of Christ in its political implications, is to teach that power does not grow out of the barrel of a gun, as some theologians seem tempted to believe, but from the lordship of the crucified. It is surely significant that neither in Eusebius nor in Don Cupitt does the cross play any significant part.

It is the Lamb with the marks of slaughter still upon him who rules the nations with a rod of iron, in a picture plainly meant to be at once a caricature and a rejection of the power of worldly empire in favour of a different conception of power altogether (Peterson, 1951), a power that is exercised in the world, and therefore fully effectively, indeed more effectively than other kinds of power, but according to a different set of rules.

It is not the place here to spell out a theory of political action on the basis of this systematic and historical reflection. That is better done by those more versed in the realities of the world of power. But the fundamental beliefs with which the Church may face an indifferent or hostile culture, or the Christian politician the inevitable clashes of loyalty he will endure in such a culture, may at least be outlined. Here some assistance is given in an important paper by Hans Schmidt. Commenting on the failure of Bonhoeffer's concept of 'world come of age' to break out of what he calls the West's 'destructive dialectic of time and eternity', he calls attention to the way in which Christianity faced its first great crisis, the devaluation of the world by Gnosticism. It had to affirm that 'this world was the work of the one God and Father of Jesus Christ', but instead of doing this by appeal to 'the prophets' testimonies to history as fulfilled and confirmed in Jesus as the Christ' it 'rather affirmed the world as the good and reasonable creation of God with the help of Stoic ideas and immanent teleology' (Schmidt, p. 253). This meant that a dualism of natural and supernatural resulted, dominating Western thought and spawning as its offspring that last effort at immanent teleology, the doctrine of the world come of age. But that is a dead end. Rather, Western Christianity must rediscover the fundamental Christian claim that 'the way in which Jesus was involved in the world and came into conflict with the lords of this world contains the decisive interpretation of this world' (p. 254). The question of the political Christ is not, then, simply a question of right action, even where that is dignified by being called praxis, but of truth: of the nature of the action and suffering of the crucified Jesus and of those who would continue to act and to suffer in his name in the real world, fallen as it is and redeemed by that very life and cross.

In this light, the pattern of relations will be very much that envisaged by the writer of the *Letter to Diognetus*:

Christians live in their own countries, but only as aliens. . . They love all men, and by all men are persecuted. They are unknown, and still they are condemned. . . When they do good, they are punished as evildoers. . . . They are treated by the Jews as foreigners and enemies, and are hunted down by the Greeks; and all the time those who hate them find it impossible to justify their enmity (Richardson, p. 217).

There is, in these antitheses, a delicate dialectic that urges neither a separation from the rest of society nor an attempted identification. The Church is for the world, but only after the manner of the cross. There is no self-conscious revolutionary posturing; indeed, the revolution consists in the fact that Christians are thought to be revolutionaries, dangerous subversives, though they do not seek to be so. The same dialectic could be said to inform the relations of Christians with members of other religious faiths. There can be no abandoning of the distinctiveness of the understanding of God and man derived from the cross. But it is precisely the humanity of God's approach that defines the way in which the distinctiveness is to be lived and presented. Elert well remarks that the legacy of the doctrine of the political Christ of the seventh century is a barrier between Christology and Islam that has still not been demolished (Elert, p. 32). If we are to behave humanly, and yet without loss of integrity, towards those who believe other than we do, our thinking and acting must be renewed at that place where God approaches us through the human Jesus of Nazareth. Once again, the renewal of Christology is to be sought not in rejecting the teaching of the tradition but in taking it further. The problem has been that Christology has not been orthodox enough, or that its lessons have not been learned.

CHRISTOLOGY AND CULTURE

As we have seen, the doctrine of the political Christ is one aspect of the many-sided relation of Christology to culture. In the kind of issues it generates, it is at one with the other parts of this book. What conclusion does this chapter have in common with those of others? The lesson of the book as a whole is that as it engages in conversation with philosophy and politics, Christology must take its centre from that place where the eternal God takes a place alongside us in time.

In this context Stephen Crites has seen, through the eyes of Hegel and Kierkegaard, what is the real challenge facing Christian theology today:

> A good deal of the tension within the churches exists between a conservative leadership attempting to perpetuate an earlier model of Christendom and bold new voices urging that Christendom be founded afresh, in alliance with whatever rough new beast may be presumed to be slouching towards Constantinople to be born. Christians are choosing sides, as they have so many times before, between a traditional culture become decadent and new social forces moving to the tune of shrill promises. But the situation may have changed more fundamentally than either party realizes. . . Christian spokesmen may proclaim their secularity as much as they please. It is quite another matter to suppose that the saeculum will ever again call itself Christian. Christendom has had its day (Crites, p. 17).

If Christendom has had its day, the situation of the theologian must be seen to be more like that of those who represent the heroes of Cochrane's account in Part 3 of his study – that is, the great exponents of trinitarian theology who out-thought the decadent classical culture of their day – than it is like those of any other era of Christianity. Their thinking was achieved by a constant struggle to allow the historical reality of God in time to break through Hellenism's rigid cosmological concepts. With Augustine, and not only in the political sphere, there was something of a return to the anti-historical concepts of classical culture, which continue to dominate Western thought-forms, particularly through the influence of Kant. The era of criticism is not so very different from that of classicism, as we have seen; and so the possibilities for a revival of Christian theological thinking depend upon the same kind of determination to think through to the end the implications for all areas of our thought of the temporal logic of the eternal love.

And so we end where we began, with a reference to a great classical scholar's evocation of an era when there was no Christendom, as there is none for all intents and purposes today. The question to contemporary Christianity, particularly in the West, is whether it has the vigour and confidence so to indwell the reality of him who was and is the temporal actuality of the eternal divine love that it may reforge its language for the conversation with an ailing, if not decadent, culture. This book is offered as a contribution to the process.

REFERENCES

Baynes, Norman H., 'The Political Ideas of St Augustine's *De Civitate Dei*' in *Byzantine Studies and Other Essays*, pp. 288–306.

Beskow, Per, *Rex Gloriae: The Kingship of Christ in the Early Church*.

Brown, Peter, *Augustine of Hippo*.

Caird, G. B., *A Commentary on the Revelation of St John the Divine*.

Cochrane, Charles Norris, *Christianity and Classical Culture: A Study of Thought and Action from Augustus to Augustine*.

Crites, Stephen D., *In the Twilight of Christendom. Hegel vs. Kierkegaard on Faith and History*.

Cupitt, Don, 'The Christ of Christendom' in *The Myth of God Incarnate*, ed. John Hick, pp. 133–47.

Dante Alighieri, *The Divine Comedy – Hell*, Eng. trans. Dorothy L. Sayers.

Elert, Werner, *Der Ausgang der altkirchlichen Christologie. Eine Untersuchung über Theodor von Pharan und seine Zeit als Einführung in die alte Dogmengeschichte*.

Eusebius Pamphili, *The Life of the Blessed Emperor Constantine*, Eng. trans. Ernest Cushing Richardson, Select Library of Nicene and Post-Nicene Fathers, 2nd series, vol. i, pp. 481–559.

Eusebius Pamphili, *Oration in Praise of the Emperor Constantine*, pp. 581–610.

Hegel, G. W. F., 1942, *The Philosophy of Right*, Eng. trans. T. M. Knox.

Hegel, G. W. F., 1949, *The Phenomenology of Mind*, Eng. trans. J. B. Baillie.

Hegel, G. W. F., 1956, *The Philosophy of History*, Eng. trans. J. Sibree.

Johnson, Paul, *A History of Christianity*.

Kierkegaard, Søren, 1941b, *Training in Christianity*, Eng. trans. Walter Lowrie.

Kierkegaard, Søren, 1944, *Kierkegaard's Attack upon 'Christendom'*, Eng. trans. Walter Lowrie.

Moltmann, Jürgen, *The Crucified God: The Cross of Christ as the Foundation and Criticism of Christian Theology*, Eng. trans. R. A. Wilson and John Bowden.

Peterson, Erik, 1935, *Der Monotheismus als politisches Problem. Ein Beitrag zur Geschichte der politischen Theologie im Imperium Romanum*.

Peterson, Erik, 1951, 'Christus als Imperator' in *Theologische Traktate*, pp. 149–64.

Richardson, Cyril C. (ed.), 'The So-Called Letter to Diognetus' in *Early Christian Fathers*, Library of Christian Classics, vol. i, pp. 213–24.

Schmidt, Hans, 'The Cross of Reality? Some Questions Concerning the Interpretation of Bonhoeffer' in *World Come of Age*, ed. Ronald Gregor Smith, pp. 215–55.

EPILOGUE

This book has begun and ended with allusions to the relationship between Christianity and culture. Culture, by which is meant the mainstream of the intellectual and artistic life of an era, inevitably provides part of the context within which theology is done. As an intellectual enterprise employing a common language, theology is part of culture, and necessarily so. But cultures change and develop, and with them theology, with the result that at a time when we are very conscious of the difference between our culture and that of the first centuries of what is called the Christian era, the very theological enterprise is called into question. In particular, we often wonder whether it is possible for us to affirm with understanding and integrity those forms of words which were for earlier generations the very essence of Christian teaching.

There is, however, also to be taken into account the other important part of theology's context, which is that of a community of worship, belief and action. Speaking of the Eucharist, J. S. Whale has pointed out that '(n)ot one Lord's Day has ever passed without this showing of the Lord's death by the Lord's people' (Whale, p. 135). It is here that we find alongside the changes of culture, and relativizing their significance, the central historical continuity in the light of which Christology has to be done. There is something here, a distinctive and recognizable *act* or series of acts which transcends not only cultural eras but spatial, racial, national – indeed, ecclesiastical – boundaries. It would be wrong to call it a fixed point, for the church is a historical reality, and subject to development, change, growth and decay. But there is, if not a fixedness, at least a continuity of central feature without which it would no longer be the Christian Eucharist. There is a consistent inner dynamic in what is there said and done.

The aim of this book has been to isolate and defend a consistent inner dynamic in the Church's teaching about Jesus Christ, in contradiction of those many contemporary voices which are saying that the cultural context is so changed that one cannot be found. That is the justification for the expending of so much argument on forging links between what is happening now and what happened in the first few centuries of Christian theology. The second and third chapters, for example, contain a detailed discussion of Christology 'from below' and 'from above' because it is in the supposed differences between the two that the breach between now and then is often held to subsist. The argument of these chapters is that the distinction is by no means clear, and that much depends upon the different ways in which the supposedly opposing methods can be understood. Although the distinction does cast some light upon the differences between the eras, a far more important and illuminating question is that of the relation of form and content in Christology. An examination of approaches to Christology in its light reveals that it is unlikely that the same or similar content will be obtained by different methods; on the contrary, the same kind of problems are seen to recur in this respect in both ages. One reason for this is that ancient and modern Christology alike face the identical problem of how they shall use the language of their culture without succumbing to that language's pressure to force their content into an alien shape.

As the argument proceeds, the kind of continuity involved in such matters becomes more manifest. It is not a static continuity, making possible the simple repetition of forms of words from the past, but a continuity within discontinuity, requiring an ever new attention to the reality of which we wish to speak today as faithfully as possible. It can be rather schematically characterized as follows: that whereas the ancient world was tempted to *eternalize* the human Jesus, we are tempted to eternalize the *human* Jesus. The one tends to abolish the genuine temporality and so humanity of the Christ, the other his origin in and reality as the eternal Word of God. Here the underlying continuity consists in a common reluctance to do what an authentic Christology must do: to think together without loss to either side and without indulging in premature appeals to paradox the temporal and the eternal as they are made known in the crucified and risen Jesus of Nazareth. Here also the importance

206

of Chapter 4 for the book as a whole becomes clear, for in the New Testament the historical and temporal foundation of Christology is laid down. But, as the chapter is designed to show, if the New Testament is to be understood, it must be accepted that we are not presented in it with a naked or purely immanent temporality. Treat it simply as a source for historical information, and it will not make sense. Amidst all the diversity of its Christology one thing remains constant, and that is the refusal to abstract the historical events from their overall theological meaning. The historical man Jesus is never construed apart from his meaning as the presence of the eternal God in time. The New Testament, if we take it seriously, will not allow us to choose between time and eternity, immanence and transcendence, in our talk about Jesus. The two are always given together.

It is at this point that Biblical teaching about the reality of God and his freedom to involve himself in the world without loss to his or the world's reality runs up against the philosophical assumptions which dominate both ancient and modern culture. Faced with a document claiming the co-presence of the temporal and eternal, the mainstream philosophical tradition tries to present us with a choice: either time or eternity. This is the phenomenon known as dualism, and the fifth chapter is devoted to showing how dualistic assumptions operate in a similar way in both ancient and modern Christology. The continuity between the eras is illustrated from the work of Schleiermacher and argued to consist in the fact that to the ancient dogma of the impassibility of God, which in its extreme form necessitated a choice between eternity and temporality, there corresponds the modern post-Kantian dogma of a world in which the eternal cannot be known to be present. The 'closed' God of antiquity is answered by the closed world of so much modern thinking.

In Chapter 6 a further continuity is established in an argument suggesting that both dogmas derive from the same source. In particular, shared features of thought can be found in a line of influence joining Augustine to Kant. The common matrix is a tendency to define time in terms of change and decay. Yet Christology is to do with the affirmation and salvation of time as a proper place for human flourishing. Such an approach to time is developed at once by the Fathers when they are able to affirm and conceive the

presence of the eternal in *Jesus* and by us when we are able to affirm
and conceive the presence of the *eternal* in Jesus. Here again there
is continuity, this time of affirmation, and it means that as we
understand Jesus as the temporal logic of the eternal God, so we
may understand and assimilate the insights of those ancient creeds
and doctrines which also resisted the reduction of eternity to time
or time to eternity.

Such a process of change of emphasis within continuity of basic
affirmation and teaching takes place partly against the stream of
modern culture, but only partly, for modern culture is not monolithic. Assistance is given from within it, in signs of the grace of God
which echo and so enable to come to expression that which is met
in Jesus. From the philosophy of music we learn of new possibilities
for understanding time, and from the philosophy of science ways of
liberation from rigid views of the relation of words and things.
These in their turn reinforce a conception of theology in which we
may assimilate the gifts of tradition without being its slave.

The lesson to be learned in all this is that, far from abandoning
the tradition, we may learn to stand on the giants' shoulders in the
cautious hope of being able to see a little further than they. A
'critical' theology which operates only or chiefly by rejection of all
that came before the modern era will be a blind theology, for it will
have lost its roots. But, as the final chapter argues, no suggestion
is being made that things have not sometimes gone wrong. The
history of Christendom, in which war and persecution were justified
in the name of the divine Christ, gives us much of which to repent.
But we shall not have the theological tools with which to combat
pagan and authoritarian distortions of Christology unless, far from
rejecting the legacy of the Fathers, we take further the process of
thinking which they began. They realized that the incarnation demanded a rethinking of the meaning of the word *God*. The God of
Christendom largely, though not entirely, escaped that rethinking,
but it was an aberration, and untrue to the main direction of
patristic theology and Christology.

Christology, like all theology, is a difficult and demanding discipline. In it, some attempt is made to think about the living Jesus
of the Church's worship and of New Testament confession. It cannot
be done without assistance from the past, nor without the great
labour of exercising thought and judgement as to where the past

was right and where it was wrong. But that is to reaffirm, not to deny, that it is the *same kind of discipline* as that engaged in by Ignatius, Athanasius and Anselm. There is a continuity of approach, method and above all of object, for Jesus Christ, the same yesterday and today and for ever, is at once the true subject and true object of Christology: the one who makes it possible, through his Spirit, and the one whose reality as truly God and truly man our human concepts strain to represent.

REFERENCE

Whale, J. S., *Victor and Victim: The Christian Doctrine of Redemption.*

BIBLIOGRAPHY

(The place of publication is London, unless otherwise indicated.)

Anderson, Ray S., *Historical Transcendence and the Reality of God: A Christological Critique.* Geoffrey Chapman 1975.

Anselm of Canterbury, *Why God Became Man*, Eng. trans. Eugene R. Fairweather, *A Scholastic Miscellany: From Anselm to Ockham.* Library of Christian Classics, vol. x. SCM Press (1956), pp. 100–83.

Athanasius, *Four Discourses against the Arians: Nicene and Post-Nicene Fathers*, vol. iv. Parker 1892.

Athanasius, *On the Incarnation of the Word*, ed. Edward Rochie Hardy, *Christology of the Later Fathers.* Library of Christian Classics, vol. iii. SCM Press (1954), pp. 55–110.

Athanasius, *'Contra Gentes' and 'De Incarnatione'*, ed. and Eng. trans. Robert W. Thompson. Oxford, Clarendon Press, 1971.

Augustine, *Confessions*, Eng. trans. R. S. Pine-Coffin. Harmondsworth, Penguin Books, 1961.

Aulén, Gustaf, *Christus Victor: An Historical Study of the Three Main Types of the Idea of the Atonement*, Eng. trans. A. G. Hebert. SPCK 1970.

Baillie, D. M., *God was in Christ: An Essay on Incarnation and Atonement.* Faber 1961.

Barrett, C. K., ' "The Father is greater than I" (John 14.28): Subordinationist Christology in the New Testament' in *Neues Testament und Kirche: für R. Schnackenburg*, ed. J. Gnilka. Freiburg, Herder (1974), pp. 144–59.

Barth, Karl, *Church Dogmatics*, vols. i–iv, Eng. trans. eds. G. W. Bromiley and T. F. Torrance. Edinburgh, T. & T. Clark, 1956–75.

Barth, Karl, *Protestant Theology in the Nineteenth Century: Its Background and History*, Eng. trans. Brian Cozens and John Bowden. SCM Press 1972.

Baynes, Norman H., 'Eusebius and the Christian Empire' in *Byzantine Studies and Other Essays.* Athlone Press (1955), pp. 168–72.

Baynes, Norman H., 'The Political Ideas of St Augustine's *De Civitate Dei*' in *Byzantine Studies and Other Essays.* Athlone Press (1955), pp. 288–306.

Beskow, Per, *Rex Gloriae: The Kingship of Christ in the Early Church.* Uppsala, Eng. trans. Eric J. Sharpe. Stockholm, Almqvist and Wiksell, 1962.

Bettenson, Henry (ed.), *Documents of the Christian Church.* Oxford University Press, 2ᵉ, 1963.

Bibliography

Bonhoeffer, Dietrich, *Ethics*, ed. Eberhard Bethge, Eng. trans. Neville Horton Smith. SCM Press 1955.

Bonhoeffer, Dietrich, *Christology*, Eng. trans. John Bowden. Collins 1966.

Braaten, Carl, 'A Trinitarian Theology of the Cross' in *Journal of Religion* 56 (1976), 113–21.

Brown, Peter, *Augustine of Hippo*. Faber 1969.

Bultmann, Rudolf, 'The Christological Confession of the World Council of Churches' in *Essays Philosophical and Theological*, Eng. trans. J. C. G. Greig. SCM Press (1955), pp. 273–90.

Bultmann, Rudolf, 'New Testament and Mythology' in *Kerygma and Myth*, ed. Hans-Werner Bartsch, Eng. trans. Reginald H. Fuller, vols. i and ii. SPCK (1972), pp. 1–44.

Bunge, Mario, *Method, Model and Matter*. Dordrecht and Boston, D. Reidel, 1973.

Butterworth, Robert, 'Bishop Robinson and Christology' in *Religious Studies* 11 (March 1975), 73–85.

Butterworth, Robert, 'Has Chalcedon a Future?' in *The Month* ccxxxviii (April 1977), 111–17.

Caird, G. B., *Commentary on the Revelation of St John the Divine*. A. & C. Black 1966.

Chadwick, Henry, 'Eucharist and Christology in the Nestorian Controversy' in *Journal of Theological Studies*, n.s. ii (1951), 145–64.

Chadwick, Henry, *The Early Church*. Pelican History of the Church, vol. i. Harmondsworth, Penguin Books, 1967.

Cochrane, Charles Norris, *Christianity and Classical Culture. A Study of Thought and Action from Augustus to Augustine*. Oxford, Clarendon Press, 2ᵉ, 1944.

Crites, Stephen D., *In the Twilight of Christendom. Hegel vs. Kierkegaard on Faith and History*. Chambersburg, Pa., American Academy of Religion, 1972.

Cullmann, Oscar, *Christ and Time: The Primitive Christian Conception of Time and History*, Eng. trans. Floyd V. Filson. SCM Press 1951.

Cupitt, Don, 'The Christ of Christendom' in *The Myth of God Incarnate*, ed. John Hick. SCM Press (1977), pp. 133–47.

Dante Alighieri, *The Divine Comedy – Hell*, Eng. trans. Dorothy L. Sayers. Harmondsworth, Penguin Books, 1949.

Descartes, René, 'Meditations on the First Philosophy' in *The Philosophical Works of Descartes*, Eng. trans. Elizabeth Haldane and G. R. T. Ross. Cambridge University Press, 2ᵉ (1931), vol. i, pp. 131–99.

Dunn, James D. G., 'Paul's Understanding of the Death of Jesus' in *Reconciliation and Hope: New Testament Essays on Atonement and Eschatology*, ed. Robert Banks. Exeter, Paternoster Press (1974), pp. 125–41.

Dunn, James D. G., *Unity and Diversity in the New Testament: An Inquiry into the Character of Earliest Christianity*. SCM Press 1977.

Dunn, James D. G., *Christology in the Making: An Inquiry into the Origins of the Doctrine of the Incarnation*. SCM Press 1980.

Elert, Werner, *Der Ausgang der altkirchlichen Christologie. Eine Untersuchung*

Bibliography

über Theodor von Pharan und seine Zeit als Einführung in die alte Dogmengeschichte. Berlin, Lutherisches Verlagshaus, 1957.

Eusebius Pamphili, *The Life of the Blessed Emperor Constantine*, Eng. trans. Ernest Cushing Richardson, Select Library of Nicene and Post-Nicene Fathers, 2nd series, vol. i. Oxford, Parker (1890), pp. 481–559.

Eusebius Pamphili, *Oration in Praise of the Emperor Constantine*, Eng. trans. Ernest Cushing Richardson, op. cit., pp. 581–610.

Fairweather, Eugene R., 'The "Kenotic" Christology' in *A Commentary on the Epistle to the Philippians* by F. W. Beare. A. & C. Black (1959), pp. 159–74.

Faraday, Michael, 'A Speculation touching Electric Conduction and the Nature of Matter' in *On the Primary Forces of Electricity*, ed. Richard Laming. 1838.

Findlay, J. N., *Hegel: A Re-examination.* Allen & Unwin, 1958.

Forsyth, P. T., *The Person and Place of Jesus Christ.* Independent Press 1909.

Forsyth, P. T., *The Cruciality of the Cross.* Independent Press, 2ᵉ, 1948.

Frei, Hans, *The Eclipse of Biblical Narrative: A Study in Eighteenth- and Nineteenth-Century Hermeneutics.* New Haven and London, Yale University Press, 1974.

Gadamer, Hans-Georg, *Truth and Method*, Eng. trans. of 2ᵉ Garrett Barden and John Cumming. New York, Seaburg Press, 1975.

Gibbs, J. G., *Creation and Redemption: A Study in Pauline Theology.* Supplement to Novum Testamentum xxvi. Leiden 1971.

Gilg, Arnold, *Weg und Bedeutung der altkirchlichen Christologie.* München, Chr. Kaiser Verlag, 1961.

Gill, Robin, 'The Suspect Approach to Christology' in *Theology* lxxi (1968), 310–16.

Grant, Robert M., 'Christian Devotion to the Monarchy' in *Early Christianity and Society.* Collins (1978), pp. 13–43.

Gregg, Robert C. and Groh, Dennis E., *Early Arianism: A View of Salvation.* SCM Press 1981.

Gregory of Nazianzus, 'Letters on the Apollinarian Controversy' in *Christology of the Later Fathers*, ed. Edward Rochie Hardie, Library of Christian Classics, vol. iii. SCM Press (1954), pp. 215–32.

Grene, Marjorie, *The Knower and the Known.* Faber & Faber 1966.

Grillmeier, Aloys, *Christ in Christian Tradition*, vol. i: *From the Apostolic Age to Chalcedon*, Eng. trans. John Bowden. Mowbray, 2ᵉ, 1975.

Gunton, Colin E., Review of J. A. T. Robinson, *The Human Face of God* in *Theology* lxxvi (1973), 486–7.

Gunton, Colin E., 'Transcendence, Metaphor and the Knowability of God' in *Journal of Theological Studies*, 31 (1980), 501–16.

Gunton, Colin E., 'The Truth of Christology' in *Belief in Science and in Christian Life. The Relevance of Michael Polanyi's Thought for Christian Faith and Life*, ed. Thomas F. Torrance. Edinburgh, Handsel Press (1980), pp. 91–107.

Bibliography

Haire, J. L. M., 'On Behalf of Chalcedon' in *Essays in Christology for Karl Barth*, ed. T. H. L. Parker. Lutterworth Press (1951), pp. 95–111.

Hanson, A. T., *Grace and Truth: A Study in the Doctrine of the Incarnation*. SPCK 1975.

Harnack, Adolf von, *History of Dogma*, Eng. trans. N. Buchanan from 3ᵉ German. Williams & Norgate 1896.

Harvey, Van A., 'A Word in Defence of Schleiermacher's Theological Method' in *Journal of Religion* 42 (1962), 151–79.

Harvey, Van A., *The Historian and the Believer: The Morality of Historical Knowledge and Christian Belief*. SCM Press 1967.

Hebblethwaite, Brian, 'The Appeal to Experience in Christology' in *Christ, Faith and History. Cambridge Studies in Christology*, ed. S. W. Sykes and J. P. Clayton. Cambridge University Press (1972), pp. 263–78.

Hebblethwaite, Brian, 'Incarnation – the Essence of Christianity' in *Theology* lxxx (1977), 85–91.

Hegel, G. W. F., *Lectures on the Philosophy of Religion*, Eng. trans. E. B. Speirs and J. B. Sanderson. Kegan Paul, Trench, Trübner 1895.

Hegel, G. W. F., *The Phenomenology of Mind*, Eng. trans. J. B. Baillie. Allen & Unwin, 2ᵉ revised, 1949.

Hegel, G. W. F., *The Philosophy of History*, Eng. trans. J. Sibree. New York, Dover Publications, 1956.

Hegel, G. W. F., *The Philosophy of Right*, Eng. trans. T. M. Knox. Oxford, Clarendon Press, 1972.

Hengel, Martin, *The Son of God: The Origin of Christology and the History of Jewish–Hellenistic Religion*, Eng. trans. John Bowden. SCM Press 1976.

Herrmann, Wilhelm, *The Communion of the Christian with God. Described on the Basis of Luther's Statements*, Eng. trans. J. Sandys Stanyon. SCM Press 1972.

Hick, J. H., 'The Christology of D. M. Baillie' in *Scottish Journal of Theology* 11 (1958), 1–12.

Hick, J. H., 'Christology at the Cross Roads' in *Prospect for Theology: Essays in Honour of H. H. Farmer*, ed. F. G. Healey. Welwyn, Nisbet (1966), pp. 139–66.

Hick, J. H., 'Jesus and the World Religions' in *The Myth of God Incarnate*, ed. John Hick. SCM Press (1977), pp. 167–85.

Hodgson, Peter C., *Jesus – Word and Presence: An Essay in Christology*. Philadelphia, Fortress Press, 1971.

Hooker, M. D., 'Interchange in Christ' in *Journal of Theological Studies*, n.s. 22 (1971), 349–61.

Hoskyns, Edwyn and Davey, Noel, *The Riddle of the New Testament*. Faber & Faber, 3ᵉ, 1947.

Hume, David, *An Enquiry Concerning Human Understanding*, ed. L. A. Selby-Bigge. Oxford, Clarendon Press, 2ᵉ, 1962.

Ignatius of Antioch, 'The Letter to the Ephesians', ed. Cyril C. Richardson, *The Early Christian Fathers*. Library of Christian Classics, vol. i. SCM Press (1953), pp. 87–93.

Bibliography

Irenaeus of Lyons, *Irenaeus Against Heresies*, Ante-Nicene Library. Edinburgh, T. & T. Clark, 1868.

Jaki, Stanley L., *The Road of Science and the Ways to God*. The Gifford Lectures 1974–5 and 1975–6. Chicago and London, Chicago University Press, 1978.

Jenkins, David E., *The Glory of Man*. SCM Press 1967.

Jenson, R. W., *The Knowledge of Things Hoped For: The Sense of Theological Discourse*. Oxford University Press 1969.

Johnson, Paul, *A History of Christianity*. Harmondsworth, Penguin Books, 1978.

Jonas, Hans, 'Origen's Metaphysics of Free Will, Fall and Salvation: A "Divine Comedy" of the Universe' in *Philosophical Essays: From Ancient Creed to Technological Man*. Englewood Cliffs, N.J., Prentice-Hall (1974), pp. 305–23.

Jüngel, Eberhard, 'Vom Tod des lebendigen Gottes. Ein Plakat' in *Zeitschrift für Theologie und Kirche* 65 (1968), 93–116.

Jüngel, Eberhard, *Gott als Geheimnis der Welt. Zur Begründung der Theologie des Gekreuzigten im Streit zwischen Theismus und Atheismus*. Tübingen, J. C. B. Mohr (Paul Siebeck), 1978.

Kähler, Martin, *The So-Called Historical Jesus and the Historic Biblical Christ*, Eng. trans. Carl E. Braaten. Philadelphia, Fortress Press, 1964.

Kant, Immanuel, *Immanuel Kant's Critique of Pure Reason*, Eng. trans. Norman Kemp Smith. Macmillan 1933.

Kant, Immanuel, *Religion within the Limits of Reason Alone*, Eng. trans. T. M. Greene and H. H. Hudson. New York, Harper Torchbooks, 1960.

Kasper, Walter, *Jesus the Christ*, Eng. trans. V. Green. Burns & Oates 1976.

Kent, J. H. S., 'The Socinian Tradition' in *Theology* lxxviii (March 1975), 131–40.

Kierkegaard, Søren, *Concluding Unscientific Postscript*, Eng. trans. David F. Swenson and Walter Lowrie. Princeton University Press 1941.

Kierkegaard, Søren, *Training in Christianity*, Eng. trans. Walter Lowrie. Princeton University Press 1941.

Kierkegaard, Søren, *Kierkegaard's Attack upon 'Christendom'*, Eng. trans. Walter Lowrie. Oxford University Press 1944.

Kierkegaard, Søren, *Philosophical Fragments*, Eng. trans. David F. Swenson and Howard V. Hong. Princeton University Press 1962.

Knox, John, *The Humanity and Divinity of Christ: A Study of Pattern in Christology*. Cambridge University Press 1967.

Kuhn, Helmut, 'Personal Knowledge and the Crisis of the Philosophical Tradition' in *Intellect and Hope: Essays in the Thought of Michael Polanyi*, eds. Thomas A. Langford and William H. Poteat. Durham, N.C., Duke University Press (1968), pp. 111–35.

Lash, Nicholas, 'Up and Down in Christology' in *New Studies in Theology I*, eds. Stephen Sykes and Derek Holmes. Duckworth (1980), pp. 31–46.

Leech, K., 'Believing in the Incarnation' in *Theology* lxxix (1976), 68–76.

Bibliography

Leontius of Byzantium, *Three Books Against the Nestorians and Eutychians*. *Migne Patrologia Graeca* 81, 1 (1865), 1267–1394.

Lessing, G. E., *Lessing's Theological Writings: Selections in Translation*, Eng. trans. Henry Chadwick. A. & C. Black 1956.

Locke, John, *An Essay Concerning Human Understanding*. New York, Dover Publications, 1959.

Lovejoy, Arthur O., *The Great Chain of Being: A Study of the History of an Idea*. Cambridge, Mass., Harvard University Press, 2ᵉ, 1964.

Lucas, J. R., *A Treatise on Time and Space*. Methuen 1973.

McIntyre, John, *St Anselm and his Critics: A Re-interpretation of the 'Cur Deus Homo'*. Edinburgh and London, Oliver & Boyd, 1954.

McIntyre, John, *The Shape of Christology*. SCM Press 1966.

MacKinnon, D. M., 'Moral Objections' in *Objections to Christian Belief*. Constable (1963), pp. 11–34.

MacKinnon, D. M., 'Subjective and Objective Conceptions of Atonement' in *Prospect for Theology: Essays in Honour of H. H. Farmer*, ed. F. G. Healey. Welwyn, Nisbet (1966), pp. 169–82.

MacKinnon, D. M., ' "Substance" in Christology – a Cross-bench View' in *Christ, Faith and History. Cambridge Studies in Christology*, eds. S. W. Sykes and J. P. Clayton. Cambridge University Press (1972), pp. 279–300.

MacKinnon, D. M., 'The Relation of the Doctrines of the Incarnation and the Trinity' in *Creation, Christ and Culture: Studies in Honour of T. F. Torrance*, ed. R. W. A. McKinney. Edinburgh, T. & T. Clark (1976), pp. 92–107.

MacKinnon, D. M., 'Lenin and Theology' in *Explorations in Theology*, 5. SCM Press (1979), pp. 11–29.

MacKinnon, D. M., Review of James D. G. Dunn, *Christology in the Making* in *Scottish Journal of Theology*, 35 (1982), 362–4.

MacKinnon, D. M., 'Prolegomena to Christology', *Journal of Theological Studies* 33 (1982), 146–60.

Mackintosh, H. R., *The Doctrine of the Person of Jesus Christ*. Edinburgh, T. & T. Clark, 2ᵉ, 1913.

Macquarrie, John, 'The Pre-existence of Jesus Christ' in *Expository Times* xxvii (1965–6), 199–202.

Macquarrie, John, 'The Humanity of Christ' in *Theology* lxxiv (1971), 243–50.

Meijering, E. P., *God Being History: Studies in Patristic Philosophy*. Amsterdam and Oxford, North-Holland, 1975.

Moltmann, Jürgen, *The Crucified God: The Cross of Christ as the Foundation and Criticism of Christian Theology*, Eng. trans. R. A. Wilson and John Bowden. SCM Press 1974.

Moule, C. F. D., 'The Manhood of Jesus in the New Testament' in *Christ, Faith and History. Cambridge Studies in Christology*, eds. S. W. Sykes and J. P. Clayton. Cambridge University Press (1972), pp. 95–110.

Moule, C. F. D., *The Origin of Christology*. Cambridge University Press 1977.

Bibliography

Newton, Isaac, *Newton's Philosophy of Nature: Selections from his Writings*, ed. H. S. Thayer. New York, Hafner, 1953.

Niebuhr, Reinhold, *The Nature and Destiny of Man*, vol. 1: *Human Nature*; vol. 2: *Human Destiny*. Nisbet 1941.

Niebuhr, H. Richard, *Christ and Culture*. Faber 1952.

Nineham, Dennis E., *The Use and Abuse of the Bible*. Macmillan 1976.

Nineham, Dennis E., 'Epilogue' in *The Myth of God Incarnate*, ed. John Hick. SCM Press (1977), pp. 186–204.

Norris, R. A. Jnr., 'Towards a Contemporary Interpretation of the Chalcedonian Definition' in *Lux in Lumine: Essays to Honour W. Norman Pittenger*, ed. R. A. Norris. New York, Seabury Press (1966), pp. 62–79.

Origen, *Origen's Commentary on the Gospel of John*, Eng. trans. Allan Menzies. Ante-Nicene Christian Library, additional volume. Edinburgh, T. & T. Clark, 1897.

Origen, *Origen's 'On First Principles': Being Koetscham's Text of 'De Principiis'*, Eng. trans. G. W. Butterworth. SPCK 1936.

Origen, *Contra Celsum*, Eng. trans. and ed. Henry Chadwick. Cambridge University Press 1953.

Owen, H. P., 'The Person of Christ in Recent Theology' in *Religious Studies* 13 (1977), 491–506.

Pannenberg, Wolfhart, *Jesus – God and Man*. Eng. trans. Lewis L. Wilkins and Duane A. Priebe. SCM Press 1968.

Pannenberg, Wolfhart, 'Analogy and Doxology' in *Basic Questions in Theology* I, Eng. trans. George H. Kehm. SCM Press (1970), pp. 211–38.

Pannenberg, Wolfhart, *Theology and the Philosophy of Science*, Eng. trans. Francis McDonagh. Darton, Longman & Todd 1976.

Peterson, Erik, *Der Monotheismus als politisches Problem. Ein Beitrag für Geschichte der politischen Theologie im Imperium Romanum*. Leipzig, J. Hegner, 1935.

Peterson, Erik, 'Christus als Imperator' in *Theologische Traktate*. München, Hochland-Bücherei, Kösel Verlag (1951), pp. 149–64.

Pittenger, W. N., *The Word Incarnate: A Study of the Doctrine of the Person of Christ*. Nisbet 1959.

Polanyi, Michael, *The Study of Man*. University of Chicago Press 1959.

Polanyi, Michael, *Personal Knowledge: Towards a Post-Critical Philosophy*. Routledge & Kegan Paul, 2ᵉ, 1962.

Quick, Oliver C., *Doctrines of the Creed*. Collins, Fontana Library, 1963.

Quine, W. V. O., 'Two Dogmas of Empiricism' in *Clarity is Not Enough*, ed. H. D. Lewis. Allen & Unwin (1963), pp. 110–32.

Rahner, Karl, *Theological Investigations*, vol. i, Eng. trans. Kevin Smyth. Darton, Longman & Todd 1961.

Rahner, Karl, *Theological Investigations*, vol. iv, Eng. trans. Kevin Smyth. Darton, Longman & Todd 1961.

Rahner, Karl, *Theological Investigations*, vol. ix, Eng. trans. Graham Harrison. Darton, Longman & Todd 1972.

Rahner, Karl, *Foundations of Christian Faith: An Introduction to the Idea of*

Bibliography

Christianity, Eng. trans. William V. Dych. Darton, Longman & Todd 1978.

Reimarus, H. S., *Reimarus: Fragments*, Eng. trans. Ralph S. Fraser. SCM Press 1971.

Relton, H. M., *A Study in Christology: The Problem of the Relation of the Two Natures in the Person of Christ*. SPCK 1934.

Richardson, Cyril C. (ed)., 'The So-called Letter to Diognetus' in *Early Christian Fathers*, Library of Christian Classics, vol. i. SCM Press (1953), pp. 213–24.

Ritschl, Albrecht, *A Critical History of the Christian Doctrine of Justification and Reconciliation*, Eng. trans. J. S. Black. Edinburgh, T. & T. Clark, 1872.

Ritschl, Albrecht, *The Christian Doctrine of Justification and Reconciliation: The Positive Development of the Doctrine*, Eng. trans. eds. H. R. Mackintosh and A. B. Macaulay. Edinburgh, T. & T. Clark, 1900.

Ritschl, Albrecht, 'Theology and Metaphysics. Towards Rapprochement and Defence' in *Three Essays*, Eng. trans. Philip Hefner. Philadelphia, Fortress Press (1972), pp. 151–212.

Ritschl, Dietrich, *Memory and Hope: An Inquiry Concerning the Presence of Christ*. Collier-Macmillan 1967.

Robinson, John A. T., *The Human Face of God*. SCM Press 1973.

Rogerson, J. W., 'The Hebrew Conception of Corporate Personality: A Re-examination' in *Journal of Theological Studies*, n.s. 21 (1970), 1–16.

Rorty, Richard, *Philosophy and the Mirror of Nature*. Oxford, Blackwell, 1980.

Rupp, George, *Christologies and Cultures – Toward a Typology of Religious Worldviews*. The Hague, Mouton, 1976.

Schillebeeckx, Edward, *Jesus: An Experiment in Christology*, Eng. trans. Hubert Hoskins. Collins 1979.

Schillebeeckx, Edward, *Christ: The Christian Experience in the Modern World*, Eng. trans. John Bowden. SCM Press 1980.

Schleiermacher, F. D. E., *The Christian Faith*, Eng. trans. of 2ᵉ, H. R. Mackintosh and J. S. Stewart. Edinburgh, T. & T. Clark, 1948.

Schlink, Edmund, *The Coming Christ and the Coming Church*. Eng. trans. Edinburgh, Oliver & Boyd, 1967.

Schmidt, Hans, 'The Cross of Reality? Some Questions Concerning the Interpretation of Bonhoeffer' in *World Come of Age*, ed. Ronald Gregor Smith. Collins (1967), pp. 215–55.

Schoonenberg, P., *The Christ*, Eng. trans. Della Couling. Sheed & Ward 1974.

Schwarz, Reinhard, 'Gott ist Mensch. Zur Lehre von der Person Christi bei den Ockhamisten und bei Luther' in *Zeitschrift für Theologie und Kirche* 63 (1966), 284–351.

Schweitzer, Albert, *The Quest of the Historical Jesus: A Critical Study of its Progress from Reimarus to Wrede*, Eng. trans. W. Montgomery. A. & C. Black, 3ᵉ, 1954.

Segundo, Juan Luis, *Our Idea of God: A Theology for Artisans of a New Humanity*, vol. iii, Eng. trans. John Drury. New York, Maryknoth, 1974.

217

Bibliography

Sellers, R. V., *Two Ancient Christologies: A Study in the Christological Thought of the Schools of Alexandria and Antioch in the Early History of Christian Doctrine.* SPCK 1954 (first published 1940).

Shaffer, E. S., *'Kubla Khan' and 'The Fall of Jerusalem': The Mythological School in Biblical Criticism and Secular Literature, 1770–1880.* Cambridge University Press 1975.

Sobrino, Jon, *Christology at the Crossroads: A Latin American Approach,* Eng. trans. John Drury, SCM Press 1978.

Stead, G. C., 'The Platonism of Arius' in *Journal of Theological Studies,* 15 (1964), 16–31.

Stead, G. C., *Divine Substance.* Oxford, Clarendon Press, 1977.

Stevenson, J. (ed)., *Creeds, Councils and Controversies: Documents Illustrative of the History of the Church A.D. 337–461.* SPCK 1972.

Strauss, David Friedrich, *The Life of Jesus Critically Examined,* Eng. trans. Marian Evans. SCM Press 1973.

Sutherland, Stewart R., 'History and Belief' in *Theology* lxxiii (1970), 4–9.

Sykes, S. W., 'The Theology of the Humanity of Christ' in *Christ, Faith and History. Cambridge Studies in Christology,* eds. S. W. Sykes and J. P. Clayton. Cambridge University Press (1972), pp. 53–72.

Taylor, Charles, *Hegel.* Cambridge University Press 1975.

Teilhard de Chardin, Pierre, *The Phenomenon of Man,* Eng. trans. Bernard Wall. Collins 1959.

Theodore of Mopsuestia, *Commentary on the Nicene Creed,* Eng. trans. A. Mingana. Woodbrooke Studies v. Cambridge, W. Heffer, 1932.

Thomasius, Gottfried, *Christ's Person and Work,* part ii, *The Person of the Mediator,* in *God and Incarnation in Mid-Nineteenth Century German Theology,* ed. Claude Welch. Oxford University Press 1965.

Thunberg, Lars, *Microcosm and Mediator: The Theological Anthropology of Maximus the Confessor. Acta Seminarii Neotestamentici Upsaliensis,* 25. Lund, 1965.

Tillich, Paul, *Systematic Theology,* combined volume. Nisbet 1968.

Torrance, T. F., 'Atonement and the Oneness of the Church' in *Scottish Journal of Theology* 7 (1954), 245–69.

Torrance, T. F., *Space, Time and Incarnation.* Oxford University Press 1969.

Torrance, T. F., *Theological Science.* Oxford University Press 1969.

Torrance, T. F., *Theology in Reconciliation: Essays towards Evangelical and Catholic Unity in East and West.* Geoffrey Chapman 1975.

Torrance, T. F., *Space, Time and Resurrection.* Edinburgh, Handsel Press, 1976.

Torrance, T. F., *Divine and Contingent Order.* Oxford University Press 1981.

Turner, H. E. W., *The Patristic Doctrine of Redemption.* Mowbray 1952.

Wainwright, Geoffrey, *Doxology: The Praise of God in Worship, Doctrine and Life. A Systematic Theology.* Epworth Press 1980.

Weingart, Richard E., *The Logic of Divine Love: A Critical Analysis of the Soteriology of Peter Abailard.* Oxford, Clarendon Press, 1970.

Weiss, Johannes, *Jesus's Proclamation of the Kingdom of God,* Eng. trans. R. H. Hiers and D. L. Holland. SCM Press 1971.

Bibliography

Welch, Claude, *Protestant Thought in the Nineteenth Century*, vol. i, 1799–1870. New Haven and London, Yale University Press, 1972.

Whale, J. S., *Victor and Victim: The Christian Doctrine of Redemption*. Cambridge University Press 1960.

Whitrow, G. J., *The Natural Philosophy of Time*. Oxford, Clarendon Press, 2ᵉ, 1980.

Wiles, M. F., 'In Defence of Arius' in *Journal of Theological Studies*, 13 (1962), 339–47.

Wiles, M. F., *The Remaking of Christian Doctrine*. The Hulsean Lectures 1973. SCM Press 1974.

Wiles, M. F., 'The Unassumed is the Unhealed' in *Working Papers in Doctrine*. SCM Press (1976), pp. 122–31.

Williams, G. H., 'Christology and Church–State Relations in the Fourth Century' in *Church History* 20 (1951), no. 3, pp. 3–33 and no. 4, pp. 3–26.

Wingren, G., *Man and the Incarnation: A Study in the Biblical Theology of Irenaeus*, Eng. trans. Ross MacKenzie. Edinburgh and London, Oliver & Boyd, 1959.

Wittgenstein, Ludwig, *Philosophical Investigations*, Eng. trans. G. E. M. Anscombe. Oxford, Blackwell, 1968.

Ziman, John, *Reliable Knowledge: An Exploration of the Grounds for Belief in Science*. Cambridge University Press 1978.

Zuckerkandl, Victor, *Sound and Symbol: Music and the External World*, Eng. trans. Willard R. Trask. Routledge & Kegan Paul 1956.

INDEX OF BIBLICAL REFERENCES

INDEX OF NAMES

The more important discussions are indicated in bold type

INDEX OF SUBJECTS

225